A Journey of Spiritual Discovery

Reflections
from the Sunroom

Sherolyn Porter

May you be rooted and established in love, and have power, together with all the Lord's holy people, to grasp how wide and long and high and deep is the love of Christ, and to know this love that surpasses knowledge, that you may be filled to the measure of all the fulness of God

ZANDER

Livonia, Michigan

Sherolyn Porter

Published by Zander
an imprint of BHC Press

Library of Congress Control Number:
2017945137

ISBN-13: 978-1-946848-51-2
ISBN-10: 1-946848-51-4

Visit the publisher at:
www.bhcpress.com

Also available in ebook

Dedication

I dedicate this book first, to my heavenly Father, who has inspired me to share his heart. He loves us so passionately and tenderly. I am grateful he has pursued me relentlessly with his love, in spite of my fears and insecurities, doubts and stubborn pride. I look forward to growing ever closer in relationship with him during my journey here on planet Earth and spending eternity with him, where I shall no longer see in a mirror dimly, and no longer know in part, but the whole. For now, I know I cannot do this life without him.

I dedicate this book to my husband, God's gift to me. You are my earthly hero. I am so thankful to have spent these last thirty-six years as your wife. You are the most unselfish, generous person I have ever known. You have always done everything in your power to help me and our children fulfill our dreams. You give me strength when I am weak. You are one of a kind.

I dedicate this book to my children: Alan, Andy, and Autumn. Being your mother has been the greatest privilege of my life. You are always in my heart, my thoughts, and my prayers. Also to my daughters- and son-"in-love": Amanda, Kassy, and Tyler. I could not be more thrilled that you are a part of our family. May we all grow in love and ever closer to our heavenly Father.

I dedicate this book to my friends and family who have encouraged me to put my musings together into a format that could be shared with many. Without your encouragement, I would not have been brave enough to try. I love you and thank you for your support.

Special thanks to my friend Frank who, as a published author of The Otherealm series, inspired me and gave me the confidence and encouragement to take the next step with my writing. I respect you immensely.

Special thanks to my editor, Allison Chamberlain. Your input and expertise was much appreciated. I looked forward to our email conversations from across the globe, and I feel like I have made a new friend.

And lastly, I dedicate this sharing of my journey to the readers of *Reflections From the Sunroom*...my fellow pilgrims, some of whom may also struggle with chronic illness. I pray for you every day, that you find encouragement in the Lover of your soul, your heavenly Father, who desires relationship with you. Seek him as hidden treasure. You will not be disappointed.

Foreword

by W. Franklin Lattimore

Life. It's a word that seems to contain so much promise: purpose, health, happiness, joy, and fulfillment. The good life. Unfortunately, though, the word can also hold a certain amount of dread, as in the phrase "a life sentence."

There is a belief among many who experience God for the first time, that he is the Great Fixer. Many have been led to believe, now that they've given their lives over to him, that He's going to start fixing all the troubles and pains of life. After all, he is supposed to be the God of the miraculous, right?

Here's a truth about life—something Jesus said—that doesn't seem to hold much hope for any of us: "In this world, you will have trouble." Not the most encouraging of declarations. But Jesus didn't leave the statement just sitting there as an indictment of life on Earth. No, he went on to say, "But be of good cheer. I have overcome the world." (John 16:33, New International Version/King James Version)

It would seem that Jesus is saying, "In the midst of the troubles that will come in this life—on this side of Heaven—be encouraged. I'm in this with you, and there are things that I will provide along the way to get you through to the end." That is what you will find throughout this book: Encouragement in the midst of pain. Love in the midst of loneliness. Faith in the midst of fear.

We live in a fallen world, and because of this we will have "fallen" experiences. We will see and experience hardships; we will feel the realities of sickness; we will hear—whether from the mouths of others or from our own inner beings—messages that will greatly discourage us. These are some of the troubles that Jesus said we would face.

We also have an Enemy. If we don't realize this, life can get very confusing. We can end up actually blaming God for the bad things that we experience. So we need to learn the Enemy's tactics and how to win against our foe.

Sherry Porter's personal experiences within these pages will help you know that you are not alone in the trials you face. Her frankness and painful honesty amidst her own battles—be they emotional, spiritual, or physical—may certainly give you momentary pause, an initial sense of misgiving, but it's the "joy in the morning" aspects of her life accounts that will help you to see that God is rich in his mercy and will be an endless source of joy when you think it otherwise impossible.

"I am leaving you with a gift—peace of mind and heart," Jesus said, "And the peace I give is a gift the world cannot give. So don't be troubled or afraid." (John 14:27, New Living Translation) With this promise, there must be a way to experience that peace.

There is.

Come alongside Sherry and experience some of her journey this side of Heaven. Hear her deepest cries for help. Feel her yearning for her Savior's comfort. Watch how Jesus responds to her innermost needs. And know for yourself the comfort of the One who created you.

W. Franklin Lattimore
Author of the Otherealm Saga

Introduction

My own journey toward the writing of this book began several years ago, after the death of a friend.

As a result of his death, I was reflecting about what heaven must be like and contemplating who I would see when I eventually got there. I thought about loved ones who had gone before me: names and faces flashed before my mind's eye—people I very much desired to see again...to hold again.

Suddenly, I realized with dismay that Jesus hadn't been first on my list...not even close!

I was struck with another thought: that although I had accepted him as my Savior years ago and considered myself "saved," I really didn't feel like I knew him very well—certainly not as well as I knew my friends and family members who had passed away. I believed in him, believed that he was the Son of God and that he had died for my sins so that I could get into heaven, and because of that, it shocked me that he was not the first one I thought about seeing when I arrived. I knew something was wrong.

Upon that realization, I resolved to seek intently a relationship with Jesus because, although I knew him as Savior, I did not know him well as Father—or as my friend.

He should be the first one I can't wait to see when I get there, and that comes only through getting to know him here in this life.

Thus began my quest. I decided to create a special spot in my home, designated for quiet time with the Lord. I chose an old sunroom at the front of the house. Although it was a bit chilly in winter months and a little warm during the summer, its walls were full of windows overlooking woods and meadows, and it was so very peaceful…the perfect place to pray, study, listen for the voice of God, and reflect.

I enlisted the help of my husband and children, who carried in furniture from other parts of the house: some comfortable chairs, a desk, and bookcases for my Bibles and study guides. I added some plants and pictures of the family.

I began to spend regular "quiet time" with the Lord—praying, studying, and reflecting about the things I felt he was speaking to me. Then, feeling prompted by God, I began to write about my journey with and insights into him.

This is a book about that journey toward a deeper relationship with God, a journal of my "reflections from the sunroom."

If you are looking for a book written by an expert, pass this one by. But if you are looking for a book of thoughts and devotions written by a fellow comrade still on the journey, maybe this will keep you company and hopefully point you to the source of strength and hope.

I would encourage you to start your own journal of reflections to be used in your quiet time with God. Wait on him with expectancy. He delights to talk with you.

My prayer for myself, as well as for you dear reader, is from Ephesians 3.

> I pray that out of his glorious riches he may strengthen you with power through his Spirit in your inner being, so that Christ may dwell in your hearts through faith. And I pray that you, being rooted and established in love, may have power, together with all the Lord's holy people, to grasp how wide and long and high and deep is the love of Christ, and to know this love that surpasses knowledge—that you may be filled to the measure of all

the fullness of God. (Ephesians 3:16-19, New International Version)

In Jesus's name, amen.

→≫≫ ✳ ≪≪←

Revelation 3:20

Here I am! I stand at the door and knock. If anyone hears my voice and opens the door, I will come in and eat with that person, and they with me.

Matthew 6:6

But when you pray, go into your room, close the door and pray to your Father, who is unseen. Then your Father, who sees what is done in secret, will reward you.

→≫≫ ✳ ≪≪←

Reflection Time

How has God been speaking to you today? Take time to write it in your journal.

Reflections
from the *Sunroom*

Chapter 1
Hidden Treasure

The Bible says to seek God as we seek hidden treasure. I think about what treasure hunters must feel like in their quest. I'm sure the excitement is overwhelming, especially when they have discovered a clue that brings them closer to the treasure.

Some treasure hunters may be tempted to give up when the road seems long and difficult and troubles get in their way. I'm sure at times they end up going in a circle and wind up back where they started. They may have doubts and question periodically whether there actually *is* treasure at the end of their quest or if they are even working with the right map.

My quest for hidden treasure is beginning in the sunroom, where I am reading and studying God's Word and praying for the needs of friends and family. I have also started a ladies' Bible study in my home for spiritual growth and fellowship with other believers.

I am noticing an ever-increasing desire to spend quiet time with the Lord and an increased hunger for reading his Word. I pray for more of that. I am looking forward to this journey. I believe there is much more available to me as a believer than I have previously experienced in my Christian walk.

Father God, I desire intimacy with you. Help me to find the treasures you have hidden for me in your Word and in the quiet times that you desire to spend with me. Please help me tune out distractions and focus on you during these times. In Jesus's name, amen.

Matthew 13:44

The kingdom of heaven is like treasure hidden in a field. When a man found it, he hid it again, and then in his joy went and sold all he had and bought that field.

Proverbs 15:6

In the house of the righteous is much treasure: but in the revenues of the wicked is trouble. (KJV)

Isaiah45:3

And I will give thee the treasures of darkness and hidden riches of secret places, that thou mayest know that I, the LORD, which call thee by thy name, am the God of Israel. (KJV)

Reflection Time

How has God been speaking to you today? Take time to write it in your journal.

Chapter 2
Friendship with God

Something I have become keenly aware of during my quiet time is the revelation that God is anxious to speak to his children. His greatest desire is for relationship with us. He wants to remove anything that would hinder that relationship. It's about friendship with a very wise and powerful being, one who has control of all things and who always has our best interests in mind. Don't take my word for it. Seek it out for yourself. He is anxious to meet with you and talk to you too. He wants to be your friend, your helper and protector, your peace and your joy. You will wonder how you ever managed without him.

Lord, help us not to make relationship with you too complicated. Give us the desire to spend time in your presence. You are our friend, our helper, and our comforter. You have the abundant life for us—not in material possessions or even freedom from trouble, but in the peace that passes understanding and in the fullness of joy despite our circumstances. In Jesus's name, amen.

Sherolyn Porter

Psalm 139:7-10

Where can I go from your Spirit?
Where can I flee from your presence?
If I go up to the heavens, you are there;
if I make my bed in the depths, you are there.
If I rise on the wings of the dawn,
if I settle on the far side of the sea,
even there your hand will guide me,
your right hand will hold me fast.

Psalm 16:1-2

Keep me safe, my God,
I say to the LORD, "You are my Lord;
apart from you I have no good thing."

Psalm 16:11

You make known to me the path of life;
you will fill me with joy in your presence,
with eternal pleasures at your right hand.

Reflection Time

How has God been speaking to you today? Take time to write it in your journal.

Chapter 3
A Sword, a Helmet, and a Shield

God uses words in the Bible that liken his people to warriors. That makes me squirm a little.

I don't see myself as a warrior. I have lived most of my life with chronic fatigue syndrome and fibromyalgia, so I am not strong. When I examine my heart, I see that there is a part of me that really wants to hang out in the beginning of Psalm 23. You know, lying down in green pastures…with still waters…God restoring my soul and all that.

I think I'd like to stay right there, while the rest of the warriors go off to war.

I am guilty of wishing God would just wave my troubles away. Instead, he tells me to put on the armor and do battle—and to be strong and courageous while doing it. In fact, I am not to fear, even if the mountains fall into the sea.

I don't like words like *battle* and *helmets, sword* and *shield.* I prefer green pastures. And still waters.

How could he possibly want me as a warrior? I'm fearful and weak. I'm weary much of the time. Not your typical warrior material.

I *try* to be a warrior. But some days I find it hard to lift the sword, let alone swing it. My sword muscles need some serious attention.

I need to practice flexing those sword muscles by spending time in the Word—inundating myself with it—because my weapons are not of this world. My sword is not silent. My sword is the Word... it *speaks*.

Instead of my typical response during hard times, when I'm tempted to say "I can't do this," I need to swing the sword which says "I can do all things through Christ who strengthens me." When I find myself saying, "I am afraid," I need to swing the sword which says, "I will fear no evil, for thou art with me." Instead of saying, "I am so exhausted," I need to swing the sword which says, "He gives power to the faint, and to them who have no might, he increases strength." When my loved one is sick, swing the sword: "And the prayer of faith shall save the sick, and the Lord will raise him up."

My Bible study this week was about the role of the church in the end times. Jesus wanted us all to be one as he and the Father are one, and he prayed for it.

In the study, we learned that God is raising up individuals in every denomination—people who have a hunger for God's Word and a desire to know him better and seek after him. It's through these believers who are seeking God through his Word that he is going to bring revival to the church in these last days. The church and God's people are going to come under fire. Many Christians are going through the fire right now because God needs to refine them for the job ahead. We are being prepared for battle *through* battle. He is going to raise up mighty warriors in his church. The persecution the church is going to go through in the last days will unify and fortify it and draw us closer to him. The things that his warriors are all going to have in common are the helmet of salvation, the breastplate of righteousness, the shield of faith, and a two-edged sword, which is the Word of God.

God is calling us—not as individual churches with doctrines and denominations, but as individuals with a heart for Christ—to rise up in the last days and prophesy, which means to speak the truth. The Sword—the *truth*—will make people free. The truth is God's Word, and we need it *in* us for the upcoming battle.

Father God, help me to remember when I am weak, you are strong, and your strength is made perfect in weakness. I'm not much to work with, but here I am. Mold me and make me. Help me to grow into a warrior for you. In Jesus's name, amen.

Hebrews 4:12
For the word of God is alive and active. Sharper than any double-edged sword, it penetrates even to dividing soul and spirit, joints and marrow; it judges the thoughts and attitudes of the heart.

Ephesians 6:10-17
Finally, be strong in the Lord and in his mighty power. Put on the full armor of God, so that you can take your stand against the devil's schemes. For our struggle is not against flesh and blood, but against the rulers, against the authorities, against the powers of this dark world and against the spiritual forces of evil in the heavenly realms. Therefore put on the full armor of God, so that when the day of evil comes, you may be able to stand your ground, and after you have done everything, to stand. Stand firm then, with the belt of truth buckled around your waist, with the breastplate of righteousness

in place, and with your feet fitted with the readiness that comes from the gospel of peace. In addition to all this, take up the shield of faith, with which you can extinguish all the flaming arrows of the evil one. Take the helmet of salvation and the sword of the Spirit, which is the word of God.

Reflection Time

How has God been speaking to you today? Take time to write it in your journal.

Chapter 4
Practicing His Presence

I was doing dishes this morning, when I kept feeling nudged to spend a little quiet time with the Lord. I finished up and went out into the sunroom and picked up a book I had just ordered last week. The acquisition of that book is a small miracle in itself. Just a few weeks ago, I had been praying that God would help me to sense his presence. That very same morning, I got a phone call from my dear friend, Debbie, who said that her sister (who I really don't know) had been praying and reading a book she had bought. The Lord kept bringing my name to her mind, and she felt impressed to call Debbie and have her tell me to get the book.

I started reading this book last week and felt overwhelmed and set it aside. The first chapter was about sitting quietly and focusing on God. (This is difficult for a woman who can be in the middle of praying and all of sudden realize she's adding items to the grocery list in her mind.)

I tried to do what the book said, but I was totally distracted by thoughts that kept pecking at my quest for stillness and silence: people to pray for, things to do, and the ever-ongoing items to be added to the grocery list. So, feeling like a failure, I didn't try it again for a few days.

This morning, in response to the nudging, I picked up reading where I had left off. The book said to sit silently and ask the Holy Spirit to make Jesus real to me.

I had a little more success quieting my mind after a few minutes of distracting thoughts and quelling the desire to jump up and do this, that, or the other. I pictured Jesus in my mind's eye, sitting across from me, and that comfortable silence one feels with a close friend… no need for conversation, just silent companionship. I looked out the windows of my sunroom, watching the pines softly swaying in the breeze and the occasional snowflake float its way to the frosty ground. Finally, I could feel the peace and joy that comes from observing nature settle over me. I became aware of the birds singing outside the window, and I thought about what a beautiful gift all of nature is to us…thought about Father, Son and Holy Spirit creating the world, in all of its awesome beauty…just for us.

Suddenly, I heard the most amazing bird song. I'm quite sure it's a song I had never heard before. It was not the range usually heard in a bird song, consisting of several notes. This song was an absolute symphony of sound…unbelievably lovely…and it went on and on. I quelled the urge to grab my cellphone to try and record the notes. I sat breathlessly still, afraid if I moved I would break the magical spell of the moment.

There, in the song of the bird, I felt the presence of Jesus, just for a moment, and I knew that the wonderful, melodious song of that bird was his special gift to me today. I could almost see him smiling. I hope to hear that song again.

Father God, thank you for your patience with my impatience. I'm sorry I struggle so hard to be still…because when I can be still and become aware of your presence, there is absolutely no place else

I would rather be. Help me to become better at waiting for you in stillness. In Jesus's name, amen.

-»»» ✳ «««-

Psalm 16:11

You make known to me the path of life; you will fill me with joy in your presence, with eternal pleasures at your right hand.

Psalm 140:13

Surely the righteous will praise your name, and the upright will live in your presence.

-»»» ✳ «««-

Reflection Time

How has God been speaking to you today? Take time to write it in your journal.

Chapter 5
Martha to Mary

The Lord awakened me to pray earlier than usual this morning. I sat in the darkness and watched the faintest tinge of light develop at the crest of the hilltop. I thought about how different the Christmas season feels to me this year. By this time, I'm usually stressed out and crazy with all my lists of things to do. This year I feel peace. Am I forgetting something on my to-do list? When I go over it in my mind, I realize the list is the same it has always been: Christmas cards to send out, holiday parties to plan and attend, presents to wrap, cooking to do, out of town guests to begin arriving in the next two weeks. Yet here I sit, with an unhurried sense of peace. I believe the difference is because I've made a conscious effort this year to start my mornings with the Lord: spending time in prayer, reading his Word, and contemplating his goodness.

Tears sting the corners of my eyes as the Scripture comes to mind: "Mary has chosen what is best, and it will not be taken from her."

I am overwhelmed with gratitude as I realize that God has answered my prayer. He has helped me to find Mary in all of my "Martha-ness."

I struggled so much in the beginning. It was hard to read the Bible—it just didn't interest me that much—and my prayers were hurried requests sent up during the course of a busy day.

It's not so much of a struggle anymore. The effort that I have put forth this year in seeking his presence has made all the difference, and nothing compares to the peace that has come with that. His Word has come alive to me, and consciously committing to early morning prayer time has left me with so much more peace throughout the day. The Lord wants us to pray continually, and I believe he loves any attempt on our part to get to know his Word.

God, I thank you for answered prayer. Sometimes I don't realize that my prayers are being answered bit by bit, a little at a time.

The greatest answer is you, because no matter what need I have, your presence is the answer to it. You are enough. Lord, help me to be disciplined in the coming year to put you first, because the abundant life is not found in my activities and my busyness. It is found in the stillness…seeking your presence. In Jesus's name, amen.

-»»» ※ «««-

Luke 10:42

But few things are needed—or indeed only one. Mary has chosen what is better, and it will not be taken away from her.

Matthew 6:33

But seek first his kingdom and his righteousness, and all these things will be given to you as well.

Philippians 4:6-7

Do not be anxious about anything, but in every situation, by prayer and petition, with thanksgiving, present your requests to God. And the peace of God, which transcends all understanding, will guard your hearts and your minds in Christ Jesus.

Reflection Time

How has God been speaking to you today? Take time to write it in your journal.

Chapter 6
Morning Moon

Awake at 5:30 a.m. on a bitterly cold morning....

I wanted so much to stay under the mound of warm blankets and drift back to sleep, but I felt the Lord nudging me to go downstairs to my sunroom, where I usually spend early morning quiet time with him. The thought of my bare feet hitting the cold wooden floor of the old house just seemed like more than my warm sleepy body could take.

Suddenly our big black-and-white alarm clock, AKA Bailey, bounded into the room with her typical doggy enthusiasm for early morning. I struggled out of bed before she could wake the whole household and went downstairs to let her outside. While I was waiting for her to make her morning rounds of chasing the squirrels away from the bird feeders, I straightened up a few things in the kitchen and began to make a mental list of things I needed to do that day.

But the gentle nudging from the Lord to spend some time with him continued. Bailey barreled back up onto the front porch, and I let her in. I made my way to the sunroom, which had begun to feel like my sanctuary. I have spent a good bit of time there this winter, working on my Bible study and listening to worship music. It was still dark outside, and the room held the chill of a winter morning, so I turned on a lamp and lit the little fire. Immediately, I sensed the Lord telling me to turn off the lamp, and when I did, I realized that the moon was still up and sinking slowly into the west behind the pines that surround our house.

Mesmerized by the scene outside my window, I backed up to the comfy chair and settled into it.

The blanket of snow covering the ground and the pine branches illuminated by the moon made the whole scene appear magical in its beauty.

I enjoyed the breathtaking scene for a few moments and then began thinking about who to pray for and which Bible verses I could meditate on.

"Be still," the Lord whispered.

Obligingly, I settled back into my chair and enjoyed the view.

As I sat there in the stillness, a precious memory from long ago crossed my mind. It was a memory of my honeymoon, when my new husband had awakened me very early one morning to come down to the beach and watch a beautiful sunrise with him. He already had chairs in place on the sand and just wanted to share that moment with me....

It struck me that the Lord just wanted to share this breathtaking dawn with me. In fact, he was pleased to show it to me.

He didn't have an agenda of Bible verses and prayer time for me; he just wanted to spend a few moments with me and share his handiwork—a gift for me, this beautiful dawn.

Father God, I fail so often to be tuned in to you. Sometimes it takes me forever to hear the melody you are singing over me.

The moments that we truly sing in harmony are too brief. Bless my ears to hear your music, because the moments that I can sing with you, those precious moments when my spirit joins with yours...that melody...that harmony...those are the moments I treasure the most.

I want your song to be the song of my life...not just a few stanzas here and there, but the whole concerto. In Jesus's name, amen.

Zephaniah 3:17

For the LORD your God is living among you. He is a mighty savior. He will take delight in you with gladness. With his love, he will calm all your fears. He will rejoice over you with joyful songs. (NLT)

Reflection Time

How has God been speaking to you today? Take time to write it in your journal.

Chapter 7
To Everything There Is a Season

When our boys were young, my husband Al and I spent countless hours at the neighborhood soccer fields watching them play soccer. The soccer fields were beside a sparsely traveled road along the river, so it has always been a favorite spot for bicyclists and walkers. Many evenings, while watching the boys practice, I would notice gray-haired couples riding their bikes along that road, and I would smile and think, "How sweet."

It was unseasonably warm this afternoon, so Al and I took a bike ride down the road by the river. We passed the soccer fields, where parents were sitting in lawn chairs, watching their children practice. I felt nostalgic, missing the days when my children were young. With misty eyes, I realized that now Al and I were the gray-haired couple riding our bikes on the river road. It was so bitter-sweet...where has the time gone?

I wondered if any of the young couples watched us and smiled. And I wondered if they knew to enjoy every second...because this time in their lives will soon be a sweet memory.

Dear Lord, I struggle so much with change and with letting go of the things in life that are precious to me. I thought by middle age I would have grown accustomed to the changes that life brings. Please help me to trust you with the latter part of my life, as well as with the lives of my children as they leave the nest. In Jesus's name, amen.

-»»» ❋ «««-

Hebrews 13:8

Jesus Christ is the same yesterday and today and forever.

Isaiah 46:4

Even to your old age and gray hairs I am he, I am he who will sustain you. I have made you and I will carry you; I will sustain you and I will rescue you.

Jeremiah 29:11

For I know the plans I have for you, declares the LORD, plans for welfare and not for evil, to give you a future and a hope. (English Standard Version)

Ecclesiastes 3:1

For everything there is a season, and a time for every matter under heaven. (ESV)

-»»» ❋ «««-

Reflection Time

How has God been speaking to you today? Take time to write it in your journal.

Chapter 8
On My Knees

God wants to speak to us continually. Many times, he will confirm what he is saying through the words of a friend, a song, or Scripture. This morning was one of those times.

I was lying in bed, praying in the early hours before dawn. As I prayed, I felt the Lord wanted me to get out of bed and onto my knees. I groaned inwardly and pulled the covers up tighter around me and continued to pray, but almost immediately, I began to feel like I was being disobedient.

So I struggled out from under the covers and knelt beside my bed. I prayed to God for strength for many of my friends and family who were going through some really tough times. Honestly, it was one of those times where I felt like my prayers weren't going any higher than the top of my head, but I still felt impressed that it was very important to God for me to be on my knees while praying this particular morning.

Later in the morning, the Scripture in my devotions was Ephesians 3:16-19.

I pray that out of his glorious riches he may strengthen you with power through his Spirit in your inner being, so that Christ may dwell in your hearts through faith. And I pray that you, being rooted and established in love, may have power, together with all the Lord's holy people, to grasp how wide and long and high and deep is the love of Christ, and to know this love that surpasses knowledge—that you may be filled to the measure of all the fullness of God.

I love that passage. I made a mental note to share it with my prayer partners and my nephew, who are going through a hard time.

After reading my devotions, my thoughts turned to the nudging I'd had from the Lord that morning to pray on my knees. I decided to look up the word "kneel" in my Strong's concordance. The Scripture reference was Ephesians 3:14, a couple of verses before the passage in my morning devotions. Interested, I turned in my Bible for the reading and started with verse fourteen. My heart thrilled within me as I read:

...for this reason I **kneel** before the Father, from whom his whole family in heaven and on earth derives its name. I pray that out of his glorious riches he may strengthen you with power through his Spirit in your inner being, so that Christ may dwell in your hearts through faith. And I pray that you, being rooted and established in love, may have power, together with all the Lord's holy people, to grasp how wide and long and high and deep is the love of Christ, and to know this love that surpasses

knowledge—that you may be filled to the measure
of all the fullness of God. (Ephesians 3:14-19, NIV)

Father, it never ceases to amaze me that the Creator of the
Universe wants to talk to me. I am so humbled…and thrilled beyond
measure. Thank you…thank you. In Jesus's name, amen.

Reflection Time

How has God been speaking to you today? Take
time to write it in your journal.

Chapter 9
Crazy World

I am a pretty simple person. I like peace and quiet, so I avoid big crowds, high traffic areas, and loud noise. It disrupts my spirit inside. If I am surrounded by busyness and noise, I can't hear myself think, let alone hear from the Lord. Even Jesus had to withdraw from the crowds and spend time alone to hear his Father's voice.

It's not too difficult to understand why this crazy world can't find God anymore. There's too much background noise to hear him.

The beautiful garden that God created and placed the first man was vastly different from what we live in now. We have developed an environment that makes it difficult to commune with our Creator.

We are in a permanent state of "rush"...trying to survive...trying to get ahead. We weave our way through traffic, getting frustrated and angry if other drivers are going too slowly. We look out of concrete buildings at other concrete buildings that obstruct the sky. We get our nourishment from fast food poisoned with artificial additives and preservatives, and we spend our evenings exhausted in front of the TV, watching shows filled with violence and sexual promiscuity...because it's more comfortable than silence.

We run or take walks with headphones in our ears and miss the sound of nature in the process. We spend any time alone texting, talking, working, or playing on our phones.

Man and woman were created and then put in a garden, where evidence of the Creator was all around them: watching the sunlight sparkle on rippling water, listening to the beautiful sounds of birds singing in the trees, enjoying the smell of warm earth and plant life, feeling the sun and wind upon their faces, enjoying the taste of wholesome foods that brought health and nourishment to their bodies.

What we seek—the desires of our hearts—can't be found in our forward motion. It can only be found in what we seem to be most afraid of: stillness.

Father God, help us not to be afraid of silence, for it is the best place to hear the still, small voice. Open our ears to hear you. In Jesus's name, amen.

→→→→ ❋ ←←←←

Psalm 46:10

Be still, and know that I am God. I will be exalted among the nations, I will be exalted in the earth! (ESV)

Job 37:14

Hear this, O Job; stop and consider the wondrous works of God. (ESV)

Isaiah 30:15

This is what the Sovereign LORD, the Holy One of Israel, says: "In repentance and rest is your salvation, in quietness and trust is your strength, but you would have none of it."

Deuteronomy 32:1-2

Give ear, O heavens, and I will speak, and let the earth hear the words of my mouth. May my teaching drop as the rain, my speech distill as the dew, like gentle rain upon the tender grass, and like showers upon the herb. (ESV)

Reflection Time

How has God been speaking to you today? Take time to write it in your journal.

Chapter 10
Is God Enough?

My husband and two of my three children are out of town this week. I have one son in town and have asked him to come and stay with me—partly because I need help with the horses, but mostly because I don't like to be alone.

The thought of them all being out of town at the same time makes me panicky, horses or no horses. I have prayed that all my children will find jobs and begin their own stories close to home so they can live nearby, but with the economy and job situation the way it is in our small town, I know that it's not very likely to happen.

I'm also coming to the uncomfortable realization that the Bible is full of instances where God calls people to leave their families. His will for their lives is in another place. It's so hard for me to take my hands off my children and trust God's will for them.

I talk to God about this fear of being alone, because someday, it may come down to just him and me. I ask myself if that is good enough for me, and if not, why isn't it? I don't *need* to be entertained or have someone beside me all the time. I always have solo projects going on—Bible study, quilting, scrap booking, gardening, and reading—and I am content to do those things alone. I just want the physical presence of someone else in the house. Even if my family is not right beside me, my heart knows when they are not at home.

I would like to be aware of God's presence all the time. There are so many Scriptures that tell me he is always with me, that he will never leave or forsake me.

Dear God, bring verses to my attention about your nearness, and open my mind and heart to see you. Take my fear of being alone and replace it with your perfect peace. In Jesus's name, amen.

Joshua 1:9

Have I not commanded you? Be strong and courageous. Do not be frightened, and do not be dismayed, for the LORD your God is with you wherever you go. (ESV)

Isaiah 41:10

Fear not, for I am with you; be not dismayed, for I am your God; I will strengthen you, I will help you, I will uphold you with my righteous right hand. (ESV)

Deuteronomy 31:6

Be strong and courageous. Do not fear or be in dread of them, for it is the LORD your God who goes with you. He will not leave you or forsake you. (ESV)

Romans 8:38-39

For I am sure that neither death nor life, nor angels nor rulers, nor things present nor things to come, nor powers, nor height nor depth, nor anything else in all creation, will be able to separate us from the love of God in Christ Jesus our Lord. (ESV)

→→⟩⟩⟩ ✳ ⟨⟨⟨←

Reflection Time

How has God been speaking to you today? Take time to write it in your journal.

Chapter 11

Processes

During my quiet time this morning, I was thinking about processes and my impatience with them.

I get frustrated with God sometimes, because he loves processes, and I am usually in a hurry. He can work instantaneously, but many times, he chooses to work through a series of events over a period of time. When I was young in the faith and learned about how awesome and powerful God was, I wanted him to use that power on my behalf and instantaneously whisk my problems away. Yet in my life, he has usually chosen deliverance through processes.

God always has something for me to learn through these processes, and if I don't learn it, the lesson usually comes up over and over again. I could save myself much heartache if I yielded to the process and asked the Lord to help me trust him through it all.

I hate winter and long for spring. Yet the Lord reminds me that the beauty is *in* the process…hidden beneath the cold and darkness of the ice and snow. When it is time, the earth will warm, and the miracle of spring will slowly begin once again.

And I trust that spring is going to come, because in my experience, it has always followed winter—every year of my life.

This same principle can be applied to my spiritual life. When the road seems long and I am discouraged about the journey, I need to focus on the times in the past that God has brought me through, and trust him. Forcing the process just frustrates me and can set things back.

When a butterfly emerges from the cocoon, the struggle it endures to be free is necessary. If we were to cut open the cocoon and spare the butterfly the struggle, it would be deformed. The stress of squeezing its body through the small opening of the cocoon pushes fluid into its wings. Without this necessary progression, the butterfly would never be able to fly. The struggle it goes through isn't just for survival; the process is essential for its completeness, for its perfection.

Processes are designed by a loving Creator who knows what is best.

Dear Lord, when I am impatient and discouraged with the journey, help me to remember that you are in control, and your ways are always best. Remind me that my strength comes in quietness and trust. In Jesus's name, amen.

James 1:2-4

Count it all joy, my brothers, when you meet trials of various kinds, for you know that the testing of your faith produces steadfastness. And let steadfastness have its full effect, that you may be perfect and complete, lacking in nothing. (ESV)

Reflections From the Sunroom

Reflection Time

How has God been speaking to you today? Take time to write it in your journal.

Chapter 12

Frustrated

Periodically, I find myself in a lot of physical pain as a result of living with a chronic illness. At times, I get very frustrated and question the Lord about it. I ask for wisdom and discernment—what I am supposed to be learning from the trial. I might as well admit my thoughts to him…he knows them anyway.

My lament usually goes something like this: "I am your child, God, and you are all powerful…so what's up with all this? There are so many Scriptures that promise victory, protection, healing…"

And then he gently reminds me that there are also many Scriptures that talk about persecution and fiery trials, Scriptures that say, "In this world you will have trouble."

He reminds me that my own infirmities create an empathy in me for my brothers and sisters in the faith who are undergoing their own "fiery trials," many of them worse than mine.

For some people, the fiery trials push them away from God. They cry out in anger and doubt his existence. I don't want that to happen to me.

I know enough of God to know that he exists…and that he is Love…and that he is good….

As I sit and reflect, the Holy Spirit reminds me of Scripture that says his ways are not my ways, his thoughts are not my thoughts…my troubles are light and momentary and will produce for me an eternal glory that far outweighs them all…he works all things together for the good of those who love him and are called according to his purpose….

So why my frustration? Because I want my "cotton candy" Jesus to "wave his magic wand"?

I'm guilty of that.

But what effect do fiery trials have on those of us who have had personal encounters with the Lord? They serve to draw us closer to the One we know is all powerful, to make us realize our complete dependence on him. If I am being totally honest with myself, I must admit that, when things are going well for me, I do not spend as much time seeking his face or delving into his Word. Although I don't forget him, I tend to use my energy to happily busy myself with many things, most of which, sadly, have no eternal value.

I have this deep sense in my spirit that, in these "last days," our total reliance on God is the only thing that is going to get us through, that we need to use our trials as nudges to seek his face, that we need to read his Word and store it up in our hearts—because someday soon, things are going to change.

Revelation says that the evil one is overcome by the blood of the Lamb and by the word of the testimony of our brothers and sisters, and a testimony—at least a really good one—doesn't come without a test.

Father God, forgive me when, in my impatience, I question your ways. Help me to remember that you work all things for my good. Keep me ever close to you. In Jesus's name, amen.

-->>>> ❄ <<<<-

2 Corinthians 4:17

For our light and momentary troubles are achieving for us an eternal glory that far outweighs them all.

Romans 8:28

And we know that in all things God works for the good of those who love him, who have been called according to his purpose.

Reflection Time

How has God been speaking to you today? Take time to write it in your journal.

Chapter 13
Seeking Him Before the Storm

The dogs woke me up earlier than usual this morning. As I went downstairs to let them out, I noticed the sky looked dark and threatening, with the promise of a spring storm. Giving up the idea of going straight back to bed, I quickly pulled on my boots and headed to the chicken coop to avoid getting caught in a downpour.

On the way, I thought of other things that needed done before the rain: a folded pile of old sheets I'd left on my garden bench from when I had covered up the strawberries the night before, a wheel barrel partially full of weeds that needed dumped before it became heavier with the rain.

Ignoring the pain in my back, I finished these tasks and headed back toward the garden gate. As I reached the gate and pushed it open, I looked over toward the horse pasture and saw a vibrant rainbow shining between the pine trees. Wow! Where did that come from? A rainbow before the storm…I smiled with pleasure.

Good morning, Lord!

I stood still for a few moments with my hand on the rusty garden gate, enjoying the beauty of the spring morning. I closed my eyes and listened to the melody of the birds and breathed in the smell of the spring breeze, rich with the promise of rain.

My thoughts turned to rainbows and how they represent God and his promises. I usually think of rainbows coming after a storm… just like I sometimes think of God after a storm of life has already overtaken me.

I know that I am better off seeking God and being strengthened by his Word *before* the storms come—because no one gets through life without troubles—and that seeking after God is not meant to be just a Sunday experience. He wants to be found by me every day…in the gift of his creation…in the beautiful melody of the birds singing in the trees…in that rainbow hiding behind my pines on this beautiful spring morning…each one waiting to reveal the treasure that is my Savior.

Father God, I desire intimacy with you—intimacy that eclipses even my most precious relationships here on Earth. Help me to cultivate that intimacy, because you are hidden treasure, just waiting to be found. Thank you for that beautiful rainbow this morning as a reminder of your promises. In Jesus's name, amen.

->>>> ❋ <<<<-

Matthew 13:44
The kingdom of heaven is like treasure hidden in a field. When a man found it, he hid it again, and then in his joy went and sold all he had and bought that field.

Proverbs 15:6
The house of the righteous contains great treasure, but the income of the wicked brings ruin.

Reflections From the Sunroom

Isaiah 45:3
I will give you hidden treasures,
riches stored in secret places,
so that you may know that I am the LORD,
the God of Israel, who summons you by name.

Reflection Time

How has God been speaking to you today? Take time to write it in your journal.

Chapter 14
Cruise Control on the Straight and Narrow

I woke up with the back pain that has been my constant companion as of late and a mile-long to-do list on my mind. I wanted to spend some quiet time with God, so I tried to hurry through my chores. As I fed the chickens—and prayed for a miracle of divine help to get everything done on my list—a bit of Scripture came to mind... something about "God worketh in me..."

"Yes," I thought. "That is exactly what I need: God working in me today to get my to-do list done. Thank you for that word, Lord." I finished up with the chickens and headed back to the house. Carrying my iPad out into the sunroom, where I spend my quiet time, I set it up to play some worship music, hoping to get myself in a "quiet time" frame of mind and redirect my thoughts from my to-do list. Realizing that the battery was nearly dead, I trudged off to find the charger and an ice pack for my back. Then I heard the still small voice whisper, "Why not sit in silence without worship music today?"

"*What?* No way! I have *so* much on my mind! I need the music to direct my focus to you, God." Tossing the ice pack onto my chair, I tried plugging the charger into the iPad, which didn't seem to fit for some reason. I sighed in frustration. "Okay, Lord...silence it is."

I settled down into my chair with my ice pack and looked out the windows, enjoying the lovely flowering trees. The snow-white blooms were strikingly beautiful against a very gray and cloudy sky.

Suddenly, the sun peeked through a break in the clouds, illuminating the highway where it met the meadow, nearly a quarter-mile below me. With striking brilliance, the sun highlighted the cargo trailer of a semi-trailer truck traveling down the highway, and I sat watching it, surprised by one thing in particular. Having traveled that section of road many times, I know that, to a driver, it seems to be a straight stretch of highway, yet observing the highlighted semi from my lofty vantage point this morning, I could see very clearly that, instead of heading south, the imperceptible curve in the road was taking it east. Strangely, I had never realized that before.

Cruise control on the straight and narrow road…yet the road is not going straight at all. I chuckled to myself.

The bit of Scripture that had come to me while doing my chores that morning nudged at the edge of my mind again…God worketh in you…what is that Scripture anyway? I got out my concordance and found it: Philippians 2:13. "For it is God who works in you to will and to act in order to fulfill his good purpose."

His good purpose…or you could be on cruise control on the straight and narrow—and going an entirely different direction than you thought.

I remembered how I have felt the Lord speaking to me in the last year about spending quiet time with him in study and writing…and I have done that, to a point—the point when my to-do list screams louder than the still small voice.

Many times, I say yes to things I want to do without praying about them first *(well, it wouldn't hurt to take a few days off from study to do this or that)* and then I find myself traveling on my own steam, with too much to do and not enough energy to do it.

Although I'm not doing ungodly things (still on cruise control on the straight and narrow), many times I am not in the center of God's will for my life.

Heavenly Father, I thank you for speaking through ordinary things. I thank you for never giving up on me, even when I am very distracted by life. You never cease to amaze me! Thank you for that *truth!* In Jesus's name, amen.

Matthew 6:31–33

Therefore do not be anxious, saying, "What shall we eat?" or "What shall we drink?" or "What shall we wear?" For the Gentiles seek after all these things, and your heavenly Father knows that you need them all. But seek first the kingdom of God and his righteousness, and all these things will be added to you. (ESV)

Proverbs 16:3

*Commit your work to the L*ORD*, and your plans will be established. (ESV)*

Reflection Time

How has God been speaking to you today? Take time to write it in your journal.

Chapter 15
The Melody of Love

I settled down into my chair for my quiet time with God this morning and was immediately filled with a rush of gratitude. Consistently spending quiet time with the Lord was very much a struggle at first. Now, I am finding that there is nothing like intimacy with someone who has been with you your entire life…someone who knows every tear you've ever cried, every secret dream you've ever cherished in your heart, every thought you've ever had (whether noble or horrible) and yet loves you unconditionally. I know that he has always had my best interest at heart, even when I have gone against his wisdom and chosen paths that have led to heartache and pain. If I could have one do-over in life, it would be to have earnestly sought after the Lord much earlier. I grieve for the time I have wasted on things that have no value, either here or in the life to come. He is hidden treasure, he turns ashes into beauty, he is the peace that passes understanding. I am so thankful that I am getting to know him better now.

My prayer for the remainder of my days is to be aware of the realm where I can hear creation singing the song of the Creator, the long forgotten song that has always been in me. I often heard that melody as a child, but as I grew older—and became distracted by many things—it faded into the background, hidden somewhere in the deepest recesses of my soul. That beautiful melody became elusive…covered up by the noise of all that clamored for my attention. Once in a great while, I could faintly hear a note or two, but the familiar song eluded me, and I wistfully thought it was one of those magical realities known only to childhood.

So many moments rush into my mind that fill me with humble gratitude, moments (gifts) in life when I didn't acknowledge God as the giver of the gift—as though I had somehow created this wonder of my own accord—such as my husband gazing into my eyes on our wedding day as he held my hands and said his vows to me, and eight years later, the feel of a little hand curling around my finger for the first time, the miraculous result of that love.

Dear God, I know I could experience even ordinary everyday moments with so much more joy and passion if I gratefully acknowledged those moments as a gift, notes in the song composed by my Creator…especially for me.

Father God, make me daily aware that the sun on my face and the wind in my hair are a part of that melody, a gift to me from a loving Creator. I want to slow down and see the gifts that are all around me: the song of a bird, the fluffy white clouds in a cornflower-blue summer sky, how the sun the sparkles on the water during the day and the moonbeams reflect a path from heaven to earth over its darkened depths at night. Let me hear the melody in the arrival of the dawn, with the morning dew sparkling like a million scattered diamonds on the grass and the trees.

Lord, also fill me with your love for mankind, your most precious creation, for that part of the melody is the most important to you. And help me to realize that the moments in my life hold a depth of richness that is lost when they are not experienced and acknowledged as gifts from a loving Creator. In Jesus's name, amen.

Matthew 7:11

If you then, who are evil, know how to give good gifts to your children, how much more will your Father who is in heaven give good things to those who ask him! (ESV)

Reflection Time

How has God been speaking to you today? Take time to write it in your journal.

Chapter 16
Cloudy Days

Today is our last day of vacation and I settle down wistfully in a chair for my quiet time with God. I am in the living room of the rented beach house this morning instead of my usual spot on the deck. I gaze out the windows, streaked with rain, and watch the wind blow over the gray and choppy water. It's hard to believe that, above this stormy, windswept sky, the sun is shining just as beautifully as it has all week. I have been in a plane and flown through a storm, so I know this to be true: above the storm, the sun is there, shining just as brightly as it always has.

I usually tend to look at what is right in front of me and see that as reality. This is something I struggle with in my spiritual life as well.

God's word tells me that what I see, hear, and feel is not always reality. He is so much bigger than my little spot on the planet, and he sees the whole picture. He knows the beginning from the end.

Father God, when I face the storms of life, sometimes I am tempted to doubt your goodness and love for me. Sometimes the darkness seems to win, and I feel like the sun will never shine again. During these times, please remind me of your Word which says that you are always with me and that nothing can separate me from your love. Remind me that, although I may not feel your presence at the moment, you are there, just as surely as the sun is still shining above the worst of storms. In Jesus's name, amen.

Romans 8:35, 37-39

Who shall separate us from the love of Christ? Shall trouble or hardship or persecution or famine or nakedness or danger or sword? ...No, in all these things we are more than conquerors through him who loved us. For I am convinced that neither death nor life, neither angels nor demons, neither the present nor the future, nor any powers, neither height nor depth, nor anything else in all creation, will be able to separate us from the love of God that is in Christ Jesus our Lord.

Reflection Time

How has God been speaking to you today? Take time to write it in your journal.

Chapter 17
Unexpected Faith

Something happened today that took me way out of my comfort zone but blessed me beyond measure in the process. My mother scolded me for it, as most mothers would, but when you feel like God is telling you to do something, you should just do it.

I was on my way home from a little farm market just down the road from my house where I'd gone to get a few things for lunch. It was a beastly hot Sunday in early June, and I was not in the mood to cook anything. As I neared home, I passed a young girl walking down the double lane stretch of highway. She was dressed all in black, with dyed pink hair and lots of tattoos, and she was wiping her eyes like she was crying.

I heard the Lord speak to my heart. "Pick her up."

I almost choked. "Say what??"

I kept driving, but felt that persistent tugging at my heart. I turned onto my driveway, but I stopped halfway up the lane and sat there questioning my sanity. "Okay Lord, I need to be sure this is you." My husband and daughter were at the house waiting for their lunch. Should I call and tell them what I was about to do? I've never picked up a stranger in my life. I felt quite sure they would tell me to come straight home, especially if I gave them a description of the stranger.

Nevertheless, sensing nothing now but a spirit of calmness, I turned around and headed back down the road, hoping someone else had already picked her up.

Part of me was thinking, *What am I doing? I have nothing to defend myself with but a sack of lunchmeat...Al is gonna kill me...what if she's far from home and someone has dumped her off and then I'm going to have to take her home with me and then Al and Autumn are both going to kill me.*

But I kept driving as if on auto-pilot, and then I saw her again. Wouldn't you know there was a perfect spot for me to pull over right in front of her.

I rolled down my window and said "Is everything okay? Do you need a ride somewhere? I thought maybe you were crying."

She looked confused. I explained, "I passed you and you were wiping your eyes." She said "Oh, I'm hot and sweaty and I got some mascara in my eyes." I asked again, "Do you need a ride? Where are you going?"

She said, "Well, that would be nice, I'm going to 2nd street." She hopped in the car, and I realized parts of her skin were dyed the same color of pink as her hair.

"I felt like the Lord told me to pick you up," I told her. She smiled, looking up towards the sky, and said, "Thank you, Lord."

Then she explained that she was walking home from church. (At this point, I am the one thanking the Lord in my head). She said she was so hot and her feet were blistered from her dress shoes and it was about an hour's walk home. I said "Well, sweetie, the Lord is looking out for you today, because I've never picked up a stranger in my life." *Let alone a pink-tattooed one,* I was thinking silently to myself.

She smiled and said, "I'll be walking back to church tonight too." We chatted a bit as I drove her home, and she thanked me again as she got out of the car.

I headed home, marveling at the Lord once again, and humbled that a young girl would walk an hour each way twice on Sundays to go to church....

Thank you, Lord, for determined faith, sometimes found in unexpected places. I pray I can heed your voice and be a help to those you bring across my path. In Jesus's name, amen.

Hebrews 4:7

Again he appoints a certain day, "Today," saying through David so long afterward, in the words already quoted, "Today, if you hear his voice, do not harden your hearts." (ESV)

Proverbs 3:5-6

Trust in the LORD with all your heart, and do not lean on your own understanding. In all your ways acknowledge him, and he will make straight your paths. (ESV)

James 1:22

But be doers of the word, and not hearers only, deceiving yourselves. (ESV)

Reflection Time

How has God been speaking to you today? Take time to write it in your journal.

Chapter 18
Great is Thy Faithfulness

I settle down in my quiet place this morning and prepare to bring my prayer list before the Lord. In the midst of all the pain and chaos in the world, there's a cozy little fire going inside, and the sun is streaming through the windows and sparkling on the frosty leaves outside. My worship music is playing softly in the background.

Suddenly, the list is not the first thing on my mind. I marvel at the breathtaking beauty of God's creation and feel the need to focus on the goodness of the Lord. Sometimes I just need to quiet myself and focus on his creation, because it is an example of his steadfastness, no matter what is going on around us. The sun comes up, the rains come down, the breezes blow—just like they did in the Garden, just like they do through all our joys and all our sorrows, just like they did when God sent his Son to Earth as a tiny baby, and just like they did when he breathed his last breath on the cross to set us free.

Father God, help me to abandon my list and my agenda sometimes. Let the cares and worries of this life fade for a little while so I can focus on your goodness and worship you for who you are...for you are good. In Jesus's name, amen.

-»»» ❊ «««-

Romans 1:20

Ever since the creation of the world his eternal power and divine nature, invisible though they are, have been understood and seen through the things he has made. So they are without excuse. (New Revised Standard Version)

Psalm 62:8

Trust in him at all times, you people; pour out your hearts to him, for God is our refuge.

Psalm 91:4

He will cover you with his feathers, and under his wings you will find refuge; his faithfulness will be your shield and rampart.

Lamentations 3:22-23

The steadfast love of the LORD never ceases; his mercies never come to an end; they are new every morning; great is your faithfulness. (ESV)

Reflection Time

How has God been speaking to you today? Take time to write it in your journal.

Chapter 19

God's Word

Anyone who knows me, knows that no one anticipates spring more than I do. I cannot wait to dig in the dirt, plant flowers, and work in my vegetable garden. After being cooped up in the house all winter, I am ready to *live* outside.

However, this year has been a little different. Although the winter was long and cold, I did not dread it as much as usual. I spent a lot of time working on Bible study and developed a real hunger for God's word. I looked forward to my time with him each morning, and the time I spent studying seemed to fly.

Now that spring has arrived, my time with God has changed. When I head out to the garden first thing in the morning, I take along my iPad and put on my praise and worship music. I enjoy the warm sun on my face and the breeze that cools my skin as I sing along, working at pulling weeds and tying tomatoes.

In early spring, I talked to God as I planted my seeds and prayed for the people who crossed my mind. When my oldest son took a job and moved to another state, I poured out my heart to God as I planted green beans and watered them with my tears.

I learned recently in my Bible studies, the word that was used for Adam tending the Garden of Eden was also the same word used later for the priests tending to their duties in God's temple. So it's no wonder I feel blessed to work in my garden.

Although this early morning time with God in the garden has been so lovely, it has thrown off my Bible study routine. By the time the sun (and my hungry tummy) chase me back in the house, there are many things that need my attention. So Bible study has gotten pushed to the back burner for the last six to eight weeks. At first I missed it, but gradually I got out of the habit that I had established, and I wasn't thinking about it so much anymore.

However, I have begun to notice some changes in myself... emotions and attitudes that had begun to appear in me, such as patience, peace, and joy, are not as prevalent as they were. I'm back to anxious thinking, impatience, and feeling a little down or sorry for myself. My attention has begun to gear more toward my own wants and needs rather than the wants and needs of others.

When the temperatures cooled this evening, I began to get ready to go back out and work in the garden...but then I stopped myself and decided to work on my Bible study instead. Though I had to discipline myself to do that, once I opened the pages, it was like a drink of cold water to a dry, thirsty throat.

Dear Lord, nothing can replace the life-giving power of your Word. Keep me hungry and thirsty for it. Let it draw and beckon me. Let me hear it call above the din of all that clamors for my attention, for *you* are the Word of life. In Jesus's name, amen.

Hebrews 4:12

For the word of God is alive and active. Sharper than any double-edged sword, it penetrates even to divid-

ing soul and spirit, joints and marrow; it judges the thoughts and attitudes of the heart.

Psalm 119:89

Your Word, LORD, is eternal; it stands firm in the heavens.

Psalm 119:105

Your Word is a lamp to my feet and a light to my path. (ESV)

Reflection Time

How has God been speaking to you today? Take time to write it in your journal.

Chapter 20
Shelter in the Storm

I rescued a tiny kitten on the side of the road one dark night years ago. Although he has been safe with me all this time, he has never lost his fear. He trusts no one and runs at the slightest hint of danger. Our back porch is enclosed by railing, and Al even installed a gate at the top of the steps, so he is safe from the dogs. Yet, when something frightens him, he flees this place of refuge instead of staying safely in the harbor that has been provided for him. He leaves the provision because his fear overcomes his trust. It frustrates me and saddens my heart, because I want to protect him.

I know in my heart that I have been just like that cat many times. Although God has proven himself faithful to me over and over again, sometimes I panic and run when I see trouble. I don't literally run like my Cocoa kitty does; rather, my mind runs away with anxious thoughts and worry. I leave my place of protection and the shelter that God offers.

God reminded me of this as I sat down for my quiet time with him this morning. I have been concerned for days about something a loved one is going through. I have continually lifted them up in prayer, and God has provided above and beyond what I asked of him.

So, as I sit in my quiet place, I am reflecting on the faithfulness of God—on the things he has brought me through and the things he carries me in the midst of. Although I prefer that he calm the storms of life, he doesn't always work that way. Sometimes the storm just continues to rage, and through it, I realize that my boat is secure. If I keep my focus on him, I am safe.

Father God, forgive me when my first response to a bad situation is fear. Help me to focus on your faithfulness, and remind me of the times you have worked all things for good. I am thankful for your provision and compassion for the things that concern me and for those I love. Help me to keep my hand in yours instead of running to something else for my security. In Jesus's name, amen.

-⟩⟩⟩⟩ ❊ ⟨⟨⟨⟨-

Isaiah 26:3

You will keep in perfect peace those whose minds are steadfast, because they trust in you.

Hebrews 10:23

Let us hold fast the confession of our hope without wavering, for he who promised is faithful. (ESV)

Psalm 91:1-2

Whoever dwells in the shelter of the Most High will rest in the shadow of the Almighty. I will say of the LORD, "He is my refuge and my fortress, my God, in whom I trust."

-⟩⟩⟩⟩ ❊ ⟨⟨⟨⟨-

Sherolyn Porter

Reflection Time

How has God been speaking to you today? Take time to write it in your journal.

Chapter 21
Words

Words. Sometimes I struggle with finding the right ones to express what's in my heart. At times I'm just too tired, or maybe I'm overwhelmed with emotion.

It's such a relief to know that God doesn't need my words. He knows each thought I have and the accompanying emotion—whether it be joy or sadness, fear or praise.

I can pour out my soul to him and he hears…even when I am too overwhelmed to speak.

Sometimes when I am in prayer, all I can do is bring names and faces before him, unable to utter a word. I know that he is intimately aware of the person I'm praying for and ultimately more acquainted with the need than I am. Even my closest and most fulfilling relationships here on Earth cannot measure up to that.

He can speak to me without words sometimes too—through his beautiful creation.

His "I love you" is in the sunrise and sunset, the fluffy white clouds, the warm sun and cool breeze, in the majestic mountains and rushing rivers.

He speaks not only through his words in the Bible but also through the encouraging words of loved ones or the gentle touch of a hand.

Dear God, make me aware of your presence each moment of the day. You created me for relationship with you, and I cannot be truly fulfilled without it. In Jesus's name, amen.

Psalm 8:3-4

When I look at your heavens, the work of your fingers, the moon and the stars, which you have set in place, what is man that you are mindful of him, the son of man that you care for him? (ESV)

Reflection Time

How has God been speaking to you today? Take time to write it in your journal.

Chapter 22
The Omnipresence of God

The Lord woke me before dawn to pray this morning. I have to admit his first attempt was not very successful. My bed was comfortable, the covers luxuriously soft and warm….

I thought, "I can pray just as well in bed." So he used one of my furry friends, who is not usually up until 8:00, to rouse me. I left the warmth of my cozy bed and headed downstairs to let the dogs out before heading to the sanctuary of my sunroom, where I lit the fire to chase away the winter chill of this old house. It was so dark, I could barely discern the silhouettes of the pine trees right outside the windows, but I knew they were there. I sat down in the chair with a warm blanket and drew my knees up under me. I gazed out the window to a distant hillside, watching as sparsely scattered lights among the trees spoke of a world beginning to wake up.

A familiar tone sounded from my iPad. It signaled a message from a friend whose father is in the hospital and taking a turn for the worse. I began to pray for her and her family, and then other people began to come to mind: my husband who is on a plane headed home across the ocean…my son who is going through a rough time and is far away from home…friends who are battling illnesses and financial difficulties. Like those pine trees outside my window, barely visible in the darkness, sometimes God is difficult to see during the hard times, but he is there nevertheless. It comforts me to know that this same God, who awakens me before dawn to pray and meets with me in my little sanctuary, is on that plane with my husband. He is in a faraway city with my hurting son and in that hospital room with my friend and her family as her father fights for his life. Whether or not we see evidence with our earthly eyes, God is there. We don't have to ask him to be with us—His Word says that he is always with us. Maybe instead, our prayer should be, "Lord, make me aware of your presence."

Father, I thank you that you are not only hearing each need I bring before you, but you are already intimately aware of it and are right there with the person I am praying for. Help us all to be aware of your presence and rest in your shadow. In Jesus's name, amen.

Psalm 139:1-18
*You have searched me, L*ORD*,*
and you know me.
You know when I sit and when I rise;
you perceive my thoughts from afar.
You discern my going out and my lying down;
you are familiar with all my ways.
Before a word is on my tongue
*you, L*ORD*, know it completely.*
You hem me in behind and before,
and you lay your hand upon me.
Such knowledge is too wonderful for me,
too lofty for me to attain.
Where can I go from your Spirit?

Reflections From the Sunroom

Where can I flee from your presence?
If I go up to the heavens, you are there;
if I make my bed in the depths, you are there.
If I rise on the wings of the dawn,
if I settle on the far side of the sea,
even there your hand will guide me,
your right hand will hold me fast.
If I say, "Surely the darkness will hide me
and the light become night around me,"
even the darkness will not be dark to you;
the night will shine like the day,
for darkness is as light to you.
For you created my inmost being;
You knit me together in my mother's womb.
I praise you because I am fearfully and wonderfully made;
your works are wonderful,
I know that full well.
My frame was not hidden from you
when I was made in the secret place,
when I was woven together in the depths of the earth.
Your eyes saw my unformed body;
all the days ordained for me were written in your book
before one of them came to be.
How precious to me are your thoughts, God!
How vast is the sum of them!
Were I to count them,
they would outnumber the grains of sand—
when I awake, I am still with you.

-»»» ❊ ««-

Sherolyn Porter

Reflection Time

How has God been speaking to you today? Take time to write it in your journal.

Chapter 23
Light

In the early morning hours when I go to the sunroom to spend time with the Lord, the sun has usually not yet broken over the hilltop. There are times that, once it's made ascent and comes through my windows with blinding brilliance, I am annoyed.

The light hurts my eyes...my windows look dirty...I can see that the floor needs swept and the furniture needs dusted.

But quite often, I turn my chair to face the sun and close my eyes, letting the light and warmth just fill my being. I imagine what it will be like when I leave this world and go to heaven. People who have had near-death experiences always talk about the bright white light that they encounter.

Perfect bright light like that chases away darkness, and its brilliance is twofold: it reveals every flaw, but it also warms and heals and gives life. Without that light, the plants in my sunroom would die... and I might overlook some things that need attention.

There are so many verses in the Bible that refer to light. The Bible says that, in heaven, there is no need for the sun because Jesus is the light.

Heavenly Father, help me never to turn away from the light or be annoyed by its illumination of any darkness in me. Help me to embrace it and allow it to lead me to you. In Jesus's name, amen.

Ecclesiastes 11:7

Truly the light is sweet, and a pleasant thing it is for the eyes to behold the sun. (KJV)

Psalm 43:3

O send out thy light and thy truth: let them lead me; let them bring me unto thy holy hill, and to thy tabernacles. (KJV)

Psalm 90:8

Thou hast set our iniquities before Thee, our secret sins in the light of thy countenance. (KJV)

1 John 2:9-10

Anyone who claims to be in the light but hates a brother or sister is still in the darkness. Anyone who loves their brother and sister lives in the light, and there is nothing in them to make them stumble.

Rev 21:23

And the city had no need of the sun, neither of the moon, to shine in it; for the Glory of God did lighten it, and the Lamb is the light thereof. (KJV)

Reflections From the Sunroom

Reflection Time

How has God been speaking to you today? Take time to write it in your journal.

Chapter 24

Prayer of Thanksgiving

What a beautiful Sunday morning it is. As I pick manna from the garden, the trees are swaying in the cool morning breeze, their arms outstretched to the heavens as if dancing to the chorus of nearby birds praising their creator. I am so thankful for my five senses this morning.

Father, I thank you for your provision: for my eyes, to behold the beauty of your creation; for the strength you give me; and for blessing the works of my hands. Thank you for the gift of hearing, so I may enjoy the sweet sounds of nature all around me. Thank you for the sense of touch, that I am able to feel the warm sun on my face and the cool breeze on my skin. Your works are wonderful. I know that full well. I thank you for your creation…the beauty of it amazes, calms, and humbles me.

I cannot even imagine the beauty of heaven…but I thank you for the gift of this Earth.

I marvel like a small child at the majesty of it—the trees that provide homes for your creatures and sheltering shade on a hot summer day, the wind that feels like your caress on my face, the sun that brightens my soul on cold winter days, and the beautiful blue sky with its fluffy white clouds. I exhilarate at the sound of the peepers in the spring when I feel I can't take one more day of winter. I love the tranquil sound of the crickets in summer as they lull me to sleep. The sweet song of the birds are a melody more precious to me than any other. I am enchanted by the way the flowers come up slowly in the spring, with small delicate buds appearing first, as I wait in delightful anticipation for the opening of their gift of fragrant blooms. I enjoy your thunderstorms, the soft sound of the rain, your rivers that turn that indescribable color at dusk, and the beautiful moon and stars at night. I love your laws of springtime and harvest— the perfect order that holds the planets in place.…God, you are awesome. The most amazing thing of all is that you—the Creator of a universe that simply abounds with intricate and masterful design— know every thought I have and every hurt in my heart. I can speak to you without voice, and you address the smallest concerns I bring to you. Thank you, Lord, for your many gifts. I am grateful…I am humbled…I am amazed. In Jesus's name, amen.

Psalm 19:1-2

The heavens declare the glory of God; the skies proclaim the work of his hands. Day after day they pour forth speech; night after night they reveal knowledge.

Psalm 111:2

Great are the works of the LORD; they are pondered by all who delight in them.

Psalm 105:1-3

Give praise to the LORD, proclaim his name; make known among the nations what he has done. Sing to him, sing praise to him; tell of all his wonderful acts. Glory in his holy name; let the hearts of those who seek the LORD rejoice.

Job 12:7-10

But ask the animals, and they will teach you, or the birds in the sky, and they will tell you; or speak to the earth, and it will teach you, or let the fish of the sea inform you. Which of all these does not know that the hand of the LORD has done this? In his hand is the life of every creature and the breath of all mankind.

Romans 1:20

Ever since the creation of the world his eternal power and divine nature, invisible though they are, have been understood and seen through the things he has made. So they are without excuse. (NRSV)

Reflection Time

How has God been speaking to you today? Take time to write it in your journal.

Chapter 25
Missing Winter

I can't believe I'm saying this…but I miss winter. My friends will be reading and rereading this in disbelief—a statement from the gal who is unofficially in charge of the Facebook countdown to spring, which I start about mid-January every year. By then, the never-ending grays and browns of earth and sky have my soul screaming for life and warmth and *color!*

Once spring arrives, I am outside at the crack of dawn, digging, planting, and planning my vegetable and flower gardens. When I stand before freshly turned earth with packets of seeds in my hands, I think I must feel the same sense of excited anticipation that a painter feels when he sees a blank canvas and a fresh palette of paints. So why in the world am I missing winter?

This past winter I spent early mornings in the sunroom, working on my Bible study and spending quiet time with the Lord. Those times became precious to me. I felt a friendship growing, replacing what had previously been a mostly academic experience. Most days this spring and summer, I still made it out to my sunroom for study and quiet time, but usually not until afternoon or evening. By that time, life had ample opportunity to intrude on my thoughts and attitudes. There is something about that early morning time with the Lord that has the equivalency of a "reboot," so to speak. My life seems to go more smoothly when I have spent the "first-fruits" of my day with him—praying for friends and loved ones, asking for wisdom and for love for others, for strength to do my tasks.

Lord, help me realize that even worthy distractions are not as important as starting my day with you. In Jesus's name, amen.

Psalm 5:3

In the morning, Lord, you hear my voice; in the morning I lay my requests before you and wait expectantly.

Lamentations 3:22-26

Because of the Lord's great love we are not consumed, for his compassions never fail. They are new every morning; great is your faithfulness. I say to myself, "The Lord is my portion; therefore I will wait for him." The Lord is good to those whose hope is in him, to the one who seeks him; it is good to wait quietly for the salvation of the Lord.

Reflection Time

How has God been speaking to you today? Take time to write it in your journal.

Chapter 26

Effective Prayer

My quiet time with the Lord today has been anything but quiet. I have been in a battle with myself this morning, and peace has eluded me. Many times I bring my prayer list before him, and my tears fall down as the requests go up. But some mornings, like this one, I have a very hard time remaining focused as I begin to pray. When I first began this routine of morning quiet time, I blamed a lack of focus on my easily distracted mind, but now I know better.

I have come to realize that when my prayers seem to go no higher than the ceiling and I am not able to focus, it may be that something in my life needs addressed. God has not turned his attention elsewhere…I have turned *my* focus elsewhere. During those times, if I ask God to search my heart, he gently shows me where I have veered off the path. Sometimes it's because I have engaged in or listened to conversation that is not edifying, or I have watched something on TV that is not godly. If you watch TV at all, then you know finding anything godly to watch is hard to do.

I'm not trying to put a bunch of rules and regulations on myself, but I have committed myself to this time of prayer, and I want it to count for something. I want my prayers to make a difference.

I don't just want to put a check in the prayer box of my spiritual life. The Word says that the effectual fervent prayers of a righteous man avail much. I know he hears me when I pray, but I want my prayers to avail much. The Word also says that he desires obedience more than sacrifice, so my sacrificial time of leaving my warm bed in the hours before dawn is not as pleasing to God as my obedience is. I believe that this morning's struggle is because of something I watched on TV last night—a series my husband Al and I have been watching for a while, and there are only a few episodes left. Although there is nothing wrong with the drama of the main storyline, there are a lot of ungodly things going on with the characters right now. I want to finish watching the series…and that is my struggle. God does not love me less because I want to watch the show. But I found that *I woke up thinking about that show this morning.*

I would rather the meditations of my heart be pleasing to God. I want my prayers to avail much.

God, help me when I struggle with following your ways. I know that your way is best. Strengthen me and help me to be obedient to your voice. In Jesus's name, amen.

-»»» ❋ ««-

James 5:16
Therefore confess your sins to each other and pray for each other so that you may be healed. The prayer of a righteous person is powerful and effective.

Philippians 4:8
Finally, brothers and sisters, whatever is true, whatever is noble, whatever is right, whatever is pure, whatever

is lovely, whatever is admirable—if anything is excellent or praiseworthy—think about such things.

Psalm 19:7-14

The law of the LORD is perfect,
refreshing the soul.
The statutes of the LORD are trustworthy,
making wise the simple.
The precepts of the LORD are right,
giving joy to the heart.
The commands of the LORD are radiant,
giving light to the eyes.
The fear of the LORD is pure,
enduring forever.
The decrees of the LORD are firm,
and all of them are righteous.
They are more precious than gold,
than much pure gold;
they are sweeter than honey,
than honey from the honeycomb.
By them your servant is warned;
in keeping them there is great reward.
But who can discern their own errors?
Forgive my hidden faults.
Keep your servant also from willful sins;
may they not rule over me.
Then I will be blameless,
innocent of great transgression.
May these words of my mouth
and this meditation of my heart

be pleasing in your sight,
*L*ORD, *my Rock and my Redeemer.*

->>>> ✳ <<<-

Reflection Time

How has God been speaking to you today? Take time to write it in your journal.

Chapter 27
Behold I Make All Things New

Yesterday on the way home from town, I saw where two animals had been hit and killed on the road, and I felt the familiar sadness grip my heart like it always does when I see something like that.

My daughter Autumn and I are animal lovers. We love our dogs, horses, cats, and even our chickens. We have bottle-fed baby goats and a tiny little kitten my son found in a dumpster at work one summer. We have taken in strays until my husband is ready to throw his hands up in the air. We worry about all the animals in our lives and try our best to give them a good and loving home.

I can't stand to see pictures of animals that have been abused; it gives me actual physical pain in my body. Autumn and I have tried to go to the shelter to volunteer, but we leave in tears because we want to bring them all home.

I can feel the pleading in their eyes when I return them to their cages and turn to walk away from them.

As I thought about my love for animals after seeing the sad scene on the road, I began to think about God creating animals.

First, he spoke into existence the heavens and the earth, with all their magnificent beauty—the expanse of the heavens, stretching farther than even our imaginations can take us…the beauty of the earth and all the provision in it to sustain life.

Then he spoke into existence animal life on earth: the birds of the air, the fish of the sea, the animals (like the ones we love so dearly), and many, many more—all of it a gift for the last of his creation…us.

He gave the animals every herb-bearing seed for meat (translated food). So there was no hunter and no prey.

And then he created man…from the dust of the earth. He didn't speak man into being like the rest of creation. He formed him with his own hands…molded the form of man like a potter molds the clay. Then, bending over that lifeless form made of clay, the Creator of the universe breathed the breath of life into man's nostrils. The hands of God formed him, and the very breath of God infused life into the body he had created. Then he placed his most prized creation into a magnificent garden, planted just for him. This garden was full of beauty, peace and harmony. He brought all the animals to the man and let him name them. What fun they must have had doing that. When a perfect helpmate for Adam was not found among the animals, God created a woman from the rib of Adam.

I imagine Adam and Eve enjoying the companionship of the animals God created—just like we do…sitting in the lush green grass, stroking the beloved pet by their side, watching the antics of the other animals in the garden.

And then I thought about how Adam and Eve were deceived by the serpent into thinking they were missing something—that God had withheld something good from them—so they disobeyed and ate the only fruit that God had told them not to eat.

When that happened, they realized they were naked and they were afraid. They tried to make a covering for themselves from fig leaves, but it didn't feel like enough…and they hid from God.

So God made them a covering from animal skins to cover their shame. How they all must have grieved the sacrifice of a beloved animal...the shedding of innocent blood.

And so it began: countless sacrifices for sin, until God made one final sacrifice—the blood of an innocent, even more precious than the blood of his beloved animal creation...the blood of his Son to cover "once for all."

Father God, I am sorry that mankind has grieved your heart. I long for the day when all will be restored as it once was, with no more death and no more sadness. Thank you for the priceless gift of your Son which makes that possible. I love you. In Jesus's name, amen.

-»»»- ❈ -«««-

Genesis 1:24-25

And God said, "Let the land produce living creatures according to their kinds: the livestock, the creatures that move along the ground, and the wild animals, each according to its kind." And it was so. God made the wild animals according to their kinds, the livestock according to their kinds, and all the creatures that move along the ground according to their kinds. And God saw that it was good.

Genesis 3:21-23

The LORD God made garments of skin for Adam and his wife and clothed them. And the LORD God said, "The man has now become like one of us, knowing good and evil. He must not be allowed to reach out his hand and take also from the tree of life and eat, and live forever." So the LORD God banished him from the Garden of Eden to work the ground from which he had been taken.

Revelation 21:4-6

"He will wipe away every tear from their eyes, and there will be no more death or mourning or crying or pain, for the former things have passed away." And the One seated on the throne said, "Behold, I make all things new." Then He said, "Write this down, for these words are faithful and true." And He told me, "It is done! I am the Alpha and the Omega, the Beginning and the End. To the thirsty I will give freely from the spring of the water of life." (Berean Study Bible)

Reflection Time

How has God been speaking to you today? Take time to write it in your journal.

Chapter 28
Not My Will

I have been praying about a certain situation for a while. However, God has not allowed me to pray for the outcome that I desire. He has led me instead to pray for his perfect will in this situation. Yesterday, it looked like the prayer was going to be answered the way I wanted. The funny thing was, the thought of receiving the answer I had desired did not bring me peace and joy. Something just didn't feel right about it.

Then, at the last minute, the prayer was answered in the way I had not wanted, yet it brought me peace...a sense that God's will would be accomplished in this situation. This morning I woke up a little sad that what I had desired did not work out. I came downstairs to spend some quiet time with the Lord and after a while, I felt peace and confidence about leaving the situation in his hands.

So I'm waiting to see what God has in store...waiting to see how his perfect will shall play out in this situation. My heart's desire may be accomplished in a totally different way than I think it should. God sees it all: past, present, and future. The desires of my heart are safe with him.

Lord, help me to rest in you when I can't see the big picture. Help me to trust you with all that concerns me, and to put my focus on you instead of on my worries. Thank you for hearing and answering prayers and for loving me. In Jesus's name, amen.

2 Timothy 1:12

That is why I am suffering as I am. Yet this is no cause for shame, because I know whom I have believed, and am convinced that he is able to guard what I have entrusted to him until that day.

Romans 8:28

And we know that in all things God works for the good of those who love him, who have been called according to his purpose.

Reflection Time

How has God been speaking to you today? Take time to write it in your journal.

Chapter 29

Insurance

Most adults have insurance policies. In fact, many of us have quite a few of them. We have insurance on our homes (and you have to add additional policies to fully cover your home), flood insurance, earthquake insurance, etc. Some people have mortgage insurance, and the bank requires we have title insurance. We have insurance on our cars and boats and campers, insurance for our health, insurance for long or short term disabilities, life insurance…and some of us even have health insurance for our pets.

Does that mean we are paranoid? Most would agree that it just makes good sense to cover ourselves with protection in case of disasters that may or may not occur without warning.

I've lived long enough to watch friends go through emotional agony when disaster struck their families. I realized that some of them had insurance for emotional strength, and they seemed to fare better than the ones who didn't. What kind of insurance is there for fortitude and support during times of turbulent, emotional upheaval in life?

It is really hard to look for an insurance policy when your world has turned upside down. It's much better to have one already in place.

My friends who fared the best during emotional upheaval in their lives were the ones who were firmly grounded in a relationship with God and spent time in his Word.

So a few years ago, I determined to invest in that kind of policy—one that would automatically come to mind when I needed it—so I began storing up God's word in my heart by daily reading and listening to Scripture and studying the Bible. It's not because I am a devout person; it's because I know my many weaknesses.

There's another insurance policy that is just as important, and it's one that we are all going to need.

Regardless of how wealthy or healthy we are, the one thing that will happen to all of us eventually is death, and after that, eternity… somewhere.

Do we have insurance for our souls? We can—and not only is it free, but having that insurance (or *assurance*) is honestly the only way to experience life to its fullest.

Giving your life to God is the only way to keep it.

I plan to continue to contribute to my spiritual insurance policy this year by storing up and absorbing God's Word in my mind and heart. I know it will give me strength for whatever comes my way. And as for my soul insurance; I already have that policy in place. Thank you, Jesus!

Lord, I thank you that you have an insurance policy better than money can buy, and yet it is free for everyone. I thank you for the gift of your Son and your Word, for they are one and the same. Keep me ever mindful of that. In Jesus's name, amen.

Reflections From the Sunroom

John 3:16
For God so loved the world that he gave his one and only
Son, that whoever believes in him shall not perish but
have eternal life.

Psalm 119:10-11
I seek you with all my heart;
do not let me stray from your commands.
I have hidden your word in my heart
that I might not sin against you.

-»»» ❊ «««-

Reflection Time

How has God been speaking to you today? Take
time to write it in your journal.

Chapter 30
New Year

It is twenty-two degrees and breezy on this frigid New Year's morning. I was glad to get back to my cozy fire after my trek outside to feed the chickens. I woke up thinking about what the new year might bring and praying for my friends and family. Having passed middle age, I tend to view the new year with a different perspective than I did when I was younger. It's not just that everyone I know is growing older; it's that the world is such a different place than it was twenty-five years ago. Things in the world that I used to rely on and have faith in are on shaky ground these days. Even though the financial markets seem solid at the moment, I know from experience that they can collapse overnight. Even though our government is one of the best in the world, many have lost faith in the people that are in authority, regardless of political party affiliation. The stability of the family has changed, and many homes are dysfunctional and broken. Drug use is rampant, and the suicide rate has steadily increased, especially among the young.

Lest I sound like doom and gloom, I know there is good news in the midst of this…there is still one thing that remains unshakable—and is alive and well for this new year.

No matter what goes on with this world in the coming year with government or finances, the Lord is ultimately in control. I'm thankful I know that, and I pray that I can hold fast to it in the midst of any storm this year might bring. I also pray that all those I know and love can come to that revelation and that it won't take a storm to help them realize that the anchor holds. It is steadfast and secure.

Lord help me to put you first this year. Reveal yourself to this hurting world through those you call your own. In Jesus's name, amen.

Deuteronomy 30:20a

And that you may love the LORD your God, listen to his voice, and hold fast to him. For the LORD is your life.

Isaiah 44:6-8

This is what the LORD says—Israel's King and Redeemer, the LORD Almighty: I am the first and I am the last; apart from me there is no God. Who then is like me? Let him proclaim it. Let him declare and lay out before me what has happened since I established my ancient people, and what is yet to come—yes, let them foretell what will come. Do not tremble, do not be afraid. Did I not proclaim this and foretell it long ago? You are my witnesses. Is there any God besides me? No, there is no other Rock; I know not one.

Reflection Time

How has God been speaking to you today? Take time to write it in your journal.

Chapter 31
The Hope of Spring

I didn't sleep well at all last night and woke up with a monster headache on this bitterly cold Monday morning. Today was the first day back to work for my husband after the Christmas holidays. The thought of the long winter, seemed to loom unendingly ahead. I decided to look through my flowery spring photos and pick a beautiful picture to start the spring countdown. As I searched through my collection of flowers and butterfly pictures, my mood began to lift. It surely doesn't seem possible in the throes of winter to imagine this sort of beauty and life will ever appear again...but there was the proof, right in front of my eyes.

It's much like an exercise in faith, this countdown to spring. Sometimes our lives seem cold, dark, and dreary. At these times, we might get tempted to think it will be this way forever. But with God as our refuge and strength, our troubles are only temporary. He can give us peace that passes understanding, joy that is unspeakable, and someday—for those who are in Christ—heaven.

One day, when we leave this earth, we will go to a place of eternal springtime, a place with no more sorrow or sickness, no more pain or suffering, no more tears, no more worry. There won't even be need of the sun, because the presence of Jesus will shine that brightly.

Father, help us in the wintry days of our lives to remember that you died to give us life abundantly. When we have trials, help us to remember that they are just for a season, and give us faith that spring will come again. In Jesus's name, amen.

John 10:10

The thief comes only to steal and kill and destroy; I have come that they may have life, and have it to the full.

John 15:9-11

I have loved you even as the Father has loved me. Remain in my love. When you obey my commandments, you remain in my love, just as I obey my Father's commandments and remain in his love. I have told you these things so that you will be filled with my joy. Yes, your joy will overflow! (NLT)

Revelation 22:1-5

Then the angel showed me the river of the water of life, as clear as crystal, flowing from the throne of God and of the Lamb down the middle of the great street of the city. On each side of the river stood the tree of life, bearing twelve crops of fruit, yielding its fruit every month. And the leaves of the tree are for the healing of the nations. No longer will there be any curse. The throne of God and of the Lamb will be in the city, and his servants will serve him. They will see his face, and his name will be on their foreheads. There will be no more night. They will not need the light of a lamp or the light of the sun, for the Lord God will give them light. And they will reign for ever and ever.

Reflection Time

How has God been speaking to you today? Take time to write it in your journal.

Chapter 32
The Veil Was Torn

My favorite passage in Scripture is one that I usually hear talked about during Easter. The Scripture is from the book of Matthew, and it talks about when Jesus died on the cross.

"And when Jesus had cried out again in a loud voice, he gave up his spirit. At that moment the curtain of the temple was torn in two from top to bottom." (Matthew 27:50-51a, NIV)

The curtain was torn from top to bottom.... Those words just do something to me every time I hear them. It's like a hushed sense of awe falls on my heart.

Until that time, the people of God depended on the high priest to go to God for them...to go behind the curtain into the Holy of Holies in the temple. No one but the high priest was allowed behind that curtain; it was a separation of God from the people, and there was a strict purification process, including multiple sacrifices of animals, to atone for the sins of the high priest before he could safely enter that part of the temple.

Through Jesus's death—through the blood that he spilled—that separation was done away with *forever!!* Jesus...Emmanuel...God *with* us....

As if that isn't enough to shout about, before he returned to heaven, he said that he needed to go so that the Comforter—the Holy Spirit—could come…and he would be *in* us.

And the benefits of having his Spirit inside is the fruit of the Spirit: love, joy, peace, patience, kindness, goodness, faithfulness, gentleness, and self-control.

Now who couldn't use some more of that?

My new study is on the Holy Spirit. I cannot wait to delve into it!

Thank you for giving your life for me, Jesus. I don't want one drop of your precious blood to be wasted. I want to experience *everything* you died to give me. Teach me. The more I learn of you, the more I want to know. You amaze me every day. Amen.

Matthew 27:50-51a

And when Jesus had cried out again in a loud voice, he gave up his spirit. At that moment the curtain of the temple was torn in two from top to bottom.

John 14:15-17

If you love me, keep my commands. And I will ask the Father, and he will give you another advocate to help you and be with you forever— the Spirit of truth. The world cannot accept him, because it neither sees him nor knows him. But you know him, for he lives with you and will be in you.

Galatians 5:22-23

But the fruit of the Spirit is love, joy, peace, forbearance, kindness, goodness, faithfulness, gentleness, and self-control. Against such things there is no law.

-»»» ※ «««-

Reflection Time

How has God been speaking to you today? Take time to write it in your journal.

Chapter 33

Prayer Soldier

My husband and I began watching an old TV series last night. It was about the women who worked in the factories making bombs during World War Two. Although they weren't in the same kind of situation that the soldiers on the front lines were experiencing, their job was dangerous, and it was a large contribution to the war effort. They were considered by many to be soldiers also.

The Lord spoke to my heart this morning about soldiers and battle.

We all serve in different capacities according to our abilities and gifts. Some are called to faraway mission fields, some are called to teach or to encourage others, some are called to spend much time in prayer...the possibilities are endless.

I sit in a cozy chair by the fire, wrapped in a soft, warm blanket. My worship music plays quietly in the background as I watch a multitude of hungry birds dart back and forth from the trees to the feeders. I am warm and comfortable on this frigid January morning. This description doesn't portray the picture of a soldier on the front lines preparing to go into battle.

However, I came downstairs to *pray*. I *am* going into battle.

God's Word talks about the battle we are in and the weapons that we fight with, and it describes places of shelter and refuge during the battle. It tells us what we must do to prepare ahead of time.

When I pray, I battle for the sick, the downtrodden, and the lost. I battle for broken relationships and broken hearts. I battle for my children and the children of others when I pray for protection from the evils of this world. I battle for souls when I pray that they would come to the saving knowledge of God. When I pray for my brothers and sisters in Christ who are dying for their faith, my prayers arm them with strength and peace. I battle with my own thoughts, worries, attitudes, and temptations. One thing I have learned is that, if I battle in my own strength, I will surely be defeated.

Father God, guide me as I battle in prayer and also in the battles I face daily. Help me to stay in the shadow of your wings and to use your Word as my sword. Keep me ever mindful of your battle instructions. Remind me that my only chance for victory is with you as my commanding officer. In Jesus's name, amen.

→>>> ❄ <<<←

Hebrews 4:12
For the word of God is alive and active. Sharper than any double-edged sword, it penetrates even to dividing soul and spirit, joints and marrow; it judges the thoughts and attitudes of the heart.

Proverbs 18:10
The name of the LORD is a fortified tower; the righteous run to it and are safe.

Ephesians 6:10-18

Finally, be strong in the Lord and in his mighty power.
Put on the full armor of God, so that you can take your
stand against the devil's schemes. For our struggle is not
against flesh and blood, but against the rulers, against
the authorities, against the powers of this dark world
and against the spiritual forces of evil in the heavenly
realms. Therefore put on the full armor of God, so that
when the day of evil comes, you may be able to stand
your ground, and after you have done everything, to
stand. Stand firm then, with the belt of truth buckled
around your waist, with the breastplate of righteousness
in place, and with your feet fitted with the readiness
that comes from the gospel of peace. In addition to all
this, take up the shield of faith, with which you can
extinguish all the flaming arrows of the evil one. Take
the helmet of salvation and the sword of the Spirit,
which is the word of God. And pray in the Spirit on all
occasions with all kinds of prayers and requests. With
this in mind, be alert and always keep on praying for all
the Lord's people.

Reflection Time

How has God been speaking to you today? Take
time to write it in your journal.

Chapter 34

Meditation in Moonlight

It was the early hours before dawn as I made my way to the sunroom for some quiet time with the Lord. As I entered, I was totally mesmerized by the breathtaking sight of the full moon. I watched it sink slowly in the western sky, its light peeking through the branches of the pine trees, magical in its beauty...and the starkness of winter was softened by its glow.

The wonderful thing about the moon is that you can stare at it. I have to close my eyes when I turn my face to the sun because its brilliance is blinding.

Although I love the silvery glow of moonlight, I know it has no true light of its own. The light it gives can only come from the reflection of the sun upon it. If I need to see the things around me clearly, its light is not enough...and life on earth needs the sun to flourish.

Sometimes our glimpses of God here on this earth are like looking at the moon instead of the sun. We listen to the "feel good" sermons that speak of God's love for us and each other. They make us feel warm and fuzzy, but when the sermon is finished and we go our way, that's all we have of God for the week. We love the glimpse of light that we had, but it's not making a discernible difference in our lives. Our Bibles gather dust on the shelves, and there are seven more days until we get our dose of God again. We leave the church parking lot as if walking in the moonlight: it is beautiful, but dim and far away.

The Word of God is like the sun: it possesses a warming, life-giving light, but its brilliance shows things clearly, shows us things that are hidden…and things that need to be cleaned up. With daily exposure to it, we can grow.

God, help me not to settle for moonlight. Help me to stay daily in the life-giving light of your Word, and use it to make me grow into exactly what you created me to be. In Jesus's name, amen.

→⟩⟩⟩⟩ ❋ ⟨⟨⟨⟨←

John 1:1-2

In the beginning was the Word, and the Word was with God, and the Word was God. He was with God in the beginning.

John 17:17

Sanctify them by the truth; your word is truth.

John 6:63

The Spirit gives life; the flesh counts for nothing. The words I have spoken to you—they are full of the Spirit and life.

Matthew 4:4

Jesus answered, "It is written: 'Man shall not live on bread alone, but on every word that comes from the mouth of God.'"

Reflections From the Sunroom

Isaiah 55:11
So is my word that goes out from my mouth: It will not return to me empty, but will accomplish what I desire and achieve the purpose for which I sent it.

Isaiah 40:8
The grass withers and the flowers fall, but the word of our God endures forever.

Jeremiah 23:29
"Is not my word like fire," declares the LORD, "and like a hammer that breaks a rock in pieces?"

Psalm 119:105
Your word is a lamp for my feet, a light on my path.

→→→→ ❋ ←←←←

Reflection Time

How has God been speaking to you today? Take time to write it in your journal.

Chapter 35
A Worthy Comparison

I opened the door to let Bailey dog out this morning and was surprised at how much warmer it felt than yesterday. Snow still covered the ground and the wind was still howling, so I went to look at the outside thermometer. When I saw it registered twenty-six degrees, I chuckled to myself. It is funny how twenty-six degrees with howling winds can be considered even remotely warm. It all depends on perspective and comparison, I guess. Compared to yesterday's subzero temps and howling winds, twenty-six is much warmer, but contrasted with temperatures of nearly sixty degrees just a few weeks ago…not so much.

As I headed to the sunroom for my quiet time, the Lord began to speak to my heart about perspective and comparison…and how it applies to my life and my Christian walk. I measure myself by what I compare myself to, and that gives me perspective on where I currently stand. If I compare myself to the depravity of this world… and use *it* as my measuring stick, I can look pretty good.

We work hard, take care of our families, believe in God, pray when we can, and try to do the right things. God's Word says that we are supposed to measure ourselves, not according to the standards of the world, but according to Jesus. He is the one we are supposed to look to as our comparison point. He became a man and was tempted in every way we are. He had a thriving ministry and was a very busy person.

He had family problems...friendship problems...problems with being misunderstood. And yet He—the Son of God—took time to be alone with God and pray.

Comparing ourselves to Jesus? That's a tough mark. But if we would compare ourselves to him instead of the world...we would no longer be tempted to "coast." God wants to make us into the likeness of his Son, and there is no way we can strive for that without his strength and power working in us, to accomplish that purpose. It is not about our works, "lest any man should boast," but about the condition of our hearts.

Some people overlook what the Bible calls sin, because it is socially acceptable. But if we allow God to make us into the likeness of his Son—through spending time with him and reading his Word—we will begin to see things from his perspective instead of the world's perspective.

We will see that the only way to "measure up" is to be in him. When the world looks at us and sees Jesus...that's the comparison we want to attain.

Dear God, help me when I am tempted to compare myself to this world and settle for "that's good enough." Help me to remember that it's not about what I do...because works are not what you desire...but about the condition of my heart.

Fill my heart with your Son, that he would overflow from me and be the only one I compare myself to. Empower me to live a holy life, because you said, "Be holy as I am holy." Your Word says that your grace is sufficient and your strength is made perfect in weakness. I confess my weakness and ask for your strength. In Jesus's name, amen.

→»»» ✳ «««←

Psalm 139:23-24

Search me, God, and know my heart;
test me and know my anxious thoughts.
See if there is any offensive way in me,
and lead me in the way everlasting.

1 Peter 1:13-16

Therefore, with minds that are alert and fully sober, set
your hope on the grace to be brought to you when Jesus
Christ is revealed at his coming. As obedient children, do
not conform to the evil desires you had when you lived
in ignorance. But just as he who called you is holy, so be
holy in all you do; for it is written: "Be holy, because I
am holy."

Hebrews 12:14

Make every effort to live in peace with everyone and to
be holy; without holiness no one will see the Lord.

Hebrews 12:1-2a

Therefore, since we are surrounded by such a great cloud
of witnesses, let us throw off everything that hinders
and the sin that so easily entangles. And let us run with
perseverance the race marked out for us, fixing our eyes
on Jesus, the pioneer and perfecter of faith.

Romans 12:1-2

Therefore, I urge you, brothers and sisters, in view of
God's mercy, to offer your bodies as a living sacrifice,
holy and pleasing to God—this is your true and proper

worship. Do not conform to the pattern of this world, but be transformed by the renewing of your mind. Then you will be able to test and approve what God's will is—his good, pleasing and perfect will.

2 Timothy 2:19
Nevertheless, God's solid foundation stands firm, sealed with this inscription: "The Lord knows those who are his," and, "Everyone who confesses the name of the Lord must turn away from wickedness."

Reflection Time

How has God been speaking to you today? Take time to write it in your journal.

Chapter 36
Lord and Friend

Today I came into my quiet time with no agenda. I snuggled up in a blanket, turned on some worship music, and watched the sun break over the hilltops. Enjoying the antics of the birds at the feeders, I just delighted in the presence of God, while the praises coming from the singers in my worship selection echoed in my own heart. Then my mind began to nag me to get out my prayer list, so I started out of the chair to get my notebook.

I almost sensed God chuckling, as he whispered to my heart, "I am well aware of every name and need on your prayer list, Sherry—even if you didn't recite it to me every morning."

I smiled and settled back to listen to the music and enjoy the view. After I had rested in his presence for a little while, he began to bring names and faces to my mind and their accompanying needs, and I lifted them up to him. What a sweet, quiet time this morning.

I have worked really hard to become more of a "Mary" and to give my quiet time with the Lord priority over my to-do list.

I realized this morning that "Martha" was creeping into my quiet time with her lists and schedules of worship, prayer, and study time. Such a sneak, that Martha....

There's nothing wrong with order, discipline to study, and my prayer lists, as long as I don't let them keep me from sitting at his feet and resting in his presence. Sometimes in focusing on his lordship, I forget about his friendship. And he is both—Lord *and* friend.

God, forgive me for always wanting to create an agenda. Help me to wait for your guidance in all that I do, even in my quiet time. I thank you for your patience, your goodness, and your love. Help me to think of you not only as the great Creator of the universe but also as Jesus on the beach, frying fish in the morning for his hungry friends. Thank you that I am a work in progress and that you are faithful to complete that. In Jesus's name, amen.

John 15:9-1

As the Father has loved me, so have I loved you. Now remain in My love. If you keep My commands, you will remain in My love, just as I have kept My Father's commands and remain in his love. I have told you this so that My joy may be in you and that your joy may be complete. My command is this: Love each other as I have loved you. Greater love has no one than this: to lay down one's life for one's friends. You are My friends if you do what I command. I no longer call you servants, because a servant does not know his master's business. Instead, I have called you friends, for everything that I learned from My Father I have made known to you.

John 21:1-12a

Afterward, Jesus appeared again to his disciples, by the Sea of Galilee. It happened this way: Simon Peter, Thomas (also known as Didymus), Nathanael from Cana in

Galilee, the sons of Zebedee, and two other disciples were together. "I'm going out to fish," Simon Peter told them, and they said, "We'll go with you." So they went out and got into the boat, but that night they caught nothing. Early in the morning, Jesus stood on the shore, but the disciples did not realize that it was Jesus. He called out to them, "Friends haven't you any fish?" "No," they answered.

He said, "Throw your net on the right side of the boat and you will find some." When they did, they were unable to haul the net in because of the large number of fish.

Then the disciple whom Jesus loved said to Peter, "It is the Lord!" As soon as Simon Peter heard him say, "It is the Lord," he wrapped his outer garment around him (for he had taken it off) and jumped into the water. The other disciples followed in the boat, towing the net full of fish, for they were not far from shore, about a hundred yards. When they landed, they saw a fire of burning coals there with fish on it, and some bread.

Jesus said to them, "Bring some of the fish you have just caught." So Simon Peter climbed back into the boat and dragged the net ashore. It was full of large fish, 153, but even with so many the net was not torn. Jesus said to them, "Come and have breakfast."

Reflection Time

How has God been speaking to you today? Take time to write it in your journal.

Chapter 37

Praising in the Storm

I was reading from the book of Psalms this morning. David, the author of the Psalms, was called the "apple of God's eye." Yet, in many of the Psalms, it seemed as if even David had a hard time discerning God's presence in his life during times of great trouble. That was a timely revelation for me, because this is something I have been asking God about. I have been praying for people who are going through excruciating pain: some with ill health, others with crumbling marriages, a few who have buried a child. I always ask the Lord to surround them and fill them with his presence. I know that the sweet presence of God makes everything else fade away. But if David, the apple of God's eye, could not always sense the presence of God, should it be any different for us?

One thing I noticed was that, when David was crying out to God at the beginning of a psalm, by the end of it, he was praising God for his goodness—either because the Lord had delivered him or because he was remembering how the Lord had delivered him in the past. Remembering how God had come through for him in the past strengthened David's faith.

Faith does not operate in the realm of things that are seen, and that is the realm we humans like to operate in. It goes against our nature to feel thankful for something we haven't received yet, but the Bible is full of instances where we are told to do just that. It is full of accounts of God's people stepping out in faith when the odds were overwhelmingly stacked against them. God places more importance on our trust and faith than he does on our present troubles. It's not that he doesn't care about our troubles; he just wants us to learn to trust him in the midst of them.

It is very difficult to praise God when we are overcome with sorrow, when we can barely lift our heads.…But that is what we are to do. God's Word says that he inhabits the praise of his people.

All of us will experience heartache and trouble at some point in our lives. If we have stored up God's Word in our hearts, it will help us through those times. A storehouse of his Word inside us will encourage us with his promises and strengthen our faith until our Deliverer arrives…because he *will* arrive.

God, I confess that I sometimes wrestle with your timetable and with the struggle it takes to strengthen my faith. Help me, like David, to trust in your unfailing love; and let my heart rejoice in your salvation. Help me to pray for my brothers and sisters who are overwhelmed with troubles and having difficulty believing for your deliverance. In Jesus's name, amen.

Psalm 13:1-6

How long, LORD? Will you forget me forever?
How long will you hide your face from me?
How long must I wrestle with my thoughts
and day after day have sorrow in my heart?
How long will my enemy triumph over me?

Look on me and answer, LORD my God.
Give light to my eyes, or I will sleep in death,
and my enemy will say,
"I have overcome him,"
and my foes will rejoice when I fall.
But I trust in your unfailing love;
my heart rejoices in your salvation.
I will sing the LORD's praise,
for he has been good to me.

James 1:2–4

Consider it pure joy, my brothers and sisters, whenever you face trials of many kinds, because you know that the testing of your faith produces perseverance. Let perseverance finish its work so that you may be mature and complete, not lacking anything.

Psalm 27:13–14

I remain confident of this:
I will see the goodness of the LORD
in the land of the living.
Wait for the LORD;
be strong and take heart
and wait for the LORD.

Reflection Time

How has God been speaking to you today? Take time to write it in your journal.

Chapter 38
Unveiled Faces

I gazed out the sunroom windows this morning at a thick, gray fog rising from the snow-covered fields. The trees and bushes in the lower meadow were covered by the fog's misty veil.

The Lord brought a Scripture to my mind about a veil, and I looked up other places in the Bible where the word *veil* was used. Sometimes a veil was used as a protection. Many times it was used to hide things and cover shame. It was also used as a separation between the glory of God and the people. Moses covered his face when he came down from the mountain after meeting with God so that the Israelites would not see the remnant of God's glory fading away from his face. When Jesus died on the cross, the veil in the temple that separated man from the Holy of Holies was torn into.

Sometimes I still see the good news of the gospel through a veil. I live like someone whose face is still covered. I don't see my freedom in Christ clearly, and the glory of God is not reflected in me for others to see.

I have been guilty of contemplating the Christian life and thinking, "Is this all there is?" Guilty of going through the motions of the Christian walk with a heavy heart…struggling to live a good life.

Second Corinthians says that, whenever anyone turns to the Lord, the veil is taken away, and if we contemplate the Lord's glory with unveiled faces, we will be transformed into his image with ever-increasing glory.

Those words—contemplate, transformed, ever-increasing—all of those suggest a process.

Dear God, help me to turn to you and remove any veil that I am living behind. Help me to persevere in seeking you. Let me not be satisfied until I receive all that you died to give me. You said that the fruit of your Spirit living in me is love, joy, peace, patience, kindness, goodness, faithfulness, gentleness, and self-control. Help me not to settle for anything less. Give me a hunger for your Word…a thirst to know you more. In Jesus's name, amen.

2 Corinthians 3:12-18

Therefore, since we have such a hope, we are very bold. We are not like Moses, who would put a veil over his face to prevent the Israelites from seeing the end of what was passing away. But their minds were made dull, for to this day the same veil remains when the old covenant is read. It has not been removed, because only in Christ is it taken away. Even to this day when Moses is read, a veil covers their hearts. But whenever anyone turns to the Lord, the veil is taken away. Now the Lord is the Spirit, and where the Spirit of the Lord is, there is freedom. And we all, who with unveiled faces contemplate the Lord's glory, are being transformed into his image with ever-increasing glory, which comes from the Lord, who is the Spirit.

Galatians 5:19-25

The acts of the flesh are obvious: sexual immorality, impurity and debauchery; idolatry and witchcraft; hatred, discord, jealousy, fits of rage, selfish ambition, dissensions, factions and envy; drunkenness, orgies, and the like. I warn you, as I did before, that those who live like this will not inherit the kingdom of God.

But the fruit of the Spirit is love, joy, peace, forbearance, kindness, goodness, faithfulness, gentleness and self-control. Against such things there is no law. Those who belong to Christ Jesus have crucified the flesh with its passions and desires. Since we live by the Spirit, let us keep in step with the Spirit.

Reflection Time

How has God been speaking to you today? Take time to write it in your journal.

Chapter 39
Search My Heart, Oh God

Lately, God has had me start my prayer time by asking him to search my heart. It's surprising, the things that come up sometimes. If I ask him to search my heart and I wait, he will bring things to my mind that I need to confess and ask forgiveness for. It might be a long-forgotten resentment from many years ago or an act of selfishness on my part that he brings to mind. Sometimes it is an emotion I am struggling with, such as envy or fear. This isn't so he can condemn me for my sins.

I confess so that I can be cleansed from unrighteousness, and then my prayers will be effective.

This morning he brought a verse to my mind that I hear prayed over our nation quite often. It is from Second Chronicles 7:14-15: "If my people, who are called by my name, will humble themselves and pray and seek my face and turn from their wicked ways, then I will hear from heaven, and I will forgive their sin and will heal their land. Now my eyes will be open and my ears attentive to the prayers offered in this place."

I used to read this Scripture and concentrate on the healing of the nation and ask for forgiveness for the sins of the nation. But this is a very personal Scripture. It starts out, "If *my* people who are called by *my* name will humble *themselves* and pray ….

He is talking to believers here…individuals.

I am not just to humble myself and pray. I am to seek his face and *turn* from *my* wicked ways. It's not just about sinning and asking for forgiveness. It's about turning away from sin.

Political correctness on the subject of sin has woven its way into our thinking and many church teachings today. We want to believe that when we sin, we just confess and our sin is forgiven. While this is true, an important part is being left out: the turning way from sin afterward. Our nation has a hard time acknowledging sin. We like to call sin "free choice" now. The voices that stand up and call sin what it is face repercussions: they are called "judgmental" and "intolerant." God's grace forgives our sin, but it is also what enables us to turn away from sin. We really don't want to turn way from our sin, so we twist the grace of God to suit our sinful natures.

We like to use the example of Jesus when he forgave and did not condemn the woman caught in adultery, but we leave out the part where he said, "Now go and sin no more."

I have to ask myself, "What is the state of *my* land?" Does it need some divine intervention? Am I brave enough to ask him to search my heart or to ask for conviction in any area of sin?

If I want God to be attentive to my prayers, I can't just pick and choose bits and pieces of Scripture from the Bible that soothe me and make me feel temporarily better.

I need to humble myself and pray, seek his face, turn away from what the Bible—*not society*—calls "sin," and ask for forgiveness.

After I have confessed, received forgiveness, and, with God's help, turned away from sin, then his Word says his eyes will be opened and his ears will be attentive to my prayers.

That is very important. The people I have on my prayer list have some very serious needs. There are people seeking healing from grave illnesses, marriages that need restored, children who are being abused, people who are strangled by cords of addiction—food, drugs, alcohol, sex—people who are so overwhelmed with heartache that they are just ready to give up, and people who will spend eternity in hell if they don't come to know God.

I need God to be attentive to my prayers. I want my prayers to be heard, and I want healing in "my land."

God, help me not to be afraid to ask you to search my heart and see if there is any wicked way in me. Forgive me for my selfishness when I really don't want to turn away from my sin. Help me to realize that anything I gain from continuing in sin is not worth nearly as much as what I have to lose. In Jesus's name, amen.

-»»»- ❋ -«««-

Psalm 139:23-24
Search me, God, and know my heart; test me and know my
anxious thoughts. See if there is any offensive way in me,
and lead me in the way everlasting.

2 Chronicles 7:14-15
If my people, who are called by my name, will humble
themselves and pray and seek my face and turn from
their wicked ways, then I will hear from heaven, and I
will forgive their sin and will heal their land. Now my
eyes will be open and my ears attentive to the prayers
offered in this place.

Psalm 66:18

If I had cherished sin in my heart, the Lord would not have listened.

John 8:2-11

At dawn he appeared again in the temple courts, where all the people gathered around him, and he sat down to teach them. The teachers of the law and the Pharisees brought in a woman caught in adultery. They made her stand before the group and said to Jesus, "Teacher, this woman was caught in the act of adultery. In the Law Moses commanded us to stone such women.

Now what do you say?" They were using this question as a trap, in order to have a basis for accusing him. But Jesus bent down and started to write on the ground with his finger. When they kept on questioning him, he straightened up and said to them, "Let any one of you who is without sin be the first to throw a stone at her." Again he stooped down and wrote on the ground.

At this, those who heard began to go away one at a time, the older ones first, until only Jesus was left, with the woman still standing there. Jesus straightened up and asked her, "Woman, where are they? Has no one condemned you?"

"No one, sir," she said.

"Then neither do I condemn you," Jesus declared. "Go now and leave your life of sin."

Reflections From the Sunroom

Reflection Time

How has God been speaking to you today? Take time to write it in your journal.

Chapter 40
The Omnipresence of God

The person I love and trust the most on this earth is my husband. I trust in his love for me and my children and in his concern for our well-being. If something needs fixed, I have faith he will figure it out and do everything in his power to remedy the situation. If one of us needs or wants something, he will move heaven and earth to get it for us.

But even the people in this world that I have the most faith in— the ones I love the most and trust with my life—cannot compare to the omnipresence and omnipotence of God. He is all powerful and can be everywhere at once…a source of comfort to everyone who needs him. That is so amazing to me.

I was praying for a friend this morning who was nervous about a visit to the doctor. As I prayed, I was overcome with gratitude for the omnipresence of God. I am so thankful that he is not only right here in this room with me but also with my friend at the doctor's office and with my son in a city far away. He is with each of the people on my prayer list: a young man who is waiting for a lung transplant; the new mother in ICU who is sitting beside her critically ill baby; the parents who have lost children and wake up with a heavy heart every morning; the lonely man who has just gone through a divorce; my friends who have chronic illness and struggle just to make it through the day. He walks beside the single parent with too many responsibilities and countless worries weighing on their hearts. He patiently waits for an invitation from those who are empty inside and longing to be filled and those who have simply lost their way.

God, I thank you for your omnipotence and your omnipresence. I thank you for your intimately personal love and concern for each one of us. Reveal yourself to each person on my prayer list and everyone reading this book. Give them a desire to know more about you and a hunger for your Word. Help us to be aware of your tender care. In Jesus's name, amen.

Psalm 139:7–10

Where can I go from your Spirit?
Where can I flee from your presence?
If I go up to the heavens, you are there;
if I make my bed in the depths, you are there.
If I rise on the wings of the dawn,
if I settle on the far side of the sea,
Even there your hand will guide me,
your right hand will hold me fast.

Psalm 34:8

Taste and see that the LORD is good; blessed is the one who takes refuge in him.

Psalm 147:3

He heals the brokenhearted and binds up their wounds.

Reflection Time

How has God been speaking to you today? Take time to write it in your journal.

Chapter 41
Nourishing the Soul

Even though I am usually very health conscious, I sure do like a drive-thru burger and fries once in a while—and realistically, sometimes that is all I have time for. But if fast food was my regular diet and something I depended on to sustain me, eventually it would be to my detriment. I would become unhealthy and malnourished. Convenient fast food is not only unhealthy for me in the long term, but I know that, even in the short term, my body and brain do not function on a fast-food meal as well as they do when I am consuming nourishing, home-cooked foods.

This principle also applies to our spiritual lives. What do we feed our souls? Do they get a steady diet of drive-thru Christianity? An hour on Sunday? Ten-minute devotionals a couple times a week? Prayer time that we fall asleep in the middle of as we drop into bed exhausted at the end of the day?

Although we might survive on this kind of diet, we will not thrive.

If we want to thrive in our spiritual lives, we need to set aside time to be in God's presence, pray, and really study his Word. When sickness enters our bodies, we have a better chance of recovering from it if we are well nourished. The same is true of our mental, emotional, and spiritual health. When troubles come, as they undoubtedly will, we are better equipped to handle them if we have sustained ourselves on nourishing, sit-down meals of God's Word on a regular basis.

God, give me the wisdom to always prioritize time with you in your Word. Give me a hunger for your Word, and help me not to be satisfied with a drive-thru version of it. I thank you that your Word is food and medicine. In Jesus's name, amen.

Proverbs 4:20-22

My son, attend to my words; incline thine ear unto my sayings. Let them not depart from thine eyes; keep them in the midst of thine heart. For they are life unto those that find them, and health to all their flesh. (KJV)

Matthew 4:4

Jesus answered, "It is written: 'Man shall not live on bread alone, but on every word that comes from the mouth of God.'"

Reflection Time

How has God been speaking to you today? Take time to write it in your journal.

Chapter 42

Refuge, Security, Shelter, and Peace

I came downstairs this morning to let the dogs out. As I opened the front door, a blast of cold winter wind hit my face, and I was extremely thankful for the shelter of my warm home. I started thinking about the things in my life that make me feel sheltered and secure. My home is one of them, but I am also fortunate to have an abundance of people in my life that make me feel secure.

Refuge…shelter…security…peace…love….

Those are all words that make us feel safe. We spend our lives looking for people, things, homes, and jobs that will bring us security, peace, and love.

Even if we are successful at finding a faithful spouse, trustworthy friends, a nice home, and a good job with financial stability, none of it is truly secure; any of it could be lost in a moment.

And the truth is, almost all of our worries center around losing these things.

When our lives are over, even if we have found temporary security in all those things, we have to leave them behind. None of them can be taken with us.

The only permanent place of refuge, shelter, security, and peace is in God. He is the only thing that we can take with us when we leave this earth, and having a relationship with him ensures that we will have all those things—not only now, but for eternity. Such a simple thing, and yet so hard for many to grasp....

Dear God, I am thankful for the things of this earth that bring me refuge, shelter, security, and peace, but I know they can all be lost in a moment. Keep me ever aware that my only fixed source of all that is good is found in you. In Jesus's name, amen.

Psalm 84:5, 11-12
Blessed are those whose strength is in you,
whose hearts are set on pilgrimage....
For the LORD *God is a sun and shield;*
the LORD *bestows favor and honor;*
no good thing does he withhold
from those whose walk is blameless.
LORD *Almighty,*
blessed is the one who trusts in you.

Reflection Time

How has God been speaking to you today? Take time to write it in your journal.

Chapter 43
Life or Death

I was thinking about potatoes the other day. I had a bag of organic potatoes and a bag of non-organic potatoes. The organic potatoes were growing "eyes" that I had to cut off. The non-organic potatoes were smooth.

I used to consider potatoes growing eyes an annoyance—until I became a gardener.

When I was young, the potatoes always sprouted eyes if we didn't eat them fast enough. You could cut off those eyes, plant them in your garden, and have a whole new potato crop. It doesn't work that way these days. Unless you buy organic potatoes, the regular ones rarely grow eyes. That's because they have been sprayed with a chemical which inhibits that growth…that sprouting of new life.

The Lord spoke to my heart about how much we do in the world these days to inhibit life and about the opportunity for abundant life in the midst of problems.

When the "eyes" (problems) of life begin to grow, we see them as an inconvenience instead of an opportunity, and we do everything we can to rid ourselves of them.

The result of this is death…in one way or another.

It is because of this get-rid-of-the-eyes mentality that we have abortion, skyrocketing divorce rates, families who are estranged from each other, persons who flit from one relationship to another, and out-of-control drug abuse. Why do we choose death more than we choose life?

Life comes with problems, and we don't feel equipped to deal with them—or we simply don't have the patience to deal with them—so we make life expendable. If something causes us trouble, our instinct is to get rid of it, leave it, take a pill, or have a drink to "make it go away."

But what if we asked God to help us with our problems before we just chucked whatever is causing them. What if we said, "God, I don't love my husband (or wife) anymore…could you bring that love back for me? I will remain faithful until you do." Or what if we said, "God, I'm tempted to get into an extramarital sexual relationship with someone, and your Word says that it's a sin…would you help me to be strong and make decisions according to your will?"

Or, "God, I'm pregnant, and I cannot handle the responsibility of this child…would you give me wisdom and courage to make the right choice."

What if instead of fighting with our parents, spouse, children, friends, or coworkers, we walked away and took some time to get down on our knees and asked for help?

What if the abundant life is to be found in the midst of the problem?

God, help us with our impatience for fast fixes that in the end lead to death. Your way is *always* best. Help us not to run from our problems or just get rid of them. Help us to give them to you and trust you to make them into something that is beautiful and life giving. You want us to have lasting peace and true joy. Help us not to settle for counterfeit. In Jesus's name, amen.

Reflections From the Sunroom

Jeremiah 29:11-13

"For I know the plans I have for you," declares the LORD, *"plans to prosper you and not to harm you, plans to give you hope and a future. Then you will call on me and come and pray to me, and I will listen to you. You will seek me and find me when you seek me with all your heart."*

Deuteronomy 30:15-16, 19

See, I set before you today life and prosperity, death and destruction. For I command you today to love the LORD *your God, to walk in obedience to him, and to keep his commands, decrees and laws; then you will live and increase, and the* LORD *your God will bless you in the land you are entering to possess... This day I call the heavens and the earth as witnesses against you that I have set before you life and death, blessings and curses. Now choose life, so that you and your children may live.*

John 16:33

I have told you these things, so that in me you may have peace. In this world you will have trouble. But take heart! I have overcome the world.

Proverbs 14:12

There is a way that seems right to a man, but its end is the way of death. (ESV)

Reflection Time

How has God been speaking to you today? Take time to write it in your journal.

Chapter 44
Blessed Are All Who Wait for Him

It's been too many days since I have awakened before dawn to spend quiet time with the Lord. Bailey-dog got me up early this morning to do just that, and I trudged sleepily down the stairs with a worry nagging at the back of my mind—the same worry I had fallen asleep with.

I have gotten better about giving my concerns to God. It's been a relief to lay down my troubles and trust him to work them out...until I don't see anything happening. Then I want to pick them back up again (with the misguided perception that I might have some control).

I sit looking out the windows of my sun room. The pines are silhouetted against the barely perceptible light of dawn breaking over the hilltop. Their emerald green branches are so still this morning...not even the hint of a breeze. Still, quiet, unmovable—those pines have stood there for decades, while their roots grow deeper into the hillside.

God brings a bit of Scripture to my mind: "In quietness and trust is your strength." (Isaiah 30:15b, NIV) And another: "Therefore we will not fear, though the earth give way and the mountains fall into the heart of the sea." (Psalm 46:2, NIV)

I wonder wistfully if it is possible for me to come to a place of trust such as that.

When I look up those Scriptures in their entirety, they seem more like a command than a suggestion.

I try to imagine a range of mountains being tossed into the sea while I watch quietly from my sun room and still trust that I will be taken care of.

I'm certainly not there yet, but doesn't his Word say I can be... that I must be?

Lord, forgive me for not trusting you with the big stuff. I believe...help my unbelief. Give me grace to remain in quietness and trust, which is where my strength lies. Fill me with your Spirit to help me trust you. In Jesus's name, amen.

->>>> ❄ <<<<-

Psalm 46:1-7

God is our refuge and strength,
an ever-present help in trouble.
Therefore we will not fear, though the earth give way
and the mountains fall into the heart of the sea,
though its waters roar and foam
and the mountains quake with their surging.
There is a river whose streams make glad the city of God,
the holy place where the Most High dwells.
God is within her, she will not fall;
God will help her at break of day.
Nations are in uproar, kingdoms fall;
He lifts his voice, the earth melts.
The LORD Almighty is with us;
the God of Jacob is our fortress.

Isaiah 30:15b

In repentance and rest is your salvation, in quietness and trust is your strength.

→⟩⟩⟩ ❋ ⟨⟨⟨←

Reflection Time

How has God been speaking to you today? Take time to write it in your journal.

Chapter 45
Vigilance

Although some of my family and friends have made fun of me lately, I have been very vigilant about hand washing and taking immune support supplements during this flu season. However, my children seem determined to give me the flu. It seems like one or the other of them have been sick since before Christmas. I diligently wipe light switches, cabinet door handles, remotes, and phones with antibacterial wipes, and keep reminding them to cover their mouths. By the time they are better, another one gets sick, and I have to start the process all over again. Sometimes I am tempted to just give up and let the germs capture me, but years ago, a bout of the flu left me bedridden and in a wheelchair for months. I have no desire to go through that again. I still suffer with after-effects of post-viral fatigue and fibromyalgia from that experience.

During flu season, I have to stay vigilant about habits like hand washing and taking good care of myself if I want to remain healthy. It doesn't do any good to practice these habits occasionally, or when I have time, or if I feel like it. I could wash my hands carefully for a week but then slack off...and become exposed.

The same is true of my spiritual life. If my time with the Lord—praying and reading his Word—is hit and miss instead of a consistent habit, I leave myself open to attacks from the enemy. The book of James says not to be hearers of the Word only, but to be obedient to what it says. First Peter tells us to be prayerful and vigilant, because the devil is like a lion roaming to and fro on the earth, seeking whom he may devour. A lion is stealthy in his attacks; his victim doesn't usually see him coming.

Dear God, give me a hunger and desire to spend time with you in your Word. Help me not to grow weary in habits that are good for me and that protect me. So many times, I am too busy or tired to be vigilant. Remind me…keep me steadfast and determined….You know what is best for me. In Jesus's name, amen.

1 Peter 5:8-9

Be alert and of sober mind. Your enemy the devil prowls around like a roaring lion looking for someone to devour. Resist him, standing firm in the faith, because you know that the family of believers throughout the world is undergoing the same kind of sufferings.

Galatians 6:9

Let us not become weary in doing good, for at the proper time we will reap a harvest if we do not give up.

James 1:22-25

Do not merely listen to the word, and so deceive yourselves. Do what it says. Anyone who listens to the word but does not do what it says is like someone who looks at his face in a mirror and, after looking at himself, goes away and immediately forgets what he looks like. But whoever looks intently into the perfect law that gives freedom, and continues in it—not forgetting what they have heard, but doing it—they will be blessed in what they do.

Reflection Time

How has God been speaking to you today? Take time to write it in your journal.

Chapter 46
A World in Need

I cannot sleep without background noise of some kind, so I always have a fan running or music or Scripture playing at bedtime. For Christmas, I received a sound machine with a selection of nature recordings, and my favorite one is the ocean waves. Somehow I've pushed a button so the machine is on a timer and the sound of my ocean waves don't last all night. I woke up shortly after 5:00 a.m. on this frigid winter morning to the low, haunting moan of the wind as it rushed through the eaves of this old house. I've never heard that mournful moan before because I always have the distraction of the fan or sound machine. My covers were snug and warm, and I burrowed under them, but instead of contentment, I felt sadness. I thought about people without homes who try to survive in weather like this. I thought about people whose spirits moan silently inside them with heartache that no one hears or sees.

How often do I miss the mournful moans of this world because of the busyness or comforting distractions that I have created around me?

Lord, I'm not much. I barely have enough energy to get through the tasks required to take care of my own family most days. But help me to be aware of any small thing I can do to make a difference. Although it makes me sad, help me to hear the mournful sounds of a world in need. Show me the part you have for me to play, even if the only thing I can do some days is bow my head in prayer. Bless the workers who hear the moans, and strengthen their hands and hearts. In Jesus's name, amen.

→››› ✳ ‹‹‹←

Romans 15:1

We who are strong have an obligation to bear with the failings of the weak, and not to please ourselves. (ESV)

Philippians 2:4

Let each of you look not only to his own interests, but also to the interests of others. (ESV)

Matthew 5:16

In the same way, let your light shine before others, so that they may see your good works and give glory to your Father who is in heaven. (ESV)

→››› ✳ ‹‹‹←

Reflection Time

How has God been speaking to you today? Take time to write it in your journal.

Chapter 47

Trustworthy and True

In the old days, people who struggled with the faith issue could be categorized as realists: they needed to see something to believe it. That is not a solid foundation for a belief system these days.

I was standing in line at the supermarket yesterday, scanning the headlines of the celebrity gossip tabloids that some people take as gospel. Every time I wait in line and see those headlines, I feel cynical, because I know that nothing they say is true. Today, however, it's not just the gossip magazines that can't be trusted. That is why fact-checking websites are so popular; everything you see and hear has to be checked out to see if it is truth.

In times past, if something was "caught on camera," it was proof. We could believe what our eyes saw; if a conversation was recorded, you could believe what your ears heard. That is no longer the case. Modern technology has brought in very clever and deceptive methods of digital editing, photoshopping, and recording. Just about anything can be altered to sway the opinion of the viewer or listener, leaving many of us skeptical and cynical about what our eyes see and our ears hear. It's no wonder this old world is in a state of confusion.

The only way to truly believe something is to trust the source... and sadly, not very many sources can be trusted anymore.

Father God, you are the only source that can be trusted. You have given us direction in your Word. In a world where instability reigns and very few things are trustworthy, you are steadfast and secure; your Word is truth and light. Help us to anchor ourselves in you. In Jesus's name, amen.

Psalm 119:89-90, 105

Your word, LORD, is eternal;
it stands firm in the heavens.
Your faithfulness continues through all generations;
you established the earth, and it endures....
Your word is a lamp for my feet,
a light on my path.

James 1:16-18

Don't be deceived, my dear brothers and sisters. Every good and perfect gift is from above, coming down from the Father of the heavenly lights, who does not change like shifting shadows. He chose to give us birth through the word of truth, that we might be a kind of first-fruits of all he created.

Reflection Time

How has God been speaking to you today? Take time to write it in your journal.

Chapter 48
Foolishness That Confounds the Wise

There is so much in the news about the Middle East these days. People are sharply divided on their opinions about Israel and how she should respond to her enemies. I am not a scholar—academically, politically, biblically, or otherwise—and I really don't understand all that has taken place.

But when I look at a map of the Middle East, I am overwhelmed at how small Israel is in comparison to the countries around her, many of which are her enemies. I find myself thinking that it is a miracle Israel has not been wiped off the map.

It makes me think about how different God's thinking is than ours…how small the nation is that he calls his chosen.

The Bible is full of Scriptures that give us these glimpses into the mind of God.

There are stories about how God chose a shepherd boy with a slingshot to slay a giant who made entire armies tremble in fear… how the King of all creation came as a baby, and instead of setting himself up as Lord of all, he gave himself to die a death reserved for the worst offenders…how Jesus took the small, basket lunch of a little boy and not only satisfied the hunger of over five thousand people with it but had plenty left over...how he said that it only takes faith the size of a mustard seed to move a mountain...and how he chose a band of simple people—not superstars or scholars or politicians, but people like you and me—to help him change the world forever.

Those are some of the reasons I know the Bible is true and was inspired by God...because we humans just don't think like that.

Lord God...you are amazing. You are lovingly patient with me, even though too often, I am slow to understand. Help me to trust you, because *that* is faith—which you consider more precious than gold. In Jesus's name, amen.

-->>>> ✳ <<<<-

1 Corinthians 1:18

For the message of the cross is foolishness to those who are perishing, but to us who are being saved it is the power of God.

2 Corinthians 12:9-10

But he said to me, "My grace is sufficient for you, for my power is made perfect in weakness." Therefore I will boast all the more gladly about my weaknesses, so that Christ's power may rest on me. That is why, for Christ's sake, I delight in weaknesses, in insults, in hardships, in persecutions, in difficulties. For when I am weak, then I am strong.

1 Corinthians 1:19-21, 25

For it is written:

"I will destroy the wisdom of the wise; the intelligence of the intelligent I will frustrate."

Where is the wise person? Where is the teacher of the law? Where is the philosopher of this age? Has not God made foolish the wisdom of the world? For since in the wisdom of God the world through its wisdom did not know him, God was pleased through the foolishness of what was preached to save those who believe....For the foolishness of God is wiser than human wisdom, and the weakness of God is stronger than human strength.

2 Corinthians 4:7-9, 16-18

But we have this treasure in jars of clay to show that this all-surpassing power is from God and not from us. We are hard pressed on every side, but not crushed; perplexed, but not in despair; persecuted, but not abandoned; struck down, but not destroyed.... Therefore we do not lose heart. Though outwardly we are wasting away, yet inwardly we are being renewed day by day. For our light and momentary troubles are achieving for us an eternal glory that far outweighs them all. So we fix our eyes not on what is seen, but on what is unseen, since what is seen is temporary, but what is unseen is eternal.

Reflection Time

How has God been speaking to you today? Take time to write it in your journal.

Chapter 49
Where Did the Time Go?

Many times I come to the end of my day and think, "Where in the world did this day go? It seems like I just got up and it's over already!" If I haven't taken time that day to be alone with God, I don't usually feel satisfied with what I've accomplished by the end of it.

Balance is a hard thing to achieve in life. Even if my life is filled with good things, I can find myself controlled and consumed by them if I am not careful.

Our families, jobs, hobbies, interests, and even our service to others can take up so much of our day that we don't leave time for God. We need time alone with him...for refreshing and renewal... time to hear him speak. It is hard to hear the still, small voice when we are in pursuit of other things—even good things.

Any relationship that we don't make one-on-one time for will not thrive, whether it is marital, parental, or a friendship. The same is true about our relationship with God.

Jesus often withdrew to a solitary place to be alone with God and pray. If the Son of God made it a habit to take time to be alone with God...how much more do *we* need it?

God, help me to start my day with you. Order my steps, for you created this day with a plan for me. Help me to align my plan with yours before the day is over and I've missed it. In Jesus's name, amen.

-»»» ❋ «««-

Psalm 63:1-5

You, God, are my God,
earnestly I seek you;
I thirst for you,
my whole being longs for you,
in a dry and parched land
where there is no water.
I have seen you in the sanctuary
and beheld your power and your glory.
Because your love is better than life,
my lips will glorify you.
I will praise you as long as I live,
and in your name I will lift up my hands.
I will be fully satisfied as with the richest of foods;
with singing lips my mouth will praise you.

Jeremiah 29:11-13

"For I know the plans I have for you," declares the LORD,
"plans to prosper you and not to harm you, plans to give
you hope and a future. Then you will call on me and
come and pray to me, and I will listen to you. You will
seek me and find me when you seek me with all your
heart."

Mark 6:45-46

Immediately Jesus made his disciples get into the boat
and go on ahead of him to Bethsaida, while he dismissed

the crowd. After leaving them, he went up on a moun-
tainside to pray.

Reflection Time

How has God been speaking to you today? Take time to write it in your journal.

Chapter 50

Come Apart

Yesterday morning, I was sitting in the sunroom watching a snowstorm. The whirlwind of snowflakes, blowing across the yard and through the pine trees made it hard to tell the difference between what was coming out of the sky and what was blowing up from the ground. Even though every snowflake is uniquely different, I sure couldn't tell it from my vantage point.

God began to speak to my heart about being apart…not blending in. The Bible says that, as a Christian, I should be different from the rest of the world.

I would say that, in the depraved state of the world today, that difference ought to be extremely noticeable.

If a Christian is to stand out in a group of people, there should be a discernable difference in the way they talk, dress, the choices they make in reading material, the movies they watch, the way they spend their money, what they do for fun, and how they conduct themselves in their relationships.

Sometimes Christians don't stand out because it's embarrassing for us to try to be different. We all want to fit in.

Sometimes we don't stand out because we want to do the same thing that non-Christians are doing. We want to wear provocative clothing, have sex with people we are not married to, or just enjoy a little "harmless flirtation" with someone when we are already married. We want to go to movies that are ungodly and read books that are risqué.

We lie (just a little) and join in with the office gossip—or maybe the gossip in Christian circles under the guise of "there's someone who needs some prayer."

Maybe we cheat—just a little—when we deem the rules unfair.

And yet, the Bible is very clear about us coming apart and being different. We are called to stand out...to be salt and light...a city on a hill.

It should not be hard to distinguish a believer from a non-believer, and if it is, then something is wrong.

It is a daily battle to try to live a life for God, but if we bring our struggle with temptation to him, he will help us live victoriously. He is not embarrassed or ashamed by the things we are tempted by. He is there to help us.

There is a well-known verse in 2 Chronicles which talks about a nation repenting and turning from its wicked ways so that God could heal their land. In this verse, the people that are supposed to be repenting are *God's* people. "If *My* people who are called by *My* name will humble themselves and pray...and turn from their wicked ways...." (2 Chronicles 7:14, NIV)

God, forgive me when I don't have the courage to be the kind of person you have called me to be. Forgive me when I don't ask for your help when I am struggling with temptation. Forgive me when I don't speak up and stand up for you and your Word because of fear. Give me gentleness...but make me bold. Make me proud of the royalty that I am in your kingdom, and help me to live worthy of my royal family. In Jesus's name, amen.

Psalm 1:1-3

Blessed is the one
who does not walk in step with the wicked
or stand in the way that sinners take
or sit in the company of mockers,
but whose delight is in the law of the LORD,
and who meditates on his law day and night.
That person is like a tree planted by streams of water,
which yields its fruit in season
and whose leaf does not wither—
whatever they do prospers.

2 Chronicles 7:14

If my people, who are called by my name, will humble themselves and pray and seek my face and turn from their wicked ways, then I will hear from heaven, and I will forgive their sin and will heal their land.

Reflection Time

How has God been speaking to you today? Take time to write it in your journal.

Chapter 51
Cleaning Out the Junk

I have a few friends that accuse me of being OCD. Although my house may look uncluttered, I have a few "junk drawers" (some closets too). Some of them are in dire need of cleaning out at the moment. My junk drawers, although hidden from view, frustrate me, because when I need something, I have to sort through the junk to find the important stuff. I hate the task of cleaning those drawers, although when I'm finished, it is wonderful feeling.

I don't know how all that junk ends up in there. It is a collection of things that need fixed, things I'm not ready to let go of yet, and things that I don't have time to deal with at a particular moment, all adding up piece by piece until one day, it's hard to get the drawer closed at all.

The same can be true of my spiritual life, and it will begin to affect my peace of mind. Junk can creep in—things that need sorted out and fixed...or tossed.

I've had a few days this week where I just felt "off"—disgruntled, frustrated, lacking peace in my quiet time, and just irritable in general.

I asked God what was going on and a mental picture of my "junk drawer" came to my mind. Then he brought to my mind a couple of episodes this week where I had not acted in a Christ-like manner. One instance in particular was my impatience on the phone yesterday with an insurance man. I was frustrated about something I felt hadn't been done right.

I sighed to myself. I hate having to apologize worse than I hate cleaning out junk drawers. But I knew God was right. I made the phone call and got a voice mail (one of the reasons I had been frustrated in the first place). Taking a deep breath, I left a message, thanking him for the time he had spent helping me and apologizing for being irritated with him. Later that day when I returned home, there was a message from him on the answering machine, thanking me for the phone call and the apology. I could hear relief in his voice, and I immediately felt my own sense of peace return.

God, thank you for showing me what is wrong when I am lacking your peace. Help me to be wise and not let "junk" pile up in my life. I don't want anything to come between you and me or to hinder the peace you give me. You are such a faithful friend to me. I love you. In Jesus's name, amen.

Matthew 5:21-24

You have heard that it was said to the people long ago, "You shall not murder, and anyone who murders will be subject to judgment." But I tell you that anyone who is angry with a brother or sister will be subject to judgment. Again, anyone who says to a brother or sister, "Raca," is answerable to the court. And anyone who says, "You fool!" will be in danger of the fire of hell. Therefore, if you are offering your gift at the altar and there remem-

ber that your brother or sister has something against you, leave your gift there in front of the altar. First go and be reconciled to them; then come and offer your gift.

Philippians 4:4-7

Rejoice in the Lord always. I will say it again: Rejoice! Let your gentleness be evident to all. The Lord is near. Do not be anxious about anything, but in every situation, by prayer and petition, with thanksgiving, present your requests to God. And the peace of God, which transcends all understanding, will guard your hearts and your minds in Christ Jesus.

Reflection Time

How has God been speaking to you today? Take time to write it in your journal.

Chapter 52
Names of God

Remember the iPhone commercial that said, "There's an app for that"? If there was anything you needed help with, there was an app that could be downloaded on your phone. There are even apps that are able to locate your car in a parking lot. (I could have used that one a few times.)

The other morning I was praying about something I was concerned about, and I felt God speak three words to my heart: "names of God."

So I looked up the names of God and found that there are quite a few—some I was familiar with and some I hadn't heard before. I read the meaning of each name and found that what God was trying to tell me is that the "names of God" are really descriptions of the attributes of his character.

So whatever I need...he "has an app for that."

Lord, I thank you that the attributes of your character describe a God who can meet all my needs. Help me to always seek your help first. In Jesus's name, amen.

-»»» ✳ «««-

Psalm 9:10

Those who know your name trust in you, for you, LORD, have never forsaken those who seek you.

Proverbs 18:10

The name of the LORD is a fortified tower; the righteous run to it and are safe.

-»»» ✳ «««-

Names of God
(just a few, in order as they appear in the Bible)

Elohim
God; Power; Strength

YHWH
The Existing One ("He Will Be")

El Elyon
The God Most High; The Most Exalted God

Adonai
Lord; Master

El Shaddai
The All-Sufficient One; Our Sustainer

El Olam
The Everlasting God

El Roi
The God Who Sees

Sherolyn Porter

YHWH Jireh
The LORD Will Provide

YHWH Nissi
The LORD My Banner

YHWH Rapha
The LORD Who Heals

YHWH Mekaddishkem
The LORD Sanctifies You;
The LORD Sets You Apart

YHWH Tzva'ot
The LORD of Hosts (Armies)

YHWH Rohi
The LORD My Shepherd

YHWH Tsidkenu
The LORD Our Righteousness

YHWH Shammah
The LORD Is There

->>>> ✳ <<<<-

Reflection Time

How has God been speaking to you today? Take
time to write it in your journal.

Chapter 53

Daily Supply

I tiptoed quietly downstairs in the darkness for my quiet time with God. Although I love my sunroom, it is not the warmest place to be on a frigid winter morning before dawn. I lit the fire and wrapped up in a blanket.

As I began to warm up, the Lord brought to my mind Scriptures about the Israelites receiving manna in the desert as they were on their way to the Promised Land. The Lord provided for them, but they were only to gather enough for that day. If they gathered more, it became spoiled and rotten before the next day. He could have just showered a bunch of manna on them and told them to stock up and store it for the journey, but he provided only enough for a day at a time.

I used to think that when a person made a decision to give their lives to the Lord, then that was it. Your path was chosen, your eternity was secured, and then you just tried your best to live a good life.

I have found that there can be so much more to it than that. God's Word says to seek him in order to find him, to ask and it will be given, to knock and the door will be opened. He's talking to people who *already* belong to him, not to people who are lost. And the verbs *ask, seek,* and *knock* are used in the sense of *ask and keep on asking, seek and keep on seeking, knock and keep on knocking.*

The verb *seek* has the connotation of seeking for hidden treasure.

Why does he want us to seek, to search with all our hearts if we already have him? Why do we need to come to him daily for our "manna" when he has the power to just give it to us all at once?

Because he *loves* us! He wants to spend time with us! The daily manna we receive will reveal hidden treasures on our way to the Promised Land!

We don't expect to receive everything all at once from any of our other relationships. We discover our love deepens and grows richer by spending quality and quantity time with someone.

Lord, I admit there are days when I would like to have an abundance of manna so I could just be lazy and stay under the covers in my nice warm bed. But I thank you for giving me the desire and hunger to spend daily time with you and time in your Word. Keep me hungry for it! I'm thankful for the hidden treasures you reveal to me a bit at a time. In Jesus's name, amen.

→⇉⇉ ❊ ⇇⇇←

Jeremiah 29:13
You will seek Me and find Me when you search for Me with all your heart. (New American Standard Bible)

Matthew 7:7-8
Ask and it will be given to you; seek and you will find; knock and the door will be opened to you. For everyone who asks receives; the one who seeks finds; and to the one who knocks, the door will be opened.

Reflections From the Sunroom

Psalm 37:4

Take delight in the LORD, *and he will give you the desires of your heart.*

Psalm 145:17-19

The LORD *is righteous in all his ways*
and faithful in all he does.
The LORD *is near to all who call on him,*
to all who call on him in truth.
He fulfills the desires of those who fear him;
he hears their cry and saves them.

Reflection Time

How has God been speaking to you today? Take time to write it in your journal.

Chapter 54
Fertile Soil

Last night I listened to a book written by a pastor who had died and gone to heaven and then was brought back. He talked about what a small percentage of people really make it, even many people who think they are Christians—people who go through all the motions of church, but then the throughout the week live like the rest of the world. He also shed light on what the Bible says about the different kinds of soil in our hearts and whether the Word of God takes root and flourishes...or just dies. Three out of four of Jesus's examples in that parable did not have the fertile soil that it took to enter the kingdom of God.

I fell asleep with a heavy heart, thinking that so many people are not in right standing with God. I even began to question my own standing, for I know in myself I am not worthy either.

Still feeling heavy-hearted as I sat down for my quiet time with the Lord this morning, I asked him to reassure me of my secure standing with him.

Then I began to pray for a friend who is going through difficult times. I messaged her to let her know I was praying for her and got an immediate response back that flooded my eyes with

grateful tears. The Lord spoke to the question in my h͏
this person who had absolutely *no idea* about the uncertainty ı w͏aͻ
experiencing this morning.

She said, "Thank you, Sherry! You are a TRUE servant of God....
You may think you are unworthy, but you shine his spirit...."

Dear Lord, forgive me for questioning my standing with you. I
am so grateful for your reassurance. Your Word tells me that when I
belong to you, you will never let me go. Thank you for your patience
with me. Father, keep the soil of my own heart fertile and help me to
sow your seed into the hearts of others. I pray that you would prepare
the soil of their hearts also. In Jesus's name, amen.

Luke 8:4-8, 11-16
While a large crowd was gathering and people were
coming to Jesus from town after town, he told this
parable: "A farmer went out to sow his seed. As he
was scattering the seed, some fell along the path; it
was trampled on, and the birds ate it up. Some fell on
rocky ground, and when it came up, the plants with-
ered because they had no moisture. Other seed fell
among thorns, which grew up with it and choked the
plants. Still other seed fell on good soil. It came up and
yielded a crop, a hundred times more than was sown."
When he said this, he called out, "Whoever has ears to
hear, let them hear...."

"This is the meaning of the parable: The seed is the word
of God. Those along the path are the ones who hear, and
then the devil comes and takes away the word from their
hearts, so that they may not believe and be saved. Those
on the rocky ground are the ones who receive the word

with joy when they hear it, but they have no root. They believe for a while, but in the time of testing they fall away. The seed that fell among thorns stands for those who hear, but as they go on their way they are choked by life's worries, riches and pleasures, and they do not mature. But the seed on good soil stands for those with a noble and good heart, who hear the word, retain it, and by persevering produce a crop."

John 10:27-29

My sheep hear my voice, and I know them, and they follow me. I give them eternal life, and they will never perish, and no one will snatch them out of my hand. My Father, who has given them to me, is greater than all, and no one is able to snatch them out of the Father's hand. (ESV)

Reflection Time

How has God been speaking to you today? Take time to write it in your journal.

Chapter 55
Your Father's Care

Brrrrrrrrrr.... *The temp* this morning was seven degrees below zero. I fuss and stew about our outside critters when it is this frigid outside. As my husband came in, stomping snow off his boots after feeding them all, I started in with a barrage of questions: "How are the horses...are the chickens ok...do they have plenty of food?" He assured me calmly that everyone was just fine. *Whew.* I went out to the sunroom and settled in my chair to spend my quiet time with the Lord. As my iPad crooned out a worship song about the names of God, I watched a variety of brightly colored birds dart happily back and forth from the shelter of the pines to the bird feeders. They looked plump and healthy from the steady diet of black oil sunflower seeds we have been providing them all winter. It sure seemed like I was the only one worrying this morning.

The Lord began to speak to my heart about provision.

If any of our animals decided to wander away from the source we supply and tried to make it on their own, they would not be faring as well right now. Our animals don't panic in these temperatures; they trust us to provide for their needs. As long as they stay near the source, they will be fine.

I know the same is true in my spiritual life. If I don't stay close to God (my source), I may survive in this life…but I will not thrive.

God, help me to bring all my needs and worries to you—no matter how small—for you care about them all. You are a source that can be trusted: YHWH Jireh, The LORD who provides. In Jesus's name, amen.

Matthew 10:29-31

Are not two sparrows sold for a penny? Yet not one of them will fall to the ground outside your Father's care. And even the very hairs of your head are all numbered. So don't be afraid; you are worth more than many sparrows.

Matthew 6:25-27

For this reason I say to you, do not be worried about your life, as to what you will eat or what you will drink; nor for your body, as to what you will put on. Is not life more than food, and the body more than clothing? Look at the birds of the air, that they do not sow, nor reap nor gather into barns, and yet your heavenly Father feeds them. Are you not worth much more than they? And who of you by being worried can add a single hour to his life? (NASB)

Proverbs 3:5-6

Trust in the LORD with all your heart and lean not on your own understanding;
in all your ways submit to him, and he will make your paths straight.

Reflections From the Sunroom

Reflection Time

How has God been speaking to you today? Take time to write it in your journal.

Chapter 56
The Name of Jesus

Sometimes we get blindsided by fear. Maybe it's being awakened by the sound of the phone at 4:30 a.m. Perhaps it's a call from the doctor's office in the middle of the day with test results, or it could be trying repeatedly to get in touch with a loved one who doesn't respond, and we imagine the worst. Our breathing quickens, our hearts pound, our palms grow sweaty, and we can't even think clearly enough to pray. Sometimes all we can say is "Jesus," and that is the perfect prayer.

There is a story in the Bible about the night Jesus was betrayed by Judas, one of his disciples. Judas brought some of the temple leaders and a group of soldiers with weapons to the garden where Jesus was praying. As the story goes, Jesus asked them who they were looking for, and they said "Jesus of Nazareth." When Jesus said "I am he," the soldiers drew backwards and fell to the ground.

When I was studying about this passage, I learned that there were some things lost from the original translation. The group of soldiers consisted of about six hundred men, and when they said they were looking for Jesus of Nazareth, his response was not "I am he" but "I AM."

When Jesus spoke his name, "I AM," the original Greek words depict the soldiers staggering and stumbling backwards as if hit by some force; they fell to the ground so hard that they appeared as dead men or corpses.

Six hundred soldiers falling to the ground when the name I AM was spoken....

I AM...the same words God used to identify himself to Moses.

There is power in the name of Jesus. The Bible says his name is above *all* names, so if all you can pray sometimes is "Jesus," rest assured...it is all that is needed.

Father God, I thank you that my prayers don't have to be long and eloquent to get your attention. When my knees quake in fear and my mouth is too dry to speak, just the whisper of the name of your Son is sufficient to bring help from above. In his name, I pray, amen.

John 18:1-6

When he had finished praying, Jesus left with his disciples and crossed the Kidron Valley. On the other side there was a garden, and he and his disciples went into it. Now Judas, who betrayed him, knew the place, because Jesus had often met there with his disciples. So Judas came to the garden, guiding a detachment of soldiers and some officials from the chief priests and the Pharisees. They were carrying torches, lanterns and weapons. Jesus, knowing all that was going to happen to him, went out and asked them, "Who is it you want?"

"Jesus of Nazareth," they replied.

"I am he," Jesus said. (And Judas the traitor was standing there with them.) When Jesus said, "I am he," they drew back and fell to the ground.

Philippians 2:9-11
Therefore God exalted him to the highest place and gave him the name that is above every name, that at the name of Jesus every knee should bow, in heaven and on earth and under the earth, and every tongue acknowledge that Jesus Christ is Lord, to the glory of God the Father.

Reflection Time

How has God been speaking to you today? Take time to write it in your journal.

Chapter 57
Thorn in My Flesh

I am a believer in prayer. I have seen God answer prayers in ways that are nothing short of miraculous. He has proven his faithfulness to me and those I love over and over.

But when he doesn't answer, in the way that I would like him to…those are the times that test my own faithfulness.

I have lived with fibromyalgia, chronic fatigue syndrome, and the depression and anxiety that go along with them for over thirty-five years. There have been times…months…even years when the pain and fatigue were tolerable and did not interfere with normal life.

There have also been years where the exhaustion smothered me, and I felt that if breathing hadn't been an unconscious effort, I surely would have stopped because I didn't have the strength to do it. I've experienced times when the constant pain made me wince to hold my loved ones close.

I have lost count of the times I have pleaded with the Lord for a miracle, for him to take this affliction from me. There is a verse in Second Corinthians where the apostle Paul talks about a thorn in his flesh…something he asked the Lord to take away from him but the

Lord did not, telling Paul that his grace was sufficient for him and that his strength was made perfect in weakness.

So Paul said he delighted in his weaknesses…in insults… in hardships.

I have to admit…I have not arrived at that place yet. However, I do know that this "thorn in my flesh" has kept me close to God, and he has been the source of my strength, even though many times, I couldn't see it in the midst of my struggle. The accomplishment of everyday tasks that most people take for granted seem monumentally overwhelming to me a lot of the time. Yet when I look back at my life, I know that it is only through God's strength that I have been able to raise a family, keep house, try my hand at running a business, and even care for a garden. To others, those things don't seem like miracles; they are just everyday life events. But to me, they are miracles indeed.

Even though I don't delight in my weaknesses, I know that because of them, I have witnessed countless miracles, rather than just one miracle of the "thorn in the flesh" being taken away. He has developed my character along the way and given me a heartfelt empathy for others who are struggling as well.

Father, I ask you for patience and strength to run the race you have set before me. I thank you for the people you have surrounded me with, who lift me up in prayer and help me when I am weak. Forgive me for the times I have questioned you and doubted. Help me to trust your heart during the times I cannot see your hand at work. Your way is perfect, and you know what is best. Keep my eyes open for the daily miracles you provide. In Jesus's name, amen.

2 Corinthians 12:8-10

Three times I pleaded with the Lord to take it away from me. But he said to me, "My grace is sufficient for you, for my power is made perfect in weakness." Therefore I will boast all the more gladly about my weaknesses, so that Christ's power may rest on me. That is why, for Christ's sake, I delight in weaknesses, in insults, in hardships, in persecutions, in difficulties. For when I am weak, then I am strong.

James 1:2-4

Consider it pure joy, my brothers and sisters, whenever you face trials of many kinds, because you know that the testing of your faith produces perseverance. Let perseverance finish its work so that you may be mature and complete, not lacking anything.

1 Peter 1:3-9

Praise be to the God and Father of our Lord Jesus Christ! In his great mercy he has given us new birth into a living hope through the resurrection of Jesus Christ from the dead, and into an inheritance that can never perish, spoil or fade. This inheritance is kept in heaven for you, who through faith are shielded by God's power until the coming of the salvation that is ready to be revealed in the last time. In all this you greatly rejoice, though now for a little while you may have had to suffer grief in all kinds of trials. These have come so that the proven genuineness of your faith—of greater worth than gold, which perishes even though refined by fire—may result in praise, glory and honor when Jesus Christ is revealed.

Sherolyn Porter

Though you have not seen him, you love him; and even though you do not see him now, you believe in him and are filled with an inexpressible and glorious joy, for you are receiving the end result of your faith, the salvation of your souls.

Reflection Time

How has God been speaking to you today? Take time to write it in your journal.

Chapter 58
Relationships

As I came to the sunroom to pray this morning, I looked at the section in my prayer list for broken relationships. It seems to grow larger all the time. So many people lack peace today—in their relationships and in their hearts. Many of the problems in our world are the result of the fallout from broken relationships....

In times past, people fixed things that were broken instead of tossing them aside. Today, most people don't seem to have the patience or even the desire to do that. In the convenience-driven, everything-is-disposable mentality of our world now, discarded relationships pile up like garbage dumps, and a world full of broken, angry, hurting people is the result.

Relationships are so important to God—not just the relationship we have with him, but the relationships we have with others. The first four commandments that God gave to Moses are about our relationship with God, and the next six are about our relationships with others. There is a reason for that order: We must first be in right relationship with God, putting him above all else and seeking his ways. Healthy relationships with others are an outgrowth of that.

If relationships are so important to God, then he is willing to help us fix them. The Bible says, "You have not because you ask not."

He is a God of healing and restoration—in us and in our relationships.

Father God, help us to put you first, to seek your will for our lives. Healing is in your hands—not just for our bodies, but for our minds, our spirits, and our relationships as well. Help us to remember that your Word says you make all things new and that we can ask for your help to fix what is broken. You promise that you will make a way in the wilderness and streams in the wasteland. Nothing is impossible for you. We believe...help our unbelief. In Jesus's name, amen.

Matthew 5:21-24

You have heard that it was said to the people long ago, "You shall not murder, and anyone who murders will be subject to judgment." But I tell you that anyone who is angry with a brother or sister will be subject to judgment. Again, anyone who says to a brother or sister, "Raca," is answerable to the court. And anyone who says, "You fool!" will be in danger of the fire of hell. Therefore, if you are offering your gift at the altar and there remember that your brother or sister has something against you, leave your gift there in front of the altar. First go and be reconciled to them; then come and offer your gift.

John 15:7

If you abide in me and my words abide in you, you will ask what you desire and it shall be done for you. (New King James Version)

Reflections From the Sunroom

2 Corinthians 5:17-19

Therefore, if anyone is in Christ, the new creation has come: The old has gone, the new is here! All this is from God, who reconciled us to himself through Christ and gave us the ministry of reconciliation: that God was reconciling the world to himself in Christ, not counting people's sins against them. And he has committed to us the message of reconciliation.

Isaiah 43:18-19
Forget the former things; do not dwell on the past.
See, I am doing a new thing!
Now it springs up; do you not perceive it?
I am making a way in the wilderness and streams in the wasteland.

Reflection Time

How has God been speaking to you today? Take time to write it in your journal.

Chapter 59
Peace That Passes Understanding

My husband Al and I were driving home from dinner out last night, listening to worship music on the radio. I felt the peace of God settle over me like a warm blanket, and I closed my eyes in thankful silence and just soaked in it.

Peace. A commodity sought after at great expense, yet something that money can't buy. Many people spend their lives trying to create an environment where they can experience it. They take an expensive vacation or try to accumulate a certain amount in their savings or retirement accounts. Some look for it in a relationship with another person—someone who creates the feeling of peace inside them. Sadly, most of the peace we try so hard to obtain from these things is short-lived and inferior…a counterfeit.

If money could buy it—or even create an environment in which one could experience it—then the rich and famous would be the most peaceful people around, but all we have to do is look at the news to know that isn't the case. If power could create it, then governments could control it, but we know that isn't the case either.

Years ago, I met peace, embodied in the person of a little old lady named Hazel. I worked on the compassionate ministries committee at church, and someone had called to let us know of her need for food. The first trip I made to Hazel's house on the outskirts of town (in an area I'd never seen before) left me feeling a little apprehensive. She lived on a tiny street of crumbling pavement that wound up a very steep hill, flanked by what could only be described as a cluster of old shacks. Her house stood out from the rest of the sadly drab and dilapidated structures around her. The tiny, postage-stamp-sized lot was full of garden statues, and plaques with Scripture adorned the outside walls of her home.

The inside of her house was composed of two rooms: a bedroom and a kitchen-living-dining combination. Her bathroom was an outhouse across the street. The kitchen consisted of a one-basin sink fed by a traditional pitcher pump and a small cupboard. The small living-dining area contained an old aluminum table and a single overstuffed chair by a stand which held a well-worn Bible. Hazel was in her eighties, with a wrinkled face that told of hard work and difficult times. I have forgotten the color of her eyes but I remember the light in them…like the sun on a warm, summer day.

In worldly terms, Hazel had very little, but in spiritual terms, she was rich indeed. She was always so thankful for everything she had and always wanted to give me a gift of some sort when I visited. I made many trips to her home over the course of a few years and even invited her to my home, which though modest at the time, seemed like a king's palace in comparison to hers.

As so often happens when the Lord is involved, things have a way of working backwards. What started out as a plan for me to be an avenue of blessing to her ended up with me feeling like the one who had been blessed. I learned that her peace and joy came from her deep trust in the Lord, and she prayed for me and my family at every visit.

I learned a great life lesson from Hazel: Peace isn't found in money or things or even other people. The peace that passes understanding...that coveted commodity...can only be found in relationship with the Lord. Hazel has long since gone to heaven, and I look forward to seeing her again someday.

God, keep me in close relationship with you. I pray that your perfect peace and joy will shine like a light from me to those around me, just like it did from my old friend, Hazel. Make me an instrument of your peace. In Jesus's name, amen.

Philippians 4:4–7

Rejoice in the Lord always. I will say it again: Rejoice! Let your gentleness be evident to all. The Lord is near. Do not be anxious about anything, but in every situation, by prayer and petition, with thanksgiving, present your requests to God. And the peace of God, which transcends all understanding, will guard your hearts and your minds in Christ Jesus.

John 16:33

I have told you these things, so that in me you may have peace. In this world you will have trouble. But take heart! I have overcome the world.

Isaiah 26:3

You will keep in perfect peace those whose minds are steadfast, because they trust in you.

Reflections From the Sunroom

Reflection Time

How has God been speaking to you today? Take time to write it in your journal.

Chapter 60
Eye Hath Not Seen

There is breathtaking beauty outside my sunroom window this morning. My breath catches in my throat at the sight of it. Behind the canopy of pine branches heavily laden with snow, the previously barren trees are thickly coated in a brilliant sparkling white, with a backdrop of the most beautiful cornflower-blue sky. The sun is reflecting off their snow-covered branches, and as it warms their heavy boughs, cascades of ice particles, like millions of tiny diamonds, fall in a shimmering spray, floating slowly to the ground. Brightly colored cardinals dart from the trees to the feeders amidst this spray of glittering crystals.

I can barely sit in my chair. I want to get up and turn in circles so that I can gaze out the windows in every direction. My heart swells, and I feel breathless with a wonder that's almost painful in its exhilaration. It's like walking through the wardrobe door and entering a magical, wintery Narnia.

The Lord speaks to my heart. "Just sit still and enjoy...."

"But that's so hard, God. I just want to share it with someone. I need to capture this moment somehow so that I can save it and experience it again and again. I have never seen anything so beautiful."

And then he speaks his Word into my spirit: "Eye hath not seen, nor ear heard, neither have entered into the heart of man, the things which God hath prepared for them that love him."

"Wow, Lord, sometimes I look forward to heaven because life can be hard on Planet Earth. Other times I cannot imagine experiencing blessings bigger than the ones you have already given me here. Thank you for this beautiful earth, and for eyes to see it. You are amazing!"

1 Corinthians 2:9

But as it is written, Eye hath not seen, nor ear heard, neither have entered into the heart of man, the things which God hath prepared for them that love him. (KJV)

Revelation 21:2-4, 10-11

I saw the Holy City, the new Jerusalem, coming down out of heaven from God, prepared as a bride beautifully dressed for her husband. And I heard a loud voice from the throne saying, "Look! God's dwelling place is now among the people, and he will dwell with them. They will be his people, and God himself will be with them and be their God. 'He will wipe every tear from their eyes. There will be no more death' or mourning or crying or pain, for the old order of things has passed away...."
And he carried me away in the Spirit to a mountain great and high, and showed me the Holy City, Jerusalem, coming down out of heaven from God. It shone with the glory of God, and its brilliance was like that of a very precious jewel, like a jasper, clear as crystal.

Sherolyn Porter

Reflection Time

How has God been speaking to you today? Take
time to write it in your journal.

Chapter 61
Receive the Gift

Gazing out the window of my sunroom this beautiful winter morning, I can see the split-rail fence that divides our yard from the upper pasture. On the other side of that fence is a thicket of assorted evergreens. I enjoy their greenery in the starkness of winter and the shade they provide in the hot days of summer. Behind the denseness of the thicket lies an open sunny meadow, but one would never know it from this vantage point. Just because I can't see it doesn't change the fact that it is there.

Last night, I was talking to a friend who is experiencing some fearful moments of health issues for herself and for a loved one. I confessed to her that one of my biggest battles is with fear also. Later, when I got into bed, I began praying for God to comfort her in this situation. I asked, "Lord, how can we experience deliverance from fear?" He spoke these words to my heart. "I've given it to you...walk in it."

"Well," I thought, "that is so much easier said than done."

I was contemplating those words again as I looked out the window this morning. I remembered hearing a sermon once about the kinds of things we pray for: God be with us; God give us your peace; Lord, fight this battle for me; Lord, give me joy. The preacher said, "We don't need to pray for things we already have."

It struck me that the things I pray for much of the time are things that God's Word says I have already been given. The Lord brought a picture to my mind of a blindfolded child behind a curtain waiting to receive a gift. The gift is on the other side of the curtain from where the child stands waiting, continuing to ask for the gift. Even if the curtain is moved aside, the blindfold must be removed before the child can see the gift. When Jesus died on the cross, the curtain in the temple that separated God from the people was torn in two. Beyond that torn curtain are *his gifts*.

Jesus told us he was leaving his *peace* with us. He said if we accepted him, the *Holy Spirit* would live in us. The *fruit* of the Spirit is love, joy, peace, forbearance, kindness, goodness, faithfulness, gentleness, and self-control. He commands us *not to fear* and tells us that *perfect love* casts out fear. Nothing can separate us from *his love*.

If all that is true, the problem is not in the provision but in the perception. We pray amiss when we ask for things that his Word says we have already been given. Instead, my prayers should be for wisdom and for revelation.

Father God, I thank you for all you have provided: peace, joy, your perfect love, freedom from fear, and victory over my enemies. God, I confess that I don't understand it all sometimes. Father, I pray you would open my spiritual eyes to see all that you have provided—everything you sent your Son to die to give me. Help me to "walk in it." God, I believe…help my unbelief. In Jesus's name, amen.

John 14:26-27

But the Advocate, the Holy Spirit, whom the Father will send in my name, will teach you all things and will remind you of everything I have said to you. Peace I leave with you; My peace I give you. I do not give to you as the world gives. Do not let your hearts be troubled and do not be afraid.

Galatians 5:22-23a
But the fruit of the Spirit is love, joy, peace, forbearance, kindness, goodness, faithfulness, gentleness and self-control.

Romans 8:38-39
For I am convinced that neither death nor life, neither angels nor demons, neither the present nor the future, nor any powers, neither height nor depth, nor anything else in all creation, will be able to separate us from the love of God that is in Christ Jesus our Lord.

2 Peter 1:3-4
His divine power has given us everything we need for a godly life through our knowledge of him who called us by his own glory and goodness. Through these he has given us his very great and precious promises, so that through them you may participate in the divine nature, having escaped the corruption in the world caused by evil desires.

Ephesians 1:17-20
I keep asking that the God of our Lord Jesus Christ, the glorious Father, may give you the Spirit of wisdom and revelation, so that you may know him better. I pray that the eyes of your heart may be enlightened in order that you may know the hope to which he has called you, the

riches of his glorious inheritance in his holy people, and his incomparably great power for us who believe. That power is the same as the mighty strength he exerted when he raised Christ from the dead and seated him at his right hand in the heavenly realms.

Isaiah 43:1b–2

Do not fear, for I have redeemed you; I have summoned you by name; you are mine.

When you pass through the waters, I will be with you; and when you pass through the rivers, they will not sweep over you.

When you walk through the fire, you will not be burned; the flames will not set you ablaze.

Reflection Time

How has God been speaking to you today? Take time to write it in your journal.

Chapter 62
Spiritual Warfare

The Christian community falls on a wide spectrum when it comes to what they think and believe about the devil. Some think the devil is responsible for anything and everything wrong in their lives, while others like to pretend that he doesn't exist at all or that he cannot do anything to them because they are Christians. The middle of the spectrum consists of those who believe the devil might cause problems but aren't sure what to do about it and those who recognize him as the enemy and are successfully waging war against him.

Sometimes the devil doesn't deserve any credit for the problems we are experiencing. In fact, he doesn't have to lift a finger to cause us misery because we do a fine job with our own self-sabotage. Blaming him for problems that are of our own making won't do a thing to alleviate them.

Those who refuse to give the devil a passing thought are the ones in the most danger. The Bible says we are in warfare and our battle is not against flesh and blood. If we don't know who our enemy is or what weapons we have available, we risk being blindsided.

Sometimes when we come under attack by the enemy, we feel like we cannot even stand to fight. We forget that we have a sword at our disposal—the Word of God. We don't have to feel strong to use this sword. The Bible doesn't say it is heavy; the Bible says it is sharp…two-edged sharp.

If you feel like you can't get up, start swinging it from where you have fallen. Call your brothers and sisters in Christ for reinforcements—people who will pray God's Word and swing their swords on your behalf.

Look up Scriptures that deal with what concerns you and turn them into prayers. God says his Word will not return void.

Father God, sometimes the attack of the enemy is so sudden or relentless, we forget that we even have weapons. Help us to swing our swords in the face of attack—for ourselves and for our brothers and sisters in Christ. Thank you that your Word is alive and active, sharper than any two-edged sword, and that it will not return void but will accomplish what you send it to do. Remind us of what you have provided to ensure our success. In Jesus's name, amen.

→⟩⟩⟩ ✳ ⟨⟨⟨←

1 Peter 5:8-9

Be alert and of sober mind. Your enemy the devil prowls around like a roaring lion looking for someone to devour. Resist him, standing firm in the faith, because you know that the family of believers throughout the world is undergoing the same kind of sufferings.

Hebrews 4:12

For the word of God is alive and active. Sharper than any double-edged sword, it penetrates even to dividing soul and spirit, joints and marrow; it judges the thoughts and attitudes of the heart.

Ephesians 6:11–17

Put on the full armor of God, so that you will be able to stand firm against the schemes of the devil. For our struggle is not against flesh and blood, but against the rulers, against the powers, against the world forces of this darkness, against the spiritual forces of wickedness in the heavenly places. Therefore, take up the full armor of God, so that you will be able to resist in the evil day, and having done everything, to stand firm. Stand firm therefore, having girded your loins with truth, and having put on the breastplate of righteousness, and having shod your feet with the preparation of the gospel of peace; in addition to all, taking up the shield of faith with which you will be able to extinguish all the flaming arrows of the evil one. And take the helmet of salvation, and the sword of the Spirit, which is the Word of God. (NASB)

2 Corinthians 10:3–5

For though we live in the world, we do not wage war as the world does. The weapons we fight with are not the weapons of the world. On the contrary, they have divine power to demolish strongholds. We demolish arguments and every pretension that sets itself up against the knowledge of God, and we take captive every thought to make it obedient to Christ.

Isaiah 55:10–11

As the rain and the snow come down from heaven, and do not return to it without watering the earth and making it bud and flourish, so that it yields seed for the sower and bread for the eater, so is my word that goes out from my mouth: It will not return to me empty, but will accomplish what I desire and achieve the purpose for which I sent it.

Reflection Time

How has God been speaking to you today? Take time to write it in your journal.

Chapter 63
Thy Will Be Done

God has been teaching me to pray differently these days. I have a lot of names on my prayer list but my requests are not as specific as they used to be. I used to pray very specifically because…well, I guess I thought I knew best how the prayer should be answered.

When God didn't answer that prayer right away, I sometimes helped him by trying to create circumstances in which that prayer had a better chance of being answered the way I thought it should be.

The more I've come to know God, the more I trust him to know the best way for a prayer to be answered. My knowledge is so limited…I can only see the here and now, whereas he sees past, present, and future all at the same time.

I've learned from the Bible that, when God's people try to manipulate circumstances to fit their timing rather than God's timing, the results can be far reaching and even catastrophic.

God promised Abraham and Sarah a baby in their old age and did not fulfill that promise for years. So Sarah took matters into her own hands and gave Abraham her slave girl to sleep with. The result was a conflict that continues in the Middle East to this day. The descendants of Ishmael, the son born of Sarah's slave girl, are still in conflict with the descendants of Isaac, the promised son God later gave Sarah and Abraham.

Jesus taught us to pray, "*Thy* will be done on earth as it is in heaven." That's a tough one, because it leaves *I, me,* and *my* out of it.

God, help me to trust that your will is not just better than mine—it is perfect. I never know all the factors involved in a prayer request, but you know everything that will result from any answer. Help me to trust when the answer I desire is a long time in coming or doesn't seem to be going my way. In Jesus's name, amen.

1 John 5:14-15

This is the confidence we have in approaching God: that if we ask anything according to his will, he hears us. And if we know that he hears us—whatever we ask— we know that we have what we asked of him.

1 John 2:16-17

For all that is in the world—the desires of the flesh and the desires of the eyes and pride of life—is not from the Father but is from the world. And the world is passing away along with its desires, but whoever does the will of God abides forever. (ESV)

Reflection Time

How has God been speaking to you today? Take time to write it in your journal.

Chapter 64
What Kind of Faith

In Hebrews, it says that, without faith, it is impossible to please God, because anyone who comes to him must believe that he exists and that he rewards those who earnestly seek him.

The prosperity gospel is all over the "rewards" part of that one—name it and claim it…God will give you what you ask for.

The problem with that mentality is that it can make our faith journey seem like a roller-coaster ride. That kind of faith is based on what God does, and if He's not doing what we have asked him to do, then our faith is shaken; we think that either he doesn't hear us or he really doesn't care that much about our problems. That kind of faith can make us doubt his love for us.

Another kind of faith is *believing* God is who he says he is—believing in the character of God. His Word says he is good, he is peace, he is love, truth, life, and so much more.

If we believed that, then our faith would stand secure, even when our prayers seemingly go unanswered.

When God promised Abraham that he would have a son and that he would make his descendants as numerous as the stars, Abraham believed God—so much so that, when God asked Abraham to sacrifice that son on the altar, Abraham did not hesitate. Abraham knew God's character and did not doubt, even when circumstances seemed to contradict God's promises.

When God was angry with the Israelites because of their disobedience, he told Moses he would give them everything he had promised their descendants: angels to drive out their enemies and a land flowing with milk and honey. But he said his presence would not go with them. Moses said if your presence doesn't go with us, then don't send us.

Do I have the kind of faith that makes the presence of God more important than *everything* else in my life? Is his presence more important than my family...my friends...my possessions...my health...my very life?

That really is the only kind of faith that can bring the peace that passes understanding. If we earnestly seek him, we will find him, and that will be the reward: God himself. And he will be sufficient.

Father God, help me to put you first in my life. Help me when I cannot see your hand at work in my circumstances to trust in your character and value your presence above all else. Help me when I don't understand what you are doing to remember that your ways are not my ways. You are God, you are good, and you are enough. In Jesus's name, amen.

Hebrews 11:1-2
Now faith is confidence in what we hope for and assurance about what we do not see. This is what the ancients were commended for.

Reflections From the Sunroom

Hebrews 11:6

And without faith it is impossible to please God, because anyone who comes to him must believe that he exists and that he rewards those who earnestly seek him.

Micah 7:7

But as for me, I watch in hope for the LORD, I wait for God my Savior; my God will hear me.

Reflection Time

How has God been speaking to you today? Take time to write it in your journal.

Chapter 65
Light for My Path

I totally messed myself up last night. I didn't feel very sleepy when I got in bed, so I went to YouTube on my iPad. Usually I listen to praise music or Scripture, but something else caught my eye and I began listening to a video made by a Christian "prepper." He was talking about the coming economic crash he believed would happen soon. He talked of all the things one needed to survive it. Then I listened to a link across from his by a non-Christian financial analyst, and their messages were eerily similar.

The next thing I knew it was 2:00 a.m. and I was still lying wide awake, overwhelmed and filled with worry. After all, I don't have any water purification tablets or gas masks or a place to "bug out" in the middle of nowhere.

Finally, I put on some Scripture (like I should have done to begin with) and fell asleep. I was awake again by 6:00 a.m. but dozed off and on until around 8:00, so I missed getting up with my husband, Al, and fixing his breakfast. I came out to the sunroom, trying to regain a sense of peace. I texted a couple of my fellow prayer warriors and my husband, telling them about my crazy night and asking them to pray for me to have the mind of Christ about the fear I had allowed in.

I prayed, "Lord, forgive me for allowing fear to overcome me like this. Please give me a message...something to help me to regain my peace."

Just then, my son came over so I could follow him to drop off his car at the shop. I left the house and headed for town, fuzzy headed and exhausted from lack of sleep.

As I stopped at a red light just down the road, my phone beeped with a text from my husband, my earthly hero.

His text read, "Just rest and let me take care of you like I always have. It will be OK. ☺"

It was like a message from my husband and God at the same time. Tears filled my eyes, and I felt peace begin to seep back in.

I finished the errand with my son and sleepily headed back home. It was rainy and gloomy, and I just wanted some hot oatmeal and a nap. As I turned in my driveway and headed up the lane, out of the corner of my eye, I saw a flickering brightness from across the meadow. What in the world was that? I slowed down and turned my head to look at a shining ribbon of light. The sun had broken through a small opening in the thick gray clouds and was shining on the neighboring lane across the field. It was the only thing illuminated, like a glistening path in the darkness. I stopped and stared in wonder.

A Scripture came to my mind. "Thy Word is a lamp for my feet and a light for my path."

A message of assurance from my other hero...Jesus.

Yes, perilous times are coming. I know this, not because of messages from doomsday preppers or financial analysts, but because God's Word says so.

I have nothing to fear when my eternal destiny is secure. The best "prepping" I can do right now is getting down on my knees in prayer for those who are lost, for the ones who can't see the shining light on the path, for those who need to wake up to what is going on around them and seek God while he may be found.

God, forgive me when I let the cares of this world lead me down the wrong path. You have marked out the way for me. Thank you for reminding me when I stray from it. No matter what happens in this crazy world, I am so thankful that my true home is with you. In Jesus's name, amen.

John 14:1-3, 6

"Do not let your hearts be troubled. You believe in God; believe also in me. My Father's house has many rooms; if that were not so, would I have told you that I am going there to prepare a place for you? And if I go and prepare a place for you, I will come back and take you to be with me that you also may be where I am...." Jesus answered, "I am the way and the truth and the life. No one comes to the Father except through me."

John 1:1-5

In the beginning was the Word, and the Word was with God, and the Word was God. He was with God in the beginning. Through him all things were made; without him nothing was made that has been made. In him was life, and that life was the light of all mankind. The light shines in the darkness, and the darkness has not over-come it.

Reflection Time

How has God been speaking to you today? Take time to write it in your journal.

Chapter 66
Sisters in Christ

I was thinking about my ladies Bible study this morning and what a blessing it has been. We have been meeting weekly at my house for three years now and have become very close to one another. Not only are we growing in God's Word, but we have become a huge support system for each other. There is a lot of learning, praying, singing, laughter, and tears. Some of these women have been through very difficult times. One has battled with cancer, one is going through a divorce. Another has recently lost a son, and one has lost her husband. Nearly everyone has a wayward child and unsaved friends and family members we pray for. I am so thankful for these sisters in Christ. They have become very precious to me.

Christians have a need for fellowship in the body of Christ in order to encourage and pray for each other. We need companions who are like minded, with the same spiritual goals and destination in mind.

Father God, I thank you for the gift of Christian fellowship… spiritual bonds that relate us as family in your kingdom. Bless my sisters in Christ, and help us to grow together—closer to you, and to each other. In Jesus's name, amen.

-»»» ✳ «««-

Matthew 18:20

For where two or three are gathered in my name, there am I among them. (ESV)

John 13:34-35

A new commandment I give to you, that you love one another: just as I have loved you, you also are to love one another. By this all people will know that you are my disciples, if you have love for one another. (ESV)

Romans 12:10

Love one another with brotherly affection. Outdo one another in showing honor. (ESV)

Colossians 2:2

That their hearts may be encouraged, being knit together in love, to reach all the riches of full assurance of understanding and the knowledge of God's mystery, which is Christ. (ESV)

Philippians 2:1-2

So if there is any encouragement in Christ, any comfort from love, any participation in the Spirit, any affection and sympathy, complete my joy by being of the same mind, having the same love, being in full accord and of one mind. (ESV)

Sherolyn Porter

Reflection Time

How has God been speaking to you today? Take
time to write it in your journal.

Chapter 67
Victory in Jesus

Walking out to feed the chickens on this chilly Easter morning, I stopped to take in the sight of the sun rising over the hilltops. Its brightness was shrouded in the cool morning mist rising silently from the ground. My thoughts turned to that Easter morning over two thousand years ago. I imagined the women making their way to the tomb of Jesus, in the early hours of the dawn. They carried spices to anoint the body of their much-loved Jesus. I pictured their heads hanging low and their shoulders drooping with the fatigue and sorrow from all they had been through in the last few days. They worried about how they were going to roll away the heavy stone, yet pressed onward to accomplish their task.

Reaching the tomb, they found it empty, with the stone rolled away and angels there instead of Jesus. The angels said, "Why do you look for the living among the dead? He is not here; he has risen! Remember how he told you while he was still with you in Galilee: The son of man must be delivered over to the hands of sinners, be crucified, and on the third day be raised again."

Then they remembered his words.

Suddenly, everything changed: the circumstances they expected to find, their entire mindset—what a whirlwind of emotions that must have been…grief and sorrow changing to ecstatic joy and elation.

Remember how he told you….

They had been a part of his ministry for years, yet traumatic events and troubles had made them forget his words…forget the hope that he had left with them.

Sometimes my walk can be like theirs: heart heavy, weighed down with the cares and sorrows of this world…and I too forget his words. I forget that he has risen, and that fact can make all the difference.

Father God, sometimes I am hard on myself when I forget to live in victory, when I've allowed my heart to be overwhelmed with my circumstances. Help me to remember your Word when my mind is focused on death instead of life. Thank you for comforting me with the realization that even your own disciples got off track too. Thank you for the victory I have in Jesus. Help me to always remember that his death gave me the power to be an overcomer. In Jesus's name, amen.

Luke 24:1-8

But on the first day of the week, at early dawn, they came to the tomb bringing the spices which they had prepared. And they found the stone rolled away from the tomb, but when they entered, they did not find the body of the Lord Jesus. While they were perplexed about this, behold, two men suddenly stood near them in dazzling clothing; and as the women were terrified and bowed their faces to the ground, the men said to them, "Why do you seek the living One among the dead? He is not here, but He has risen. Remember how He spoke to you while He was still in Galilee, saying that the Son of Man must be delivered into the hands of sinful men, and be crucified, and the third day rise again." And they remembered His words. (NASB)

John 14:1-6

"Do not let your heart be troubled; believe in God, believe also in Me. In My Father's house are many dwelling places; if it were not so, I would have told you; for I go to prepare a place for you. If I go and prepare a place for you, I will come again and receive you to Myself, that where I am, there you may be also. And you know the way where I am going." Thomas said to him, "Lord, we do not know where You are going, how do we know the way?" Jesus said to him, "I am the way, and the truth, and the life; no one comes to the Father but through Me." (NASB)

Reflection Time

How has God been speaking to you today? Take time to write it in your journal.

Chapter 68
Quest for the Good Life

I love going out to feed the chickens in the peaceful, early-morning hours. Nature is just waking up…the cool mist rises silently from the earth to greet the sun, and the birds begin their chorus of praise for a new day. If I wait until a little later in the morning to feed, the peaceful melodies of the dawn are accompanied by the sounds of a steady stream of traffic on the highway, over a quarter of a mile below us. I will be thankful when the buds on the trees have become clouds of leafy green, because the traffic noise will be greatly softened.

Nature is rarely in a hurry, and that is the pace that soothes my soul. I was thinking this morning about the "progress" that has been made over the last fifty years. I imagine most of it was in the quest to make all of our daily tasks quicker, to enable us to have more free time, yet it seems to have had the opposite effect. We are more rushed than we ever have been because our gadgets and gizmos come with a price, and we kill ourselves trying to make the money to pay for them. Our cell phones and computers, while keeping us in touch through cyber space, have us constantly checking emails and messages instead of looking into the eyes of the people who are all around us. Our time with God is a hurried ten-minute devotion (if we are lucky) and a few short prayers breathed out between muttered frustrations at the other drivers on the road. We come home exhausted at the end of the day and spend the evening flipping channels on the TV, where the media brainwashes us away from godly values and morals…and before we know it, things that we once considered sinful don't seem so bad anymore.

When we were children, we rode our bikes and played outside from morning until night. We laid on our backs under the trees and actually talked to the person right beside us. We read books, swung on rope swings, or maybe played baseball or Frisbee with the neighborhood kids.

Too many of our young people spend their summers behind closed blinds and curtains playing video games full of violence or being rushed by exhausted parents to a schedule of endless activities of dance, gymnastics, music lessons, and sport practices. Our quest for the good life has robbed us of our peace and threatens to steal our very souls. It reminds me a bit of the Scripture in Deuteronomy that says, when God brings you into a good land and when you eat and are satisfied, be careful that you do not forget the Lord.

God, help us to slow down and realize that what our hearts long for cannot be found in the rush. Help us to make the good life work for us and not against us. Give us wisdom in the management of our time and resources, and most of all help us to put you first. In Jesus's name, amen.

Deuteronomy 6:5–12
Love the LORD your God with all your heart and with all your soul and with all your strength. These commandments that I give you today are to be on your hearts. Impress them on your children. Talk about them when

you sit at home and when you walk along the road, when you lie down and when you get up. Tie them as symbols on your hands and bind them on your foreheads. Write them on the doorframes of your houses and on your gates. When the LORD your God brings you into the land he swore to your fathers, to Abraham, Isaac and Jacob, to give you—a land with large, flourishing cities you did not build, houses filled with all kinds of good things you did not provide, wells you did not dig, and vineyards and olive groves you did not plant—then when you eat and are satisfied, be careful that you do not forget the LORD, who brought you out of Egypt, out of the land of slavery.

Reflection Time

How has God been speaking to you today? Take time to write it in your journal.

Chapter 69

True Worship

God was talking to me about worship this morning. I love to sit in my sunroom, during my time with him, and listen to worship music. Sometimes all distractions fade completely away, and my heart becomes full of thankfulness for the goodness of the Lord and all he has done for me. I feel so humbled and amazed. That worship is a wonderful thing to experience.

There are many definitions of worship. Some define worship as a sense of adoration for a deity. For many the definition of worship includes Sunday Service…songs, offering, the message….

According to Webster's 1828 Dictionary, worship is "to honor with extravagant love and extreme submission."

Submission….

I had to think about that. Many times, worship makes *me* feel good, and I worship God for the good things he has done for *me*….

But true worship is not the songs and poems and prayers that make me feel happy and warm and fuzzy inside.

True worship is living a life in submission to God, making him first on my priority list. True worship is living a life of holiness, not a life that fulfills my own human desires—a life that serves God, whether things are going my way or not.

The meaning of true worship was expressed by Job when, after having lost everything, he fell to the ground in worship and said, "Naked I came from my mother's womb, and naked I will depart. The Lord gave and the Lord has taken away; may the name of the Lord be praised."

Wow! I am afraid I fall short in light of that example of worship.

Job could worship the Lord like that because he trusted in the goodness of God, even when things "took a turn for the worse." This is evident when he said, "Though he slay me…yet I will trust him."

Job depended on God…he trusted in God…and he waited on God.

Lord, I confess that I have a long way to go when it comes to true worship. Forgive me for the times when I *think* I'm making it "all about you" when, in reality, it's all about me. I confess that I fear I wouldn't have enough trust in you if I did lose it all. Help me to trust in your ultimate goodness no matter what goes on around me. In Jesus's name, amen.

Job 1:20-22

At this, Job got up and tore his robe and shaved his head. Then he fell to the ground in worship and said: "Naked I came from my mother's womb, and naked I will depart. The LORD gave and the LORD has taken away; may the name of the LORD be praised." In all this, Job did not sin by charging God with wrongdoing.

Reflections From the Sunroom

Psalm 27:13-14

I remain confident of this: I will see the goodness of the
Lord in the land of the living.
Wait for the Lord; be strong and take heart and wait
for the Lord.

Reflection Time

How has God been speaking to you today? Take
time to write it in your journal.

"American Dictionary of the English Language." Websters
Dictionary 1828. Accessed July 01, 2017.
http://webstersdictionary1828.com/.

Chapter 70
Prayers That Avail Much

Ask my children… they will tell you that their mama has no qualms about "gettin' in their bizness." If I see them heading down a path that I know will not be for their good, I don't hesitate to let them know my heart on the matter. I know that's not the "politically correct" thing to do these days, but I really don't care. My children might not like what I have to say sometimes, and they don't always follow my advice, but they *know* I love them.

There is a Scripture in the Psalms that says, "Search me, God, and know my heart; test me and know my anxious thoughts. See if there is any offensive way in me, and lead me in the way everlasting." I know I don't pray that prayer often enough.

In reality, if God's people prayed that prayer every day and confessed what he brought to mind, lives would be transformed…relationships would be transformed…the world would be transformed.

Why? Because the Word says that the prayers of a *righteous* man availeth much. Unless God is convicting and cleansing us from our sin, our prayers are not as effective. That's scriptural.

So why don't we pray it? Maybe because we don't want God in our "bizness"…and because it will mean change for us.

We live in a world where authority is not respected, whether it be parental, police, governmental, or God's.

If people respected God's authority, they would be living how the Bible tells them to live, and there would be peace—or at least a lot more of it: peace in our homes, in our neighborhoods, on our planet.

We also live in a world that has brainwashed us into thinking that humility is a bad thing and that the truth of the Bible is judgmental and offensive, so we keep quiet. We don't admonish one another, and we don't submit ourselves to God for his admonishment.

Whenever I pray that prayer, God often has something to talk to me about—and I don't always like it. If he brings to my mind an "offensive way in me," it will mean humbling myself…or giving up something that my flesh desires.

Yet if I want my prayers to be effective—and I do—I have to humble myself before God, ask him to find the offensive ways in me, and cleanse me.

People need effective prayers. There is so much pain and suffering in the world, much of it needless.

Father God, speak to your people. Help us to humble ourselves and invite your searching of our hearts. You have only our best in mind, and anything that we have to give up will only be for our good and our gain. You are good, and you desire good for us. Thank you, in the name of Jesus. Amen.

Psalm 139:23-24
Search me, God, and know my heart; test me and know
my anxious thoughts.
See if there is any offensive way in me, and lead me in
the way everlasting.

James 5:19-20

My brothers and sisters, if one of you should wander from the truth and someone should bring that person back, remember this: Whoever turns a sinner from the error of their way will save them from death and cover over a multitude of sins.

1 John 1:8-9

If we claim to be without sin, we deceive ourselves and the truth is not in us. If we confess our sins, he is faithful and just and will forgive us our sins and purify us from all unrighteousness.

James 5:16b

The prayer of a righteous person is powerful and effective.

Reflection Time

How has God been speaking to you today? Take time to write it in your journal.

Chapter 71
God's Word is Medicine

You've heard the old saying, "A spoonful of sugar helps the medicine go down." That came about because sometimes the cure is "hard to swallow."

The Bible says God's Word is like medicine. At times, it very sweetly comforts and encourages us. Other times, his Word is hard to swallow, and it is difficult to be obedient to it. But it is always medicine, always beneficial for all our needs.

Sometimes in life we are treated unjustly and unfairly by other people. Selfishness, greed, or jealousy triumph over love and loyalty. Our human nature gets angry and wants to retaliate. We want to be vindicated, to let others know how we have been cheated and mistreated. But that is the way of the world…and we have to be careful not to be drawn into it.

As Christians we are told to "come apart," that we are not of this world, that we cannot give the devil a foothold in our response.

So what should we do when our flesh threatens to overwhelm our spirit?

We must turn to the Word of God. It is a lamp for our feet and a light for our path.

Father God, help me when everything in me wants to fight and the desires of my flesh do not line up with your Word. I thank you for the gift of your Son whose death overcame the world. By his strength, I am able to be an overcomer. Help me always to keep my eyes on you. Remind me of your Word, which has direction for every area of my life. In Jesus's name, amen.

Ephesians 4:20-27, 29-32
That, however, is not the way of life you learned when you heard about Christ and were taught in him in accordance with the truth that is in Jesus. You were taught, with regard to your former way of life, to put off your old self, which is being corrupted by its deceitful desires; to be made new in the attitude of your minds; and to put on the new self, created to be like God in true righteousness and holiness.

Therefore each of you must put off falsehood and speak truthfully to your neighbor, for we are all members of one body. "In your anger do not sin." Do not let the sun go down while you are still angry, and do not give the devil a foothold....

Do not let any unwholesome talk come out of your mouths, but only what is helpful for building others up according to their needs, that it may benefit those who listen. And do not grieve the Holy Spirit of God, with whom you were sealed for the day of redemption. Get rid of all bitterness, rage and anger, brawling and slander, along with every form of malice. Be kind and compassionate to one another, forgiving each other, just as in Christ God forgave you.

-»»» ❋ «««-

Reflection Time

How has God been speaking to you today? Take
time to write it in your journal.

Chapter 72
Pity Party

I usually eat a fairly healthy diet, but every once in a while, I'll go a few days and eat whatever I want: fried food, sugar, lots of carbs, or too much meat. Every time I do that, I *always* think, "That was *so* not worth feeling like this!"

There are always consequences to my bad food choices. When I've made the wrong ones and feel awful as a result of it, I know I have to get back to eating healthfully. The same thing can happen in my spiritual life. I can choose servings of peace and joy...or bitterness, anger, and pride. And I will feel either good or awful as a result of those choices.

I have had a really bad day today. Let me rephrase that. I have *chosen* to have a really bad day today. I allowed my feelings to be hurt by someone, and then I took off on a tangent of my own—anger, resentment, pride...oh, I just let them all in.

I did not take it to the Lord...because...well, I guess I just wanted to wallow in it for a while, have my own little pity party. And so I ruined my whole day.

By dinner time and just before Bible study, I decided I had been miserable long enough and I needed to spend some time with the

Lord in repentance and prayer. Even though I had been the one who was hurt, I needed forgiveness for allowing resentment, self-pity, and pride to control my thought life for the whole day. I also asked for help with my own low self-esteem that had led me to buy into the words that had hurt my feelings.

After about twenty minutes in my quiet place with the Lord, his cleansing peace began to seep back in. I sure wished I would have done that to start with.

Father God, thank you for always being there, even when I sometimes take the roundabout way to find you. Help me to be better about seeking your wisdom first in every situation. I know your way will save me from heartache. In Jesus's name, amen.

->>>> ❋ <<<<-

2 Corinthians 10:3-5

For though we live in the world, we do not wage war as the world does. The weapons we fight with are not the weapons of the world. On the contrary, they have divine power to demolish strongholds. We demolish arguments and every pretension that sets itself up against the knowledge of God, and we take captive every thought to make it obedient to Christ.

Philippians 4:4-7

Rejoice in the Lord always. I will say it again: Rejoice! Let your gentleness be evident to all. The Lord is near. Do not be anxious about anything, but in every situation, by prayer and petition, with thanksgiving, present your requests to God. And the peace of God, which transcends all understanding, will guard your hearts and your minds in Christ Jesus.

215

Sherolyn Porter

→»»» ❋ «««←

Reflection Time

How has God been speaking to you today? Take
time to write it in your journal.

Chapter 73

An Aroma Pleasing to the Lord

Fragrance is a booming industry these days. We have fragrance diffusers for our homes and cars, tart warmers, candles, room sprays, incense, essential oils, and aroma therapies.

All these are lovely, and I have many of them.

Smells are a wonderful part of our world. There is nothing like coming home to the smell of dinner in the oven or freshly laundered sheets.

But some of our favorite fragrances can't be bottled, made into a candle, or cooked on a stovetop. We love the smell of our loved ones…they have a certain scent unique to them. I used to love the smell of my babies as I held them close. I would close my eyes and just breathe them in. I love the smell of my husband. When he used to go out of town for extended periods of time, I would wear one of his t-shirts to sleep in because it brought me comfort. When he hugs me before he leaves for work in the morning, I smell the faint hint of his cologne on me for hours afterward.

God loves fragrance too. It is obvious by all the wonderful scents he created on planet earth—all the beautiful things that bloom…the smell of fresh earth…a spring rain…the autumn leaves…the clean crisp smell of a snowy winter morning.

But did you know that God loves our smell too? The Bible says that those who are *in* Christ smell *like* Christ to God…so his fragrance must rub off on us too, like the scent that my husband's cologne leaves on me after our morning hug.

The Bible also says that our prayers are like incense to God. The gifts we give to one another also create a pleasing aroma to him.

Father God, I thank you for the wonderful sense of smell. I pray that my scent will be pleasing to you. Help me to stay in close relationship with your Son, to be faithful in prayer, and to be generous in my gifts to your people. In Jesus's name, amen.

Philippians 4:18b-19

They are a fragrant offering, an acceptable sacrifice, pleasing to God. And my God will meet all your needs according to the riches of his glory in Christ Jesus.

2 Corinthians 2:14-15

Now thanks be unto God, which always causeth us to triumph in Christ, and maketh manifest the savor of his knowledge by us in every place. For we are unto God a sweet savor of Christ, in them that are saved, and in them that perish. (KJV)

Revelation 5:8

And when he had taken it, the four living creatures and the twenty-four elders fell down before the Lamb. Each one had a harp and they were holding golden bowls full of incense, which are the prayers of God's people.

-»»» ✳ «««-

Reflection Time

How has God been speaking to you today? Take time to write it in your journal.

Chapter 74
Familiar With the Father

Today, I saw a video in which blindfolded children were told to pick their own mother out of a group of silent women.

The children always chose the right woman, even without their sense of hearing or sight.

Without exception, they knew their mother; they knew her touch…her essence. No scientific proof or DNA test was needed. They didn't have to see her to believe she was their mother. They knew her because they were so familiar with her. They knew who had met their needs and the touch of the one who had comforted them. It brought tears to my eyes.

The Holy Spirit whispered a Scripture to my heart:

"I am the good shepherd; I know my sheep and my sheep know me—just as the Father knows me and I know the Father."

It is so important that we spend daily time in our relationship with God so it will be easier to determine when we have strayed outside of it.

The Bible says in the last days, many will be deceived by false prophets—even by the anti-Christ. If we are not familiar with our heavenly Father before these things come to pass, we will be deceived.

Father God, thank you for revealing your truth to me today. I want to be so close to you that it would be no trouble for me to discern you from anything that would seek to deceive me. Keep me close, in Jesus's name, amen.

→⇒⟩⟩ ❋ ⟨⟨⟨←

Colossians 2:8

Be careful that no one takes you captive through philos-ophy and empty deceit based on human tradition, based on the elemental forces of the world, and not based on Christ. (Holman Christian Standard Bible)

2 Timothy 3:13-14

But evil people and impostors will go from bad to worse as they deceive others and are themselves deceived. But as for you, continue in what you have learned and found to be true, because you know from whom you learned it. (International Standard Version)

Luke 21:8

He said, "Be careful that you are not deceived, because many will come in my name and say, 'I AM' and, 'The time has come.' Don't follow them." (ISV)

Matthew 24:24

For false messiahs and false prophets will appear and perform great signs and wonders to deceive, if possible, even the elect.

→⇒⟩⟩ ❋ ⟨⟨⟨←

Reflection Time

How has God been speaking to you today? Take time to write it in your journal.

Chapter 75
Self-control

I was feeling unsettled this morning as I came out to my sunroom to spend some quiet time with the Lord. I was ashamed of the frustrated, angry thoughts I was having about some situations over which I have no control.

"Lord," I lamented, "I feel like I am so far from obtaining the fruit of the Spirit sometimes. You surely must get tired of working on me."

I put on some praise and worship music and settled down in my chair with a sad sigh.

As I sat listening to the music and trying to quiet my thoughts, the words of a song I had listened to dozens of times before began to wrap themselves around my heart in a new way.

My spirit began to settle down within me, and then the next verse brought tears to my eyes as it talked about how the Father makes us like Jesus…how he brings beauty for ashes and frees us from guilt and shame.

Thank you, Jesus.

The Lord began to speak to my heart. He showed me how anxiety comes from wanting control over things that I cannot control.

When I am trying to control circumstances, I am not trusting him. In truth, my struggle to obtain control causes the loss of everything I am striving to gain: love, joy, peace, forbearance, kindness, goodness, faithfulness, gentleness, and self-control.

Self-control....

The only control I truly have is self-control.

I can exercise that by choosing to trust God for the things I can't control and asking him to help me with my response to those things.

Father, I thank you for your tireless patience and faithfulness to complete the good work you have begun in me. Help me to cooperate with you. In Jesus's name, amen.

Galatians 5:22–23

But the fruit of the Spirit is love, joy, peace, forbearance, kindness, goodness, faithfulness, gentleness and self-control. Against such things there is no law.

Philippians 1:6

Being confident of this, that he who began a good work in you will carry it on to completion until the day of Christ Jesus.

Revelation 3:5

He that overcometh, the same shall be clothed in white raiment; and I will not blot out his name out of the book of life, but I will confess his name before my Father, and before his angels. (KJV)

Reflection Time

How has God been speaking to you today? Take time to write it in your journal.

Chapter 76
No Root of Bitterness

There is a lot of work to gardening. I start my seeds indoors when it is still cold and snowy outside. I have more control in those conditions, to protect my seedlings in regards to temperature and light. Even though the seedlings need regular care and maintenance inside, it is a lot more work when I move them outside. Then my garden is at the mercy of nature...and I don't have as much control.

I am having a frustrating battle with thistles this year. My garden beds were literally full of them. I have spent hours digging them out, and I have found that, if I don't get deep enough to remove the whole root, then they come right back up and are nearly impossible to remove without harming my vegetables.

A few weeks ago, as I was digging them up for about the third time, I thought, "Lord, I just bet you have a lesson in this for me somewhere."

Last night as I was digging thistles yet again, one of their little barbs sliced my toe, and this morning it is red, sore, and festering.

So important to get those roots out....

It reminded me of some bitterness I thought I had dealt with a long time ago; it recently resurfaced, as I am still struggling to forgive someone. It reminded me of the deep roots of those thistles.

Father God, give me grace to forgive when I feel unforgiving. Help me to recognize and get rid of any root of bitterness in me. In Jesus's name, amen.

Hebrews 12:15
See to it that no one fails to obtain the grace of God; that no "root of bitterness" springs up and causes trouble, and by it many become defiled. (ESV)

Reflection Time

How has God been speaking to you today? Take time to write it in your journal.

Chapter 77

Land That Drinks Rain From Heaven

I was reading in my Bible this morning, and something in Deuteronomy jumped out at me about gardening.

The Israelites were about to cross into the Promised Land, and God said:

> The land you are entering to take over is not like the
> land of Egypt, from which you have come, where
> you planted your seed and irrigated it by foot as in a
> vegetable garden. But the land you are crossing the
> Jordan to take possession of is a land of mountains
> and valleys that drinks rain from heaven. It is a land
> the LORD your God cares for; the eyes of the LORD
> your God are continually on it from the beginning of
> the year to its end. (Deuteronomy 11:10-12, NIV)

Wow! Land that drinks rain from heaven…land that the Lord cares for….

It spoke to my heart about my spiritual walk. A few years ago, I came to the realization that there was more to my walk with God than I was experiencing.

Reflections From the Sunroom

I was determined to find a place of rest with the Lord, determined to seek his presence.

It took the discipline of countless quiet times, but when I began to experience his sweet presence, it was like drinking rain from heaven.

However, there is a prerequisite for that sweet fellowship: obedience. Deuteronomy goes on to say:

> So if you faithfully obey the commands I am giving you today—to love the LORD your God and to serve him with all your heart and with all your soul—then I will send rain on your land in its season, both autumn and spring rains, so that you may gather in your grain, new wine and olive oil. I will provide grass in the fields for your cattle, and you will eat and be satisfied. (Deuteronomy 11:13-15, NIV)

I tend to be stubborn. This stubbornness carries over in my walk with the Lord. The Word is a guide for how I am to behave as a believer (even in my thought life), but sometimes I struggle with obedience to it. I know when I am being disobedient to his word—letting anger, resentment, or bitterness toward others invade my thought life—because it has an effect on my fellowship with the Lord.

Dear God, I don't want anything to hinder my sweet fellowship with you. Help me to be obedient to your ways. I want your sweet rain in the land of my soul. In Jesus's name, amen.

->>>> ❋ <<<<-

Deuteronomy 11:8-15

Observe therefore all the commands I am giving you today, so that you may have the strength to go in and take over the land that you are crossing the Jordan to possess, and so that you may live long in the land the

*L*ORD *swore to your ancestors to give to them and their descendants, a land flowing with milk and honey. The land you are entering to take over is not like the land of Egypt, from which you have come, where you planted your seed and irrigated it by foot as in a vegetable garden. But the land you are crossing the Jordan to take possession of is a land of mountains and valleys that drinks rain from heaven. It is a land the* LORD *your God cares for; the eyes of the* LORD *your God are continually on it from the beginning of the year to its end.*

So if you faithfully obey the commands I am giving you today—to love the LORD *your God and to serve him with all your heart and with all your soul— then I will send rain on your land in its season, both autumn and spring rains, so that you may gather in your grain, new wine and olive oil. I will provide grass in the fields for your cattle, and you will eat and be satisfied.*

Reflection Time

How has God been speaking to you today? Take time to write it in your journal.

Chapter 78
Praying for the Stranger

My husband Al and I were coming back from Pennsylvania last weekend, and we stopped at a restaurant for supper. While we were eating, I was people watching. In two different booths across the aisle, I saw single dads (I assumed by the ring-less left hand), each with a small son, probably having a last Sunday evening meal before they took them home from their weekend visit.

One father seemed thoroughly engaged with his son, and the child was well behaved. The other father spent most of the meal texting on his cell phone, and that child was bouncing off the walls.

It made my heart sad for their struggles. At the table directly behind me, I could overhear bits and pieces of a conversation that a family was having. The father, trying to take advantage of a teachable moment, said, "Well, the Bible says…" and his young teenage daughter interrupted him with a short tone to her voice, "Dad, don't start. I don't want to hear it." He drifted off into silence, and their conversation lagged. My heart ached for him, and I wanted to reach over the booth and place a comforting hand on his shoulder.

As I finished up my prayer list this morning, the Lord brought each of those families to my mind. I don't know their names and will never see them again, yet I can pray for them—for the healing revelation of God to be brought forth in their lives, for restoration of broken relationships....

What a wonderful God, who knows every intimate detail about every person in each of these situations.

I don't know how my prayers will make a difference, but I need to be obedient to his leading.

Father God, you are not limited by time and space. You are here in my prayer time with me and also with each person on my list. I trust that my prayers will make a difference, and I thank you for the privilege of bringing them before you. In Jesus's name, amen.

Colossians 4:2
Devote yourselves to prayer, being watchful and thankful.

1 John 5:14-15
This is the confidence we have in approaching God: that if we ask anything according to his will, he hears us. And if we know that he hears us—whatever we ask— we know that we have what we asked of him.

John 14:13
And I will do whatever you ask in my name, so that the Father may be glorified in the Son.

Reflection Time

How has God been speaking to you today? Take time to write it in your journal.

Chapter 79
They Do Not Fear Bad News

I have been worried today. We had our ladies Bible Study last night, and after the study, one of my closest friends mentioned that she needed to lose some weight. I had noticed the last couple of weeks that she was gaining a lot of weight in her stomach area, but who wants to tell anyone they are looking bigger around the middle....

However, when she said that, I encouraged her to go to the doctor. "You're not gaining weight anywhere else. I just think you need to be checked out."

She took my words to heart and made an appointment with her doctor for today. The doctor was also alarmed, and has scheduled a scan for tomorrow.

I am trying not to let fear influence my thinking, instead asking God for a good report for her. I remember when another gal in our group was diagnosed with cancer a couple of years ago...and all the uncertainty and fear that went with it. But God was faithful to hear our prayers, and she made it through a double mastectomy and chemo and is now doing fine.

Still, a cold fear seems to wrap itself around my heart....

Father God, please help me when uncertainty and fear of what the future may hold overshadow my confidence in your ability to carry me and those I love, no matter what. Help my dear friend as she awaits her test results. Help us to keep our minds stayed on you and to trust in you so that we can remain in the only place of perfect peace. In Jesus's name, amen.

→→⟩⟩⟩ ❄ ⟨⟨⟨←

2 Timothy 1:7
For God has not given us a spirit of fear and timidity, but of power, love, and self-discipline. (NLT)

Psalm 34:7
The angel of the LORD encamps around those who fear him, and he delivers them.

Matthew 10:31
So don't be afraid; you are worth more than many sparrows.

John 14:27
I am leaving you with a gift—peace of mind and heart. And the peace I give is a gift the world cannot give. So don't be troubled or afraid. (NLT)

Joshua 1:9
This is my command—be strong and courageous! Do not be afraid or discouraged. For the LORD your God is with you wherever you go. (NLT)

Psalm 56:3
When I am afraid, I put my trust in you.

Reflections From the Sunroom

Psalm 91:4-8

He will cover you with his feathers. He will shelter you with his wings. His faithful promises are your armor and protection. Do not be afraid of the terrors of the night, nor the arrow that flies in the day. Do not dread the disease that stalks in darkness, nor the disaster that strikes at midday. Though a thousand fall at your side, though ten thousand are dying around you, these evils will not touch you. (NLT)

Psalm 112:7

They do not fear bad news; they confidently trust the LORD to care for them. (NLT)

⤗⤗⤗ ❋ ⤖⤖⤖

Reflection Time

How has God been speaking to you today? Take time to write it in your journal.

Chapter 80
But the Spirit Intercedes for Us

My husband had the day off today, and I joined him to run some errands in town. We stopped at a hardware store, and as he talked to the man at the counter, I wandered around aimlessly, my mind seemingly a million miles away. My phone rang, and I saw that it was my dear friend who had gone for a scan earlier today. Her voice was flat and emotionless as it uttered two words: "ovarian cancer."

The thudding of my heart threatened to drown out her voice as I made my way hurriedly out of the hardware store to the car.

"What????" I said, feeling a surge of anger that someone would even tell her such bad news. I was in a panic to get into the car before the tears that threatened to overwhelm me actually did so. "How can they possibly know that with just a scan and no biopsy?" I stammered.

"They can tell from the scan," she said, her voice still flat. "Surgery is scheduled for next week...."

I felt so helpless as I said, "I'm praying...I love you...." We hung up and I sat in stunned silence for a moment, before a torrent of tears began. "God...WHY??" I wailed.

I saw the alarmed face of my husband as he opened the car door. "What is WRONG?"

"Jenny got her test results" I sobbed. "It's ovarian cancer!"

"Oh no," he responded softly, and I could see my own sorrow reflected in his eyes.

We drove home in silence. I thought about how she must be feeling. My own fear and grief were overwhelming; I could not imagine the depth of hers. Funny how just a few words can change a life.

Father God, sometimes I don't even know how to pray. Holy Spirit, please pray for my dear friend.... In Jesus's name, amen.

Romans 8:25-27

But if we hope for what we do not see, we wait for it with patience. Likewise the Spirit helps us in our weakness. For we do not know what to pray for as we ought, but the Spirit himself intercedes for us with groanings too deep for words. And he who searches hearts knows what is the mind of the Spirit, because the Spirit intercedes for the saints according to the will of God. (ESV)

Reflection Time

How has God been speaking to you today? Take time to write it in your journal.

Chapter 81
Keeping My Eyes on You

I get motion sickness so easily anymore. No one calls "shotgun" at our house these days (on the rare occasion that we are all getting in the same vehicle). They already know that Mom is the one who needs that position. This from a girl who used to love to ride roller coasters. One of the downsides of aging I guess....

Even when I ride "shotgun," I have to fix my eyes straight ahead. If I look to the side, my stomach begins to churn.

The Lord reminded me of this equilibrium problem as I sat down for my quiet time with him this morning. My heart was heavy as I put on my praise and worship music, and I stared out the windows at a dark and gloomy sky.

Yesterday, one of my dearest friends in the world received some frightening and unsettling news from the doctor, and she has been constantly on my heart and in my thoughts since.

This morning, I woke up to a text from my sister about the earthquake in Nepal. I thought about the fear and confusion the victims and rescue workers must be feeling.

I breathed a prayer for supernatural strength and peace for those in Nepal.

I prayed for God to flood my sweet friend with a sense of his presence.

As my mind was consumed with these thoughts, the lyrics from a song that was playing in the background began to capture my attention. They reminded me that God can calm the storm for me, that when I keep my eyes on him, it *will* be well with my soul, no matter what is going on around me.

Many times in life, our worlds can go reeling—whether it's from an earthquake or a phone call—and things can begin to feel as if they are spinning out of control.

Father God, when the world is shaken, help me to fix my eyes on the one secure thing…the only thing that doesn't change. It seems more and more like you are the only safe place to be. Keep my eyes firmly fixed on you today. Help me to take fearful thoughts captive, and please help all those who are struggling to do the same. Help me to remember when my eyes are fixed on you, I can regain my balance. The waves and wind still know your name. In Jesus's name, amen.

Hebrews 12:1c-2a
And let us run with perseverance the race marked out for us, fixing our eyes on Jesus, the pioneer and perfecter of faith.

2 Corinthians 4:18
So we fix our eyes not on what is seen, but on what is unseen, since what is seen is temporary, but what is unseen is eternal.

Sherolyn Porter

Reflection Time

How has God been speaking to you today? Take
time to write it in your journal.

Chapter 82

Prepare in Advance

In order to be successful at something, one must prepare in advance. Athletes prepare ahead of time for their sport or event by practicing the same drills again and again until their responses become second nature. They can act without consciously thinking about it.

The same needs to be true of our spiritual lives.

I got up early this morning, but instead of my usual quiet time with the Lord, I got ready to go to the hospital. One of my dearest friends was having serious surgery today, and I wanted to sit with her family while they waited.

My dear friend's response to a frightening diagnosis just two weeks ago has been nothing short of amazing. Although she has been afraid at times, I have watched her counter that fear with faith over and over again.

As I showered, dressed, and packed my bag with a few things to take with me, some anxious thoughts began to pass through my mind. The funny thing was, I noticed that—in my spirit, beneath the anxious thoughts—there flowed a steady stream of familiar praise and worship tunes, even though no music was playing at the time.

As each worried thought was countered—without any conscious effort from me—by bits of Scripture or words from a praise and worship song, the anxious thoughts began to fade away, calmed by the music in my soul…God's Spirit, giving me strength and peace.

I am so thankful for the quiet times I have spent with the Lord. There is nothing more important we can do for ourselves than saturate our minds with the things of God.

Sometimes life is just going to blindside us, and things can spiral out of control. If the Word of God has saturated our minds and hearts, we can regain our balance.

I was at the hospital for a good part of the day with my friend's family and friends. As we waited for our loved one to get out of surgery, it was so good to be with other believers—people for whom praying together was second nature, despite a crowded waiting room.

I'm sure it won't be our last battle with fear over this situation, but I am so glad our response is second nature. We don't have to scramble to look for answers.

Father God, fill that hospital room with your peaceful, healing presence tonight. I pray your sweet rest for my dear friend and for her husband, as he spends the night sitting by her bedside. Comfort her children and her parents, and bless their rest tonight as well. I thank you for your faithfulness, that even in the midst of fear, uncertainty, or pain, we can say, "Through it all, my eyes are on you. It is well with my soul." In Jesus's name, amen.

Colossians 3:1-3, 15-17
Since, then, you have been raised with Christ, set your
hearts on things above, where Christ is, seated at the
right hand of God. Set your minds on things above, not

on earthly things. For you died, and your life is now hidden with Christ in God....

Let the peace of Christ rule in your hearts, since as members of one body you were called to peace. And be thankful. Let the message of Christ dwell among you richly as you teach and admonish one another with all wisdom through psalms, hymns, and songs from the Spirit, singing to God with gratitude in your hearts. And whatever you do, whether in word or deed, do it all in the name of the Lord Jesus, giving thanks to God the Father through him.

Reflection Time

How has God been speaking to you today? Take time to write it in your journal.

Chapter 83

You Perceive My Thoughts From Afar

My morning started in the garden with the flowers and the chickens, as it has for the last three weeks. I worked on the chicken coop door, which has been giving me some trouble, watered the garden, transplanted some sweet potatoes, and moved my tomato plants outside.

Then I went in to shower and get dressed for the day. As I was putting on my makeup, the Lord spoke to my heart. "So…do you want to talk about it?"

"Talk about what, Lord?"

"Talk about Jenny," he whispered.

My throat immediately constricted. "Not really," I said and went back to fixing my hair, feeling hot tears behind my eyes.

The Lord persisted. "You haven't spent quiet time with me since Jenny was diagnosed with cancer.…"

"What? That can't be true.…"

I finished getting ready, went downstairs, and put the beginnings of dinner in the crockpot. I started the dishwasher and opened the front door to call the dogs in. Noticing how beautiful the falling flower petals were on the sidewalk, I went inside to get my iPad and take some pictures.

"So, do you want to talk about it?" I heard the whisper again. "You're angry...."

"I'm not angry."

I went back inside and started some laundry. The washer door hadn't closed completely, and I gave it a satisfying extra-hard slam... then I kicked some laundry that was lying on the floor.

"You really need to talk with Me about this...." the still small voice came again.

Remembering what the Lord had said earlier about the last time I had spent quiet time with him, I went to check the dates of my last writing. There was only one since the day after Jenny's diagnosis: the day of her surgery, when we got the news that the cancer was stage 3. It was not only on her ovary, but in her lymph nodes, on her stomach and intestines, and in her blood...Jenny was going to have a very long grueling fight ahead of her.

I sighed and went to the sunroom, sat down somewhat defiantly, and turned on some music.

"Okay. What, Lord? You want me to tell you that I'm angry? Okay. I'm ANGRY! I feel like You let my friend down!!"

"Cry," said the still small voice.

My aching throat threatened to choke me as a few tears began sliding down my cheeks, and then a flood of them....

I began to sob and pound the chair with my fists.

A few minutes later, with puffy eyes, a headache, and stuffy nose, my spirit began to fill with a sense of peace.

I opened my devotional to read and a bit of Scripture jumped out at me:

> For we do not want you to be unaware, brethren,
> of our affliction which came to us in Asia, that we
> were burdened excessively, beyond our strength,

so that we despaired even of life; indeed, we had the sentence of death within ourselves so that we would not trust in ourselves, but in God who raises the dead; who delivered us from so great a peril of death, and will deliver us, he on whom we have set our hope. And he will yet deliver us. (2 Corinthians 1:8-10, NASB)

Wow. I've got to share that with my Jenny....

Father God, I thank you that you never leave me, that you stay right with me—even when I am running from you. Forgive me when I don't bring my concerns to you. With you, all things are possible; help me to put my trust in that promise. Your Word says that you work all things for the good of those who love you and are called according to your purpose. Thank you for encouraging me to cry on your shoulder. In Jesus's name, amen.

Psalm 139:1-2
You have searched me, LORD,
and you know me.
You know when I sit and when I rise;
You perceive my thoughts from afar.

Reflection Time

How has God been speaking to you today? Take time to write it in your journal.

Chapter 84
"Guardening"

I worked out in the garden this morning in the coolness of early dawn. The weeds are horrendous this year—not just the little garden-variety, easily-pulled-up weeds, but the thistles and the morning glory vines.

They are choking my plants—and prickling me if I'm not careful.

I was enjoying yanking and chopping...for some reason, I felt particularly vengeful toward the unwanted intruders today.

Some of them I had let go too long, and they were especially difficult to pull up.

God began to speak to my heart about vigilance.

He showed me that prayer is like gardening...or "guardening." One must be vigilant to keep the enemy at bay.

I hear people say, "Oh, so and so is a prayer warrior...call them to pray for you."

But biblically, we are *all* called to pray—about *everything*.

Prayer is also warfare...it is our frontline defense. A soldier stationed on the frontline in battle does not neglect his post, because all the forces behind him are depending on him to do his job. If a soldier decides she is too tired or needs to do other things, or maybe she is not happy with some decisions allowed by the commander in chief…whatever the reason, if the soldier decides to abandon his/her post, it leaves others vulnerable to enemy attack.

Two of the analogies used over and over again in God's Word are gardening and warfare.

We are all called to be vigilant and faithful in prayer—not just the "prayer warriors." The prayer warriors are simply those soldiers who take their position on the frontline seriously.

Father God, I confess I have been lax in my prayer life lately. I am sorry. As your child, I know you hear me when I pray…help me not to take that responsibility lightly. Bring those with needs to my mind, and help me to be vigilant in my "guardening." I thank you for the authority you give your children to come against the enemy in the name of Jesus. Amen.

Luke 18:1-8a

Then Jesus told his disciples a parable to show them that they should always pray and not give up. He said: "In a certain town there was a judge who neither feared God nor cared what people thought. And there was a widow in that town who kept coming to him with the plea, 'Grant me justice against my adversary.' "For some time he refused. But finally he said to himself, 'Even though I don't fear God or care what people think, yet because this widow keeps bothering me, I will see that she gets justice, so that she won't eventually come and attack me!'" And the Lord said, "Listen to what the unjust judge says. And will not God bring about justice for his chosen ones, who cry out to him day and night? Will he keep putting them off? I tell you, he will see that they get justice, and quickly."

Philippians 4:6
Do not be anxious about anything, but in every situation, by prayer and petition, with thanksgiving, present your requests to God.

Colossians 4:2
Devote yourselves to prayer, being watchful and thankful.

1 Thessalonians 5:17
Pray continually.

James 5:16b
The prayer of a righteous person is powerful and effective.

Ephesians 6:12
For our struggle is not against flesh and blood, but against the rulers, against the powers, against the world forces of this darkness, against the spiritual forces of wickedness in the heavenly places. (NASB)

Ephesians 6:18
With all prayer and petition pray at all times in the Spirit, and with this in view, be on the alert with all perseverance and petition for all the saints. (NASB)

2 Corinthians 10:3-4
For though we walk in the flesh, we do not war according to the flesh, for the weapons of our warfare are not of the flesh, but divinely powerful for the destruction of fortresses. (NASB)

→⟩⟩⟩ ✻ ⟨⟨⟨←

Reflection Time

How has God been speaking to you today? Take time to write it in your journal.

Chapter 85
Anchor of My Soul

Whenever we put our boat in the river, I get into the boat while my husband backs the boat and trailer down into the water. Then it is my job to back the boat off the trailer, while he takes the truck and trailer back up to the parking lot.

I don't really like that job. If the engine stops running once I'm in the river…unless I have an anchor down, I am at the mercy of the current; if it is swift, it can be frightening.

Life (our boat) can be like that. Sometimes the engine unexpectedly stalls out, the current grows swift, and we can go careening out of control—mentally, emotionally, and spiritually.

Dangers lie ahead…things that are unknown and out of our control.

But if we remember the anchor, we can ground ourselves in the midst of the current…and the anchor holds.

Father God, when things seem to spin out of control, help me to focus on you, my Anchor. You were there in the beginning. You will be there in the end. You are the same yesterday, today, and tomorrow. You are steadfast and true. You spoke the great universe into being, and you know the very number of hairs on my head. You hem

me in behind and before. You are with me wherever I go. Calm me
when my heart is afraid. In Jesus's name. Amen.

→→≫ ❊ ᛕᛕᛕ⟵

Psalm 139:1-18
You have searched me, LORD,
and you know me.
You know when I sit and when I rise;
you perceive my thoughts from afar.
You discern my going out and my lying down;
you are familiar with all my ways.
Before a word is on my tongue
you, LORD, know it completely.
You hem me in behind and before,
and you lay your hand upon me.
Such knowledge is too wonderful for me,
too lofty for me to attain.
Where can I go from your Spirit?
Where can I flee from your presence?
If I go up to the heavens, you are there;
if I make my bed in the depths, you are there.
If I rise on the wings of the dawn,
if I settle on the far side of the sea,
Even there your hand will guide me,
your right hand will hold me fast.
If I say, "Surely the darkness will hide me
and the light become night around me,"
Even the darkness will not be dark to you;
the night will shine like the day,
for darkness is as light to you.
For you created my inmost being;

you knit me together in my mother's womb.
I praise you because I am fearfully and wonderfully made;
your works are wonderful,
I know that full well.
My frame was not hidden from you
when I was made in the secret place,
when I was woven together in the depths of the earth.
Your eyes saw my unformed body;
all the days ordained for me were written in your book
before one of them came to be.
How precious to me are your thoughts, God!
How vast is the sum of them!
Were I to count them,
they would outnumber the grains of sand—
when I awake, I am still with you.

Reflection Time

How has God been speaking to you today? Take time to write it in your journal.

Chapter 86
What is Happening?

Jenny's cancer diagnosis prompted all the girls in the Bible Study to make their own appointments for check-ups (some of us long overdue). Our collective appointments are all spread out over the next two months.

Peggy's was the first one scheduled. We sat in stunned silence when she told us that her mammogram showed something suspicious and that she had to have a biopsy. She didn't want anyone with her, but Jenny and I went and sat in the lobby the morning of her biopsy, unbeknownst to her, while she underwent the procedure. I know it was hard for Jenny, having been in this same situation a few short weeks before. We prayed for strength, peace, and a favorable result. When she came out the door from the procedure room, we were the first people she saw, and we could tell by the look on her face that she was glad we had come. We embraced and chatted, and we soon decided that the three of us should have lunch at my house. We visited all afternoon in the sunroom—listening to worship music… praying…laughing…and trying to quell the fear that kept rising up in each of us.

A few days later, I had gone to the chicken coop to let the chickens out into the yard so they could roam a little bit. I was enjoying the smell of early summer, breathing deeply of the cool evening air, as I walked over to meet my husband who had just come home from work. My cell phone buzzed and I answered.

"Are you sitting down?" The voice belonged to my friend Peg, and my heart sank at her words. "The biopsy was positive...I have breast cancer."

"Oh, Peggy," I breathed. "What in the world is happening?"

She told me that she had an appointment to schedule her surgery. Her voice sounded strong and determined, and I took courage from it. I don't even remember what I said after that. My brain felt numb, and I could see that my husband was questioning the look on my face. I got off the phone with Peggy and began to cry as I told him her diagnosis. He tried to comfort me, and I just kept thinking how unbelievable it all was.

Suddenly the thought of my own checkup, scheduled for a couple weeks from then, loomed like a dark, threatening mountain in front of me.

Father God, I feel like my world is rocking right now. Please help my friends...give them strength...give them peace. Lord, please intervene...bring healing and guidance and wisdom. Help me with this fear that is threatening to suffocate me right now. In Jesus's name, amen.

Isaiah 43:2
When you pass through the waters,
I will be with you;
and when you pass through the rivers,
they will not sweep over you.

Sherolyn Porter

When you walk through the fire,
you will not be burned;
the flames will not set you ablaze.

-»»» ❋ «««-

Reflection Time

How has God been speaking to you today? Take time to write it in your journal.

Chapter 87
Praise Him in the Storm

There are many things we hold onto in this life that give us security: our spouses, families, friends, our homes, good health, our jobs, our financial portfolio....

Yet no matter how tightly we grasp these things, none of them are permanent security. Any and all of them can be taken away from us without a moment's notice. Holding on to any of them too tightly can just lead to fear.

Another of my closest friends has been diagnosed with cancer in the last week...two beautiful women that I love and respect with all my heart...diagnosed within the last month.

My own emotions have been on a roller coaster ride, going up and down, back and forth between a stunned sort of numbness to fear, then peace, grief, and then hope.

I had barely finished reeling from the news of my first friend's diagnosis when I got the news of my second friend's diagnosis. "Are you sitting down?" were the words she started with....

And no, I wasn't. I have not "sat down" for a while. I have kept myself extremely busy to the point of falling exhausted into bed every night and waking up to another list of "must-be-dones" the next day. I have not had consistent quiet time with the Lord for over a month.

Yet the Lord has been whispering to my heart through all my busyness. The words of a song have played in the background of my mind throughout every busy day. In the song, the Lord is calling to his beloved child to come into his courts…into his presence.

Yesterday evening was our ladies Bible study. The Lord spoke to my heart that afternoon. "You need to have praise and worship tonight." I texted my friend Em, the musical one in the group, and asked if she could bring some music and play the piano for us to sing.

The women of our group gathered near the piano and surrounded my two treasured friends while our beautiful Em played, and we sang until we were nearly hoarse—praise to the Giver of life, the Lion of Judah, Jehovah Rapha, the LORD who heals….

When I could sing no more, I just stood there listening to them, with eyes closed and tears streaming down my face.

Both of my friends have a deep faith, and I have been in awe of how they have handled their worlds being rocked to the core. God is truly faithful. When we cannot see his hand, we must trust his heart. It's going to be a rough year, but we will trust, and we will speak life.

God, I've missed you. Forgive me for shutting you out, the one true thing I need. In order for me to be of any help to my friends, I know that I have to be filled up with you. Give me a hunger for your Word again and for time with you. I love you. In Jesus's name, amen.

Philippians 4:13
I can do all this through him who gives me strength.

Philippians 4:19

And my God will meet all your needs according to the riches of his glory in Christ Jesus.

Ephesians 3:14-21

For this reason I bow my knees before the Father, from whom every family in heaven and on earth derives its name, that He would grant you, according to the riches of His glory, to be strengthened with power through His Spirit in the inner man, so that Christ may dwell in your hearts through faith; and that you, being rooted and grounded in love, may be able to comprehend with all the saints what is the breadth and length and height and depth, and to know the love of Christ which surpasses knowledge, that you may be filled up to all the fullness of God. Now to Him who is able to do far more abundantly beyond all that we ask or think, according to the power that works within us, to Him be the glory in the church and in Christ Jesus to all generations forever and ever. Amen. (NASB)

Reflection Time

How has God been speaking to you today? Take time to write it in your journal.

Chapter 88
Outdoor War Room

My prayer room today is outdoors, where the sanctuary smells like honeysuckle and the music consists of the sweet melody of numerous bird songs.

In the peace of this place, I love to sit back for a little while and bask in what seems like a tiny glimpse of heaven. I enjoy thinking about the Lord and spending time in his presence.

But I am not just here for my enjoyment. Although I would like to linger in the tranquility of these moments, I must go to battle. This is my wartime.

In the midst of the fragrant smells of early summer, the cool wind brushes the tears from my face as I bring my prayer list to the Father.

The enemy is the master of deception, stealing what we once held dear right out from under our noses and unraveling the very fabric of our families, our churches, and our government...and one day, they will barely be recognizable.

The definitions that used to characterize who we were and what we stood for have become confused and a source of contention and division. What once was evil is now called good, and taking exception to that is now labeled intolerant. *Choice* is a word that has made the murder of millions of babies acceptable. Marriage no longer means the union of a man and a woman.

Those who come out as transgender are called heroes while the veterans who fought for our freedoms have a difficult time receiving adequate health care.

This deception has even spread to the church, where the word *grace* is used as an excuse to have sex outside of marriage or divorce without biblical grounds. When godly people take exception, the word *judgmental* is thrown out to shut them up.

Our grandchildren will not have the comparisons we have. They don't know how things used to be. Their measuring stick starts in the here and now.

I know that I have brothers and sisters in Christ who are battling alongside me in their own war rooms right now. We pray against the lying and deceptive spirits that are eroding the very foundations of our nation and threatening the souls of our children. In our war rooms we battle for families, for marriages on the edge of destruction, for children who have gone astray, for health issues, and for estranged relationships. We ask for comfort for those who have lost loved ones. We plead for strength and peace for Christian brothers and sisters all over the world who are facing tremendous persecution for their faith. We pray against corruption in government and against the liberties that schools take as they shout, "separation of church and state!" and try to shape the moral values of our children.

I pray the promises in Scripture, for that is my weapon in this battle. The Word of God is sharper than a two-edged sword. It does not return void but will accomplish what God sends it to do.

Father, forgive me when I am lax in battle. You have given me the responsibility of prayer. Help me to remain vigilant. I thank you that, although I bring my prayers and petitions to you, the battle is ultimately yours…you bring the victory. In the name of Jesus, amen.

Ephesians 6:18

Praying at all times in the Spirit, with all prayer and supplication. To that end keep alert with all perseverance, making supplication for all the saints. (ESV)

Isaiah 5:20

Woe to those who call evil good and good evil, who put darkness for light and light for darkness, who put bitter for sweet and sweet for bitter.

Galatians 6:7-10

Do not be deceived: God cannot be mocked. A man reaps what he sows. Whoever sows to please their flesh, from the flesh will reap destruction; whoever sows to please the Spirit, from the Spirit will reap eternal life. Let us not become weary in doing good, for at the proper time we will reap a harvest if we do not give up. Therefore, as we have opportunity, let us do good to all people, especially to those who belong to the family of believers.

Reflection Time

How has God been speaking to you today? Take time to write it in your journal.

Chapter 89
The Place of Balance

We have a hammock that we hang between a couple trees, and it is a peaceful place to relax…as long as you are balanced.

I have taken more than one tumble out of it when additional weight I wasn't expecting was suddenly added—from an enthusiastic pet…or a mischievous child…or husband….

When that happens, I have to scramble to find the place of balance again if I don't want to hit the ground.

This morning I am lying awake in that deep darkness before dawn, sleep eluding me.

I have listened to Scripture and now some praise and worship music. My day will be starting out at the hospital—again—sitting with the husband of another precious friend while she undergoes surgery to remove cancer.

I am also awaiting some test results of my own, which have me a little unnerved, given the events of the last month. I have to admit, "my hammock" has been swinging precariously recently, and I have been scrambling to find the center.

Yet my spirit is calm with the peace that passes understanding—the kind that comes only from God…my place of balance.

Many times, in God's kingdom, things work backwards, and I am finding that, sometimes, victory in battle comes not by fighting the enemy but by resting in the Lord.

I long for the day when finding that center of balance is second nature to me and I don't have to panic and scramble while looking for it.

Father God, you are the center...the calm in the eye of the storm. Help me to remain in you when life has things rocking precariously. In Jesus's name, amen.

Psalm 62:1-2

Truly my soul finds rest in God;
my salvation comes from him.
Truly he is my rock and my salvation;
he is my fortress, I will never be shaken.

2 Chronicles 20:9

If calamity comes upon us, whether the sword of judg-
ment, or plague or famine, we will stand in your pres-
ence before this temple that bears your Name and will
cry out to you in our distress, and you will hear us and
save us.

Reflection Time

How has God been speaking to you today? Take time to write it in your journal.

Chapter 90
When Prayers Are Not Answered Our Way

I spent most of my day at the hospital waiting while my precious friend was in surgery to remove her breast cancer. While there, I was scrolling through Facebook and saw a post by a woman on a pastor's page. She was upset about the fact that she had prayed healing Scriptures out loud for three years and she was still not healed. She then wondered if it was because she had not tithed, so she tithed for a year and she was still not healed. She said she was coming to the conclusion that maybe Christianity was no different than any other religion.

That's tough stuff, and the "name it and claim it" people can make it hard for someone who does not receive what they prayed for. Either *they* feel like a failure for not doing something right…or they will see *God* as a failure.

At the end of the day, my friend's cancer surgery was a success, and her prognosis was very good. She shouldn't have to have chemo. Yet my other friend with cancer is facing a year of chemo. Lots of prayers have gone up for *both* of these women. If I based my belief in God on what he was *doing* in this situation, I could become very confused.

I believe in healing; there are many Scriptures to back it up. There are also a lot of Scriptures about sorrow and suffering too. I know God has the power to heal—or do anything else for that matter—but the fact is, he doesn't always do it the way we think he should. Sometimes that can shake our faith.

There have been times in my walk with the Lord that I have been angry when I haven't received an answer to prayer, whether it be for healing or something I have prayed for someone else. I have questioned God about it, and I don't always receive a definitive answer.

But I know this: God is very good about getting out of any "box" I try to put him in.

The longer I walk with God, the less important having him answer all my prayers the way I want seems, and the more important having a personal relationship with him becomes.

And *that* is where Christianity differs from other religions. It is not just about the rules ("do this and you will receive that"). God does have rules for his children, but first and foremost, he wants relationship with us. He created us for love—He would love us and would be loved in return. If we truly spend time in his presence—get to know and love him—then the rules are not so hard to follow. We want to please him because we love him, not because we will get some reward for it.

It's not just because of victories and answers to prayer that I know my God is real; it's because of my troubles and weaknesses.

If I had plenty of my own strength, how could I know about his?

If I didn't have any troubles, how would I know that he could help me through them?

Father God, when you don't answer prayer the way I think you should, help me to focus on who you are and not what you are doing. I cannot see the big picture, the other side of my life's tapestry which you are weaving. Help me to trust you. I pray you would give people a hunger for *relationship* with you. Reveal yourself to us Lord. In Jesus's name, amen.

John 16:33

I have told you these things, so that in me you may have peace. In this world you will have trouble. But take heart! I have overcome the world.

Psalm 40:17

As for me, I am poor and needy, but the Lord takes thought for me. You are my help and my deliverer; do not delay, O my God! (ESV)

Romans 8:28

And we know that for those who love God all things work together for good, for those who are called according to his purpose. (ESV)

2 Corinthians 12:8-9b

Three times I pleaded with the Lord to take it away from me. But he said to me, "My grace is sufficient for you, for my power is made perfect in weakness."

Reflection Time

How has God been speaking to you today? Take time to write it in your journal.

Chapter 91

The Pain No One Sees

My daughter, Autumn, has a favorite horse named Rodeo, a huge white horse splashed with red and gray. He has the most beautiful blue eyes that allow you to see his expressions and give him a lot of personality. Rodeo has a heart as big as Texas, and it is full of love for Autumn, even though he can drive her crazy with his orneriness. Rodeo was rescued from an abusive situation, by our friends Tonia and Bill, who later drove him all the way from Oklahoma to give him to Autumn...and forever changed our lives for the better.

Tonia told us after she rescued him, she was very pleased with his disposition...until she tried to ride him. Then he would go crazy. She was very frustrated until a friend of hers told her to try a horse chiropractor. Turns out Rodeo had some misalignment, so weight on his back was causing him a great deal of pain. Once that was fixed, he was like a different horse under saddle.

I was talking to the Lord this morning about some heartache I'd been feeling because of something someone said and did. He brought Rodeo to my mind. Then, he spoke to my heart.

"When people are unkind, many times it has nothing to do with you. You cannot see the wounds or misalignment that causes their behavior. That is why I ask you to pray for those who hurt you. They may be carrying pain you know nothing about."

Jesus was able to say about his persecutors and tormentors, "Forgive them Father, for they know not what they do," because he knew all about their pain and misalignments.

Father God, forgive me when I make it all about me. Help me to show mercy to others, as you have shown mercy to me…in Jesus's name, amen.

Psalm 86:5

For You, LORD, are good, and ready to forgive, And abundant in lovingkindness to all who call upon You. (NASB)

Psalm 145:9

The LORD is good to all: and his tender mercies are over all his works. (KJV)

Luke 6:36

Be you therefore merciful, as your Father also is merciful. (American King James Version)

Ephesians 2:4

But God, who is rich in mercy, for his great love with which he loved us. (AKJV)

Titus 3:5

Not by works of righteousness which we have done, but according to his mercy he saved us, by the washing of regeneration, and renewing of the Holy Ghost. (AKJV)

Hebrews 4:16
Let us therefore come boldly to the throne of grace, that
we may obtain mercy, and find grace to help in time of
need. (AKJV)

Reflection Time

How has God been speaking to you today? Take
time to write it in your journal.

Chapter 92

Deep Water

I don't like deep water. When I was young and spent time at the public pool, I would start at the shallow end and walk slowly toward the deep end. When I had to get on my tiptoes to keep my head above water, I would feel panicky, turn around, and head back for the shallows. I could swim basic strokes—enough to get myself to the side or from one end of the pool to the other—but I was never comfortable in the deep end.

When I was in Junior High, we had swimming at the YMCA in place of gym class one semester. There I was taught different swim strokes, but what I struggled with the most was learning how to float. You were supposed to lay face up in the water, arch your back, and just relax. I could never relax with the water just a few inches away from covering my face. My body always felt as stiff as a board. Watching my struggle one day, the instructor put her hands under the small of my back for support while I floated, and I instantly relaxed.

Last week, I went for my (long past due) mammogram. The woman who took my mammogram said that they were able to get good images and would be sending me a card in the mail in about a week. Whew. I was glad that was over and didn't really give it another thought.

A day and a half later, I was standing at my kitchen sink washing dishes, and the phone rang. Drying my hands off, I glanced at the caller ID and recognized the number of the doctor's office. *Crap. That's not a card in the mail....*

Answering, I heard the receptionist say (in a normal receptionist sort of way), "Hello, Sherolyn. We are going to need you to come in for further testing, because something showed up on your mammogram. The other office will be calling you to set up an appointment...." Her voice faded into the background, and I thought, "How do you keep a normal tone of voice when you call people to tell them that sort of thing?" The sing-song voice went on to explain what to expect, and I mumbled, "Okay...okay," as icy fingers of fear began to wrap themselves around my mind and heart. *What are the chances?* I thought. *Two of my best friends have been diagnosed with cancer in the last six weeks...this is probably nothing* Yet as I hung up the phone, I began to feel that panicked sensation of deep water only inches from my face....

I was finding it hard to breathe, and my heartbeat began to escalate. I called my husband and my mother and texted a few of my prayer partner friends, most of whom immediately responded, "DO NOT GIVE IN TO FEAR," and said they would pray.

Do not give into fear....I have struggled with anxiety for most of my life, even in times when there was nothing to be anxious about.

But within seconds after requesting prayer from my friends, I felt the peace that passes understanding begin to fill me and I relaxed... like floating when the instructor's hands were supporting my back.

What a lesson in the importance of prayer...the difference it makes when we lift one another up. One of the greatest treasures we can have in this life is friends who "have our backs" in prayer—

friends who go boldly into the throne room on our behalf, to lift us up to the Father.

It gave the prayers I pray for others a whole new significance because I've experienced the results of my friends' prayers for me.

My second round of testing is still over a week away, but I'm doing ok at the moment. I am enjoying time with family and friends, trusting that my Jesus has me in his hands and he hears my prayers and the prayers of those who love me.

Father God, I thank you that you are an ever-present help in times of trouble. Lord, help me to continue to rest, trusting in your strong arms to keep me afloat. I thank you for precious friends who pray for me. Keep me ever mindful to pray for others. In Jesus's name. Amen.

Philippians 4:6-7
Do not be anxious about anything, but in every situation, by prayer and petition, with thanksgiving, present your requests to God. And the peace of God, which transcends all understanding, will guard your hearts and your minds in Christ Jesus.

Reflection Time
How has God been speaking to you today? Take time to write it in your journal.

Chapter 93

Round Two

I went for my second mammogram today. I figured I'd be in and out just like the first one. I was a little nervous but doing ok. After the mammogram was finished, I went into the waiting area and sat with my precious friend, Peggy, who had come with me. She had just been through all of this herself a month before. Al had to stay out in the main lobby because it was a "no boys allowed" area.

The nurse came back and said the radiologist now wanted me to get an ultrasound. Peg and I looked at each other nervously.

Well…I wasn't expecting that….

I followed the nurse to a dark room, and she had me lie down on a small bed by the ultrasound machine. She said, "The gel will be warm," and I lay there quietly as she ran the ultrasound machine. I listened to the soft clicking as she took picture after picture, lingering in some spots for what seemed like an eternity. My throat tightened, wondering why she had to take so many images.

Taking a deep breath, I closed my eyes, and my mind flashed back to another dimly lit room nearly twenty-eight years ago…a warm ultrasound probe gliding over my distended belly, my husband

and I excitedly watching the image of our first child coming into focus on the black and white screen.

And then two sons and nine years later, when the ultrasound showed a baby girl....

Such happy memories...seems like yesterday....

But today the click and whir of the machine in the darkened room did not hold excited anticipation for me...today they are looking for cancer.

A few tears slid down my cheeks, and I stared at an empty chair a few feet in front of me, trying to picture Jesus sitting in it. *Lord, I know you are here with me...none of this is a surprise to you...but I sure wish I could see your face right now.*

The tests were finally over...still no definitive answers...the radiologist tells me he needs to do a biopsy to be sure...they will be in touch to set up an another appointment.

So, more waiting...more practicing my float...more learning to rest in the Lord.

For my Bible reading tonight, I turned to the book of Revelations:

> Then the angel showed me the river of the water of life, as clear as crystal, flowing from the throne of God and of the Lamb down the middle of the great street of the city. On each side of the river stood the tree of life, bearing twelve crops of fruit, yielding its fruit every month. And the leaves of the tree are for the healing of the nations. No longer will there be any curse. The throne of God and of the Lamb will be in the city, and his servants will serve him. They will see his face....(Revelation 22:1-4, NIV)

Sigh… "They will see his face…." I look forward to that day when I can see his face, but until then, I will have to trust in his promises. He promises that he will never leave me or forsake me. He works all things for the good of those who love him and are called according to his purpose. He will keep in perfect peace those whose minds are fixed on him because they trust him.

Father God, give me the mind of Christ in all my circumstances. Holy Spirit reveal truth to me. Help me to keep my mind fixed on Jesus and keep me in perfect peace. Help me to be aware of your presence…for your presence is better than life. In Jesus's name, amen.

→→>>> ❋ <<<←

Deuteronomy 31:8
The LORD himself goes before you and will be with you; he will never leave you nor forsake you. Do not be afraid; do not be discouraged.

Isaiah 26:3
You will keep in perfect peace those whose minds are steadfast, because they trust in you.

Romans 8:28
And we know that in all things God works for the good of those who love him, who have been called according to his purpose.

Isaiah 41:10
So do not fear, for I am with you;
do not be dismayed, for I am your God.
I will strengthen you and help you;
I will uphold you with my righteous right hand.

Reflections From the Sunroom

→≫≫≯ ❋ ≮≪≪←

Reflection Time

How has God been speaking to you today? Take time to write it in your journal.

Chapter 94
A Light to My Path

My writing room today is outside under the trees, facing the hilltop where I like to watch the sunrise. I'm listening to beautiful music and the song of the birds. The heavy sweet smell of the meadow below speaks of mid-summer, and the morning air is pleasant and soothingly cool on my skin.

I've been awake since 4:30 a.m. I couldn't get back to sleep so I began to talk to the Lord.

"Father, I don't want to have cancer...."

In my mind's eye, he showed me a fork in the road: one path looked light and open—no roadblocks; the other path was narrower—with twists and turns, places of shadows and light.

It was almost as if I got to choose.

"Do I get to choose, Father?"

He spoke to my heart, "What if the difficult path was the one that led to the true desires of your heart? What if the difficult path accomplished the greater good?"

I hesitated, weighing the options....

"Do I have cancer, Father?" There was no answer. Hesitantly, I said, "I want the path that you are on." He said, "I am always with you."

"But I'm afraid of the difficult path."

"What I want from you, Child, is trust—on whatever path I guide you through in this life."

I lay there thinking about it. "Father, help me to trust you...no matter what."

The Lord began to bring people to my mind to pray for. At about 5:30, I messaged a friend who will undergo serious heart surgery later today, to let her know I was thinking about her and praying for her. She said things weren't looking good. I tried to reassure her. "God's got this," I said.

"I know," she replied, "but his plan may not be my plan. I do trust him though...I am attempting to listen to and hear all that he is saying."

Father God, I thank you for this example of faith and trust. Increase *my* faith and trust...my spirit is willing, but my flesh is weak. Guide every hand that touches my faithful friend today. I pray for healing for her heart. Help my mind to stay focused on you today, Lord, and not on what may come across my path. In Jesus's name, amen.

Of course my devotion today was about paths....

Psalm 119:105
Your word is a lamp to my feet and a light to my path.
(ESV)

Proverbs 3:5-6
Trust in the LORD with all your heart
And do not lean on your own understanding.
In all your ways acknowledge Him,
And He will make your paths straight. (NASB)

-»»» ❄ «««-

Reflection Time

How has God been speaking to you today? Take time to write it in your journal.

Chapter 95
Above the Clouds

I did my outside chores in the early morning hours, shaking my head in frustration as I checked on the flowers and plants. My petunias look absolutely pitiful. I've given them especially good care this summer—put them in a good location, made sure they had adequate fertilizer...I've done everything I know to do. What they need is something I have no control over: sunshine.

I'm sure a lot of gardeners are feeling like me this summer. It seems like the sun will never shine again.

We just have to keep doing everything we know to do to help our plants until the sun decides to break through.

The Lord began to speak to my heart about cloudy skies. The fact is that the sun *is* shining just as brightly as it ever has; we just can't see it for the cloud cover. If we could see above the clouds, we would see that the sun hasn't changed at all.

Sometimes, when the storms of life threaten to overwhelm us, it seems like God is not there and it feels like we will never see the sun again.

But nothing has changed except our perspective. God says he will never leave us or forsake us. He is there, whether we can see his hand or not.

I thought of the words to a beautiful song that talks about hiding under his wings and being still…focusing on who he is. The lyrics brought comfort to my heart.

Oh Lord, at times I don't understand your ways. Sometimes this path is hard. Help me to be still, find the place of quiet, and wait for you. There are times you help me to soar with you above the storm, and other times you just shelter me in your hand. I do trust you. Help me to rest in that trust. In Jesus's name, amen.

James 1:2-4

Consider it pure joy, my brothers and sisters, whenever you face trials of many kinds, because you know that the testing of your faith produces perseverance. Let persever-ance finish its work so that you may be mature and complete, not lacking anything.

Reflection Time

How has God been speaking to you today? Take time to write it in your journal.

Chapter 96
Live For Today

I was so glad to get the biopsy over with yesterday. I was amazed at the amount of friends who were praying for me, and I could truly feel the prayers being spoken on my behalf. The relief I experienced at that hurdle being crossed almost felt like the end of the journey.

This morning, when I went to roll out of bed, the stinging tenderness at the biopsy site awakened the nagging worry at the back of mind…three to five days for test results.

I went downstairs and let the dogs out. The early morning air was surprisingly cool, and I put on my flip flops, slipped on a light jacket, and decided to try my hand at some morning chores. Grabbing some apples and carrots for the horses, I turned on some praise songs using my iPhone, slipped it in my pocket, and made my way toward the barn, worry beginning to fill my conscious thoughts. As I rounded the fence by the riding arena, the Lord spoke to my heart.

"Hush, child.… *Today* there are crystal blue skies, and the sun is breaking over your beloved hilltop."

I paused for a moment and looked up. The heavy gray clouds that have been the pattern for most of this summer's skies were nowhere to be seen. The sky was cornflower blue with faint wisps of white clouds, as if trailed by the finishing brush of the Creator. I breathed deeply of the chilly morning air and turned to look at the sun breaking over the hilltop. I noticed with the delight of a child the cold, morning dew on my feet and heard the welcoming nicker of my pony as he caught sight of me. The birds were singing along with me as I joined the praise song coming from the iPhone in my pocket. I fed the horses and chickens and made my way back to the house.

Lord, I have prayed for a deeper walk with you…I had no idea what that would entail.…Please Father, help me to have the faith of a little child—delighting in what is right in front of me and living in the present moment. When troubles come in this life, help me to take your hand, trusting with absolute certainty in your help and care. In Jesus's name, amen.

Matthew 6:34a
Therefore do not worry about tomorrow, for tomorrow will worry about itself.

Philippians 4:8
Finally, brothers, whatever is true, whatever is honorable, whatever is just, whatever is pure, whatever is lovely, whatever is commendable, if there is any excellence, if there is anything worthy of praise, think about these things. (ESV)

Isaiah 41:10
Fear not, for I am with you; be not dismayed, for I am your God; I will strengthen you, I will help you, I will uphold you with my righteous right hand. (ESV)

Reflection Time

How has God been speaking to you today? Take time to write it in your journal.

Chapter 97

Distraction

In the quest for distraction the other day, Al and I test drove a convertible just for fun. I had never driven one before and I loved it.

The wind in my hair, the smell of the outdoors…it felt like my worries just blew away with the breeze.

"Really," I said to Al, "this is like therapy…but a convertible isn't that practical for us. I have hot flashes, and you are deathly allergic to bees." We laughed.

Last night after dinner we were driving home and saw a cute little convertible parked outside the frozen-custard shop. "If I have cancer," I said, "I'm buying a convertible."

I will be glad when that worry is no longer always at the back of my mind.

Father God, thank you for the fun distraction. I love the wind in my hair and the smell of a summer evening. Please help me to live in the present moment without worrying about what tomorrow could bring. You hold my future in your hands. Help me to trust you with it. In Jesus's name, amen.

Reflections From the Sunroom

Philippians 4:8

Finally, brothers and sisters, whatever is true, whatever is noble, whatever is right, whatever is pure, whatever is lovely, whatever is admirable—if anything is excellent or praiseworthy—think about such things.

Matthew 6:27

Can any one of you by worrying add a single hour to your life?

Reflection Time

How has God been speaking to you today? Take time to write it in your journal.

Chapter 98

A Beautiful Word

I was standing at the kitchen counter this afternoon, chopping vegetables. The ticking of the clock on the wall was unnerving me for some reason. Waiting on the test results has been agonizing. We are supposed to be going to the mountains of Tennessee with our good friends, John and Teresa, in a few days. I'm not sure if I want the test results before we go because if the results are bad, it will ruin my trip. On the other hand if they are good, I would be elated.

I know this wait has seemed endless because I feel like I have been waiting with bated breath all spring. Waiting on test results for my two friends…waiting on surgeries for them…waiting for the chemo to start…and now waiting on my own test results.

It makes all the other things I've worried about seem very unimportant.

My son, Andy, walked in the back door, and I smiled and hugged him…a welcome distraction. He was telling me about his day when the phone rang. I reached for it and saw on the caller ID that it was the doctor's office. I froze. He looked at me strangely as I stared at the phone without answering. "It's the doctor," I said.

"Answer it, Mom!" I hesitated, knowing that the voice on the other end had the power to change my life. Time seemed to stand still. Finally I pushed the answer button and said a breathless hello. I listened as my son watched intently. I thanked the doctor and hung up.

There are some beautiful words in the English language. Dr. Cooper just said one of them to me: *benign.*

Oh, thank you, Jesus! My son was all smiles as I grabbed the phone again to call my husband.

I couldn't get ahold of Al. He was on a four-hour conference call. He texted me, "Did you try to call?"

"Yes," I typed back. "Dr. Cooper called. It's benign!!"

"Praise God! Amen! Hallelujah!" he responded.

I was smiling as I texted him back. "I still want a convertible...."

Tennessee mountains, here I come. I don't think I have ever looked forward to a vacation so much!

Father God, I thank you for a good report. I pray for my friends who didn't receive one, and I continue to ask you for their complete healing. Thank you for helping me in my weakness. In Jesus's name, amen.

-->>>> ※ <<<<-

1 Peter 5:10

And the God of all grace, who called you to his eternal glory in Christ, after you have suffered a little while, will himself restore you and make you strong, firm and steadfast.

Isaiah 43:2

When you pass through the waters, I will be with you; and when you pass through the rivers, they will not sweep over you. When you walk through the fire, you will not be burned; the flames will not set you ablaze.

Reflection Time

How has God been speaking to you today? Take time to write it in your journal.

Chapter 99
Passing the Test

The last few months have been an emotional roller coaster ride for me: watching two of my best friends receive a diagnosis of cancer and worrying about and praying for them through tests, surgeries, and chemo.

Then, there have been health uncertainties for myself: going through testing of my own (some of it painful), battling the fear that comes when waiting on test results, uncertainty about the outcome, dreading the phone call that could change the course of my life....

When I was finally given a clean bill of health, I was elated and couldn't wait to share the news with all who had been praying for me.

My friend, Frank, a precious brother in Christ, messaged me and said, "So how did you do with the test? (not the one the doctor gave you.)"

I have been contemplating that—my experience, from a spiritual standpoint, on this test—quite a bit over the last few weeks. On that test grade, I would probably give myself a C. I passed...could have done better...but I certainly did better than on previous tests. Am I being hard on myself? I don't think so....

I have not yet measured up to the attitude the apostle Paul had when he said, "Therefore I will boast all the more gladly about my weaknesses, so that Christ's power may rest on me," or James, when he said, "Consider it pure joy when you face trials of many kinds"
But I did learn some things that will help me on the next test.... What have I learned?

~ Don't sweat the small stuff. Everyday annoyances are nothing compared to what some people are going through.

~ To a certain extent—even with outside support—there are some things in life that come down to me and God. Death will be one of those. It's a comfort to have eternal security.

~ That God is my strength when I have none—and when I allow him to be.

~ That I need some improvement in the trust department...although I did better than I thought I would. I want to trust God—not just for the outcome I desire, but also when my prayers aren't answered in the way I would like.

~ That I have God-given authority to do spiritual battle—something that I have never made good use of in the past. I showed some improvement in this area.

~ That the prayers of others are more precious than gold. It has renewed my fervor to pray for people. Prayer moves the heavenlies. I need to be vigilant in prayer. Don't be afraid to ask for prayer support.

~ That worship is a powerful and effective weapon against the enemy. It may not be what I feel like doing when circumstances are scary and over-whelming, but it is extremely important. It's where God reveals himself to me. Worship of the Lord brings strength and healing to my heart.

~ That I am loved—by my Creator and by my family. I am humbled and amazed by the love shown me in hundreds of messages I received from friends.

I am blessed.

Father God, I thank you that you love me, not because I am a perfectly finished work, but because I am yours. I thank you for your promise that you have begun a work in me and you will be faithful to complete it. I thank you for your Word—a powerful weapon against the enemy—and I thank you for all the love and support you have surrounded me with here on this earth. In Jesus's name, amen.

James 1:2-4

Consider it all joy, my brethren, when you encounter various trials, knowing that the testing of your faith produces endurance. And let endurance have its perfect result, so that you may be perfect and complete, lacking in nothing. (NASB)

Romans 5:3-4

And not only this, but we also exult in our tribulations, knowing that tribulation brings about perseverance; and perseverance, proven character; and proven charac-ter, hope. (NASB)

Isaiah 48:10

Behold, I have refined you, but not as silver, I have tested you in the furnace of affliction. (NASB)

→⟩⟩⟩ ❋ ⟨⟨⟨←

Reflection Time

How has God been speaking to you today? Take time to write it in your journal.

Chapter 100
The Journey

I'm gazing out over a mountaintop in the smoky mountains of Tennessee. It is early morning. Everyone else was still asleep when I tiptoed out onto the balcony of the condo to watch the sunrise. From my vantage point on the summit, I can see a huge range of mountain peaks with pockets of fog in the valleys that look almost like lakes. The wind is whipping, threatening to blow my iPad out of my hand as I try to take pictures of the ever-changing sky, which is a kaleidoscope of misty gold and gray. My spirit is overwhelmed with the majestic grandeur of this place.

When we travel to Tennessee, we love to go off the beaten path...find scenic routes and drive through the mountains, pausing to picnic and wade in cool mountain streams. We make numerous stops to admire and take pictures of God's handiwork: rocky mountain streams, beautiful waterfalls, wild flowers tenaciously growing in the crevices of rocks. Sometimes we just stop and stare up into the forest, hoping for a glimpse of black bear. Thank heavens there are plenty of places to pull off to enjoy these gifts on our adventure.

There are other travelers on the roads we choose in our journey. It surprises me how many of them seem to be in a hurry. We always pull over to let them go around us. It makes me sad for them; they don't realize what they are missing in their haste.

The Lord began speaking to my heart about this even before I joined him on the balcony for the sunrise this morning.

Whether mankind acknowledges it or not, our journeys all begin the same, and they will end the same: with the hand of the Creator.

We will all arrive at the same destination at the end of our travels: the end of life here on this earth. Sadly, many will not have used their time to even acknowledge God, let alone get to know the Creator of their journey. For those, the eternal road will take a different turn, and it will be too late. It will all have been for nothing…the waste of a precious, beautiful gift.

Father God, I thank you for the breathtaking beauty of your creation. I thank you for your Word as a guide on my pilgrimage. But most of all, I thank you for your presence as you guide me toward my final destination. Help me to use the time you've given me on this earth to draw ever closer to you, until I arrive at my forever home in heaven. Forgive me when I become hurried and miss the gifts you have placed for me all along my path. In Jesus's name, amen.

Revelation 4:11

You are worthy, our Lord and God, to receive glory and honor and power, for you created all things, and by your will they were created and have their being.

Psalm 139:13b–15

You knit me together in my mother's womb. I praise You, for I am awesomely, wonderfully made!…My frame was not hidden from You when I was made in the secret place, when I was woven together in the depths of the earth. (Tree of Life Version)

Ephesians 2:10

For we are his workmanship, created in Christ Jesus unto good works which God has before ordained that we should walk in them. (King James 2000 Bible)

2 Timothy 4:7

I have fought the good fight, I have finished the course, I have kept the faith. In the future there is reserved for me a crown of righteousness, which the Lord, the righteous judge, will award to me on that day—and not to me only, but also to everyone who has longed for His appearing. (TLV)

Reflection Time

How has God been speaking to you today? Take time to write it in your journal.

Chapter 101
Journey's End

Yesterday, Al and I decided to "get lost" in Tennessee. We found the address of a farm we'd seen for sale in a homes magazine that advertised, "Have your very own waterfall!" And so we journeyed out to the middle of nowhere. We ended up on a road marked with a "Dead End" sign, but the sign beside it, which said "Serenity Falls," was too tempting to pass up.

We turned down the old lane and eventually came upon a charming old gray farmhouse with a tin roof. Across the small lane were four old log cabins—the picture of Americana—with rocking chairs and American flags on their porches and country curtains at the windows. Just past the house at the end of the lane was the waterfall: "Serenity Falls."

Al came to a stop, gravel crunching under the tires, and we opened the car doors. Immediately, we could hear the sweet melody of the waterfall. It was as beautiful as anything we had seen or heard this week on our Tennessee vacation.

There was a lush, grassy area to one side, complete with a swing and some concrete benches, inviting one to sit a spell and enjoy the peace. The larger falls turned into several smaller falls that cascaded into a stream that flowed behind the old cabins.

A gentleman sat in an old, whitewashed swing on the porch, which ran the entire length of the farmhouse. He yelled a friendly "Hello!" and we walked up to the porch. His wife came outside, drying her hands on a dishtowel and wearing a welcoming smile. We all introduced ourselves and shook hands. They were so very friendly and invited us to sit in the white wooden rockers across from the porch swing. We said we had seen the ad in a homes magazine and were intrigued by the waterfall. She told us the story of how her mother and dad had bought the place thirty years prior. Back in the mid-1800s, the old dead-end lane had been a state route that came to an end in a little town consisting of the four cabins across the road. They had been the mill, the post office, the grocery store, and a stable.

It had long since been abandoned when her mother happened upon it those many years ago.

She went into the house and brought out an old photo album for me to look at, which was full of pictures from when her parents had first bought the place.

"Mama loved the mountains," she said, "and Daddy loved Mama...."

I opened the album, which showed the old farmhouse in dilapidated condition and the old cabins looking in sadder shape still. There was a picture of a young couple (her mother and father). The handwritten caption above the woman said, "God has given me the desire of my heart," and the caption above the man said, "This is going to be a challenge."

I smiled and grew misty eyed as I turned the pages of the album, seeing pictures of hard work, dedication, and smiling faces as the couple's dreams became reality. The handwritten captions spoke of deep faith in God and love for each other.

"I would have loved to have known your mother" I said.

We spent the next half hour chatting, and then she invited us to look through the cabins and the farmhouse, full of antiques and memories of the past.

How much richer the experience was, knowing the history behind it.

After a nice visit, we said goodbye. She hugged me and told us to come back anytime.

I was thinking about the experience today, and the thought struck me…I *will* meet her mother someday in heaven, and I can say, "Hey! I saw your waterfall!!"

Father God, I thank you that when we are in your family, there are no goodbyes, only "see you laters," and that people we have never even met in this life will be part of our family in eternity. I thank you for the new friends we made and for the inspiration of their heritage. In Jesus's name, amen.

--->>>> ※ <<<<--

Ephesians 2:19
Consequently, you are no longer foreigners and strangers, but fellow citizens with God's people and also members of his household.

Galatians 6:10
Therefore, as we have opportunity, let us do good to all people, especially to those who belong to the family of believers.

Reflections From the Sunroom

Romans 12:5

So in Christ we, though many, form one body, and each member belongs to all the others.

1 Corinthians 3:9

For we are co-workers in God's service; you are God's field, God's building.

Reflection Time

How has God been speaking to you today? Take time to write it in your journal.

Chapter 102
Letting Go

We are on our way home from Tennessee. My sweetie is driving and I am lost in thought, trying to choose some of my favorite moments from the week. There are so many to pick from, but I think yesterday would have to be the most special day.

I wish I had taken a picture of the sign at the beginning of the gravel road that we decided to explore. It read:

> Travel at your own risk.
> Road is unimproved.
> High-profile, 4-wheel drive vehicles recommended.
> Limited emergency services available.
> One way…no turn around.

Our good friend, John, was driving our Acadia, and I was up front with him. Al and Teresa were in the back seat.

We turned off the main road onto the gravel road and sat staring at the sign for a moment. It seemed a little ominous…then we all began talking at once.

Al: Go for it!
Me: Doesn't *high-profile* mean a truck?

John: Yep.

Al: Go for it!

Me: Wonder how often they check these back roads….

Al: Maybe once a month.

John hits the gas.

Woohoo!!

Eight miles of gravel back roads at ten miles an hour. It took all wonderful afternoon. The road was narrow, rocky, and rutted. The trees were massive in the deep, thick mountain forest, with shafts of sunlight filtering through. Teresa was setting her camera for the lighting in her persistent hunt for the perfect bear shot. The first time we came to a waterfall, its stream crossed the road right in front of us. I could barely contain a squeal. John slowed to a stop, and Teresa and I jumped out with our phones and cameras to take pictures. We stepped out of our flip flops immediately and waded into the blissful, but shockingly frigid, water. My feet were aching from the cold within minutes, but I loved it. The guys were patient, allowing us to snap pictures to our hearts' content. We snapped pictures of the woods, the waterfall, and of each other snapping pictures.

I lost count of how many streams with waterfalls crossed that road in those eight miles, but I know my bare feet were in most of them. We never knew what was over the next rise or around the next bend…which added to the sheer enjoyment.

The tightly wrapped cords of stress and worry that had held me bound for the last couple of months had loosened their hold on me the day we arrived in Tennessee. Yesterday afternoon, they fell completely off, washing away down those cold mountain streams.

At the end of the rocky mountain road, we came out on the section of highway called the "Tail of the Dragon." There were hundreds of hairpin turns within an eleven-mile stretch of road, punctuated by overlooks boasting of breathtaking mountain and valley views. We ate supper at a great little restaurant, drinking ice-cold water out of mason jars, and arrived back at the condo after dark, happy and exhausted. Teresa and I sat down to look at all of our pictures, and I was in awe. It wasn't just the breathtaking beauty of the place, although God was surely showing off when he created Tennessee.

I was shocked to see *myself* in the pictures. The woman in the photos was mid-fifties, with graying hair and creases at the corners of her eyes….

But the girl on the rocky mountain road on that perfect summer afternoon, with her bare feet in the waterfalls, had been no more than seventeen.

And I realized why I am so in love with Tennessee….

Father God, I thank you for this week in your beautiful creation. The mountains of Tennessee are only a glimpse of the beauty of heaven, I'm sure. I thank you, Lord, for this much-needed time of refreshing. Help me to store it up in my heart. In Jesus's name. Amen.

Psalm 36:5-6

Your love, LORD, reaches to the heavens,
Your faithfulness to the skies.
Your righteousness is like the highest mountains,
Your justice like the great deep.
You, LORD, preserve both people and animals.

Reflection Time

How has God been speaking to you today? Take time to write it in your journal.

Chapter 103
Joyful Mindset

One thing I always notice during our vacations in Tennessee is the warm friendliness of the people. Total strangers welcome and speak to you like old friends. Another thing I notice is that, nearly everywhere you turn, there is some sort of reference to the Lord, whether it is Scripture on a plaque outside a building or restaurant or some kind of Christian-themed t-shirt on a passerby. In every store we visited, there was Christian-themed material for sale.

Yesterday was the last day of vacation. When I woke up, I saw on the dresser the little business card given to me by the couple we met who owned the cabin rentals by the waterfall. I noticed a Scripture reference at the bottom of it.

I went out and sat at the dining room table in the condo, picked up my Bible, and turned to the Scripture:

"Trust in the LORD with all thine heart and lean not unto thine own understanding. In all thy ways acknowledge him and he shall direct thy paths." (Proverbs 3:5-6, KJV)

Then I read my devotional for today, which said that God speaks to his children in many ways.

"Lord, guide my path today," I prayed. "Help me to be attentive to your messages in whatever form they come. Amen."

When Al woke up, we decided to go check out a couple little general stores we had seen on the way home the previous day. Our friends, John and Teresa, had gone for an early morning motorcycle ride, and we made plans to meet up with them at the first general store.

My anticipation was high, especially since I had specifically prayed for God to direct my path that morning. I had experienced so many blessings from him on my travels this week.

The first general store was adorable. I took a "selfie" in a chair that looked like a bear and found a neat tin cross that was adorned with little stones to add to my collection. They had a variety of pickles and sauces, and I found some yummy ones to take home. The clerk in the sauce department was a bit grumpy, so I moved on to look at some little bear statues.

At the second general store, I didn't find anything I wanted, but there were a lot of neat things to look at, especially some hand-carved walking sticks that each had a little notch with a possum face sticking out of them as the artist's insignia. John and Teresa didn't find anything either, and we wandered out onto the front porch of the general store. Al and I sat in a double-seated log swing. The angle was just right for my back, and there was a little built-in table to hold your drinks. The price seemed very reasonable, and we were contemplating a purchase.

At that moment, the storeowner came out and told John in a grumpy, growly voice that he needed to move his motorcycle out of the driveway, which seemed strange because the driveway was as wide as the entire parking lot and John was parked on the very end of it.

John and Teresa headed for the parking lot.

Al and I got up from the swing and headed for the car.

On the way back to the condo, we decided that instead of leaving in the morning, we would go ahead and pack up and leave that afternoon.

I felt sad about leaving, as the day had been sort of a downer—no great revelations from the Lord, no directing of my path.

I cried when we left Tennessee and headed for Ohio.

This morning I woke up early and headed out to do the chores: feeding my pony and the chickens, picking some garden veggies, and watering the flowers.

The meadows and hills surrounding our property looked especially beautiful today, and I drank in the beauty as I went about my morning duties.

On the way back to the house, I noticed a bag on the back stoop. I lifted it up and realized it was a bag of rocks. My mind went back to an afternoon a few days previous, by a waterfall in the Tennessee forest, where my sweet Al had gathered rocks for me to take home and put by my own waterfall. I remembered saying, "Do you suppose the people that live here notice this beauty every day, or do they just drive right by it?"

"They probably take it for granted," Al said.

The Lord brought to my mind the grumpy clerk and store owner from the day before.

Then he began to speak to my heart.

"People have problems…stresses and worries…no matter where they live.

Put these stones in your waterfall as a reminder of the carefree moments you had in the mountains. Those moments are just as possible here. It's not about your location…it's not about your age… it's about your mindset.

Go off the paths you are familiar with. Hidden treasures await you there."

Sherolyn Porter

Father, I thank you for your wisdom and guidance. Keep my eyes and ears open for your messages. Keep my heart tuned to yours, for in your presence is fullness of joy. In Jesus's name, amen.

Psalm 121:1-2
I lift up my eyes to the mountains—
where does my help come from?
My help comes from the LORD,
the Maker of heaven and earth.

Reflection Time

How has God been speaking to you today? Take time to write it in your journal.

Chapter 104
Deceptive Current

Al pulled the camper to Pennsylvania this week, and we spent a few days visiting my sister. She lives on a small farm off a myriad of country backroads dotted by larger farms, and the scenery is just gorgeous. Since it is north of us, the weather was much cooler and less humid, and it was a refreshing change.

On Thursday we took Autumn, her friend who had come with us, my niece, and my nephew even farther north to Niagara Falls.

It was a long walk through the park to enjoy the boat ride on the "Maid of the Mist." The boat takes its passengers right up to the falls, which cascade from a height of 176 feet into the churning, rolling waters of the Niagara River, which has a depth of 170 feet. When we got in line to board the boat, we were given rain ponchos to keep us dry from the "spray" off the falls. It was a bit windy that day, and the spray from those towering falls was more akin to a torrential rainstorm than a spray. It was thrilling!

After our boat ride, we climbed a concrete staircase and then took an elevator ride back up to the top. We walked through the beautiful park along the river. Al and the kids wanted to hike across a bridge to a small island upriver from the falls. I was already tired from all the walking we had done thus far, so I opted to rest contentedly on a bench near the river, under the welcoming shade of a nearby tree.

The turbulent river, with its churning rapids of aquamarine and white, mesmerized me. It was exciting and beautiful, but it didn't look particularly dangerous—not like some I've seen that people go white water rafting on. From my vantage point on the bench, one would never guess those deadly falls loomed just a short distance away.

As I sat there quietly, God began to speak to my heart.

Sin doesn't always have the appearance of evil. Sometimes it seems harmless—even beautiful and exciting—and before you know it, you are caught in a dangerous current, unaware that you are heading toward a deadly precipice.

God doesn't give us rules to take all the fun out of our lives. He gives us rules for our protection and to set us apart as his children. He tells us that we are to be "in this world" but not "of it." We cannot fulfill our calling—the reason he placed us here on Planet Earth—if we are not listening to his voice, and his voice is found in his Word. If we listen to any other voice that contradicts God's Word (even if it looks and sounds good), then we are in danger of being immersed in a seductive current that will have a fatal outcome.

I remembered my pastor's words from the previous Sunday. He said there are people who call themselves "Christians" who do not live any differently than the rest of the world. We are called to be different. The world has the right to expect us to live differently.

Father God, I want to live as your child. Help me to recognize your voice and be obedient only to it. I pray, Lord, that I am different, that I am *in* the world but not *of* the world. I know I can't accomplish any of this without your help. I thank you for your help and your strength in Jesus's name, amen.

Reflections From the Sunroom

James 1:22-25

Do not merely listen to the word, and so deceive yourselves. Do what it says. Anyone who listens to the word but does not do what it says is like someone who looks at his face in a mirror and, after looking at himself, goes away and immediately forgets what he looks like. But whoever looks intently into the perfect law that gives freedom, and continues in it—not forgetting what they have heard, but doing it—they will be blessed in what they do.

1 Peter 2:9

But you are a chosen race, a royal priesthood, a holy nation, a people for his own possession, that you may proclaim the excellencies of him who called you out of darkness into his marvelous light. (ESV)

Philippians 2:15

That you may be blameless and innocent, children of God without blemish in the midst of a crooked and twisted generation, among whom you shine as lights in the world. (ESV)

Colossians 3:1-5

If then you have been raised with Christ, seek the things that are above, where Christ is, seated at the right hand of God. Set your minds on things that are above, not on things that are on earth. For you have died, and your life is hidden with Christ in God. When Christ who is your life appears, then you also will appear with him in glory. Put to death therefore what is earthly in you: sexual immorality, impurity, passion, evil desire, and covetousness, which is idolatry. (ESV)

→⟩⟩⟩⟩ ✳ ⟨⟨⟨⟨←

Reflection Time

How has God been speaking to you today? Take time to write it in your journal.

Chapter 105
What is Man That You Are Mindful of Him?

I was driving to a nearby town today, listening to the Christian radio station, and suddenly thankfulness and gratitude for God's tender loving care flooded over me. At one point, I lifted my hand in the air in praise and agreement with the words of the worship song playing on the radio.

In the car ahead of me, I noticed another hand held up in the air out the car window, but I realized it was an angry gesture meant for the driver who was traveling very slowly in front of him.

When I looked at the speedometer, I realized we were only going 30 in a 45-mph zone. I hadn't even noticed.

We were travelers on the same road at the same speed, but the atmospheres in our cars were totally different based on what we were focused on. We were looking at things from different perspectives.

I have believed in God since I was a young girl and have seen evidence of his involvement in my life for years. But it doesn't grow old for me. In fact, I feel the amazement in a fresh, new way every time I see his hand at work and with every new revelation of himself. I feel so humbled that the Creator of the universe is interested in me…knows the very number of hairs on my head…saves my tears in a bottle when I cry…it's just unfathomable.

It brought to mind a Scripture from the Psalms: "What is man that you are mindful of him, the son of man that you care for him?" (Psalm 8:4, NIV)

I know it's not just me that he cares for. He cares for the angry driver in that car ahead of me today. The only thing I can do is pray for a revelation of God for that angry man…and for this hurting world.

Father God, do whatever it takes to wake people up to your loving pursuit of them. I do not pray this prayer lightly, because I know that sometimes it takes a great shaking for men to stop and look for you. Make yourself known, Lord. Reveal your truth. Help us to realize your great love for us. In Jesus's name, amen.

Romans 11:33a
Oh, the depth of the riches of the wisdom and knowledge of God!

John 3:16
For God so loved the world, that he gave his only Son, that whoever believes in him should not perish but have eternal life.

Reflection Time

How has God been speaking to you today? Take time to write it in your journal.

Chapter 106
Prayers of Protection

I just have to give God some praise right now! I had called my friend Peggy this morning about a prayer request and she said, "God woke me up some time after 1 a.m. this morning, and I just saw your daughter's name…like it flashed in front of me."

I said, "Wow! Autumn was driving home from a rodeo really late last night with the truck and horse trailer. Did you pray for her?" She said, "Yes, I prayed for her protection."

"That's awesome!" I said. "Who knows what your prayers could have protected her from?"

We went on to chat for a few minutes and then Autumn, who had been out running an errand, came home, opened the door of the sunroom, and walked in. She said "Hey, I forgot to tell you—I almost hit a deer last night."

I blinked my eyes in disbelief and put Peggy on speaker phone. She went on to say, "It was so foggy, I had the fog lights on, and I decided to hit the brights to see if I could see better…and there was the deer. I hit the truck brakes hard…the anti-locks kicked in.…I barely missed it."

"Did you hear that, Peggy?" I asked.

We both said, "What time was it?"

"I don't know…sometime after one…."

Thank you, Father, for your hand of protection and for my friend, Peg, who is obedient to pray in the wee hours of the morning. I stand amazed.

Psalm 5:11

But let all who take refuge in you be glad; let them ever sing for joy. Spread your protection over them, that those who love your name may rejoice in you.

Psalm 20:1

May the LORD answer you when you are in distress; may the name of the God of Jacob protect you.

Psalm 46:1

God is our refuge and strength, an ever-present help in trouble.

Reflection Time

How has God been speaking to you today? Take time to write it in your journal.

Chapter 107

Foreign Environment

Yesterday we were invited to lunch at a club we used to be members of nearly thirty years ago. It was a perfect afternoon in August. There were picnic tables set up in the shade, and we were periodically treated to a refreshing breeze that spoke of summer's end. Country music played in the background, and the smell of barbecued chicken from the nearby smoker was tantalizing and mouthwatering.

All of that was "right up my alley."

But the atmosphere felt foreign to me, and I realized it was because I had not been in that kind of environment for a long time. Alcohol flowed freely, as did curse words and the use of the Lord's name in vain. I had to keep myself from physically wincing at the raucous laughter and at each time I heard the Lord's name used in vain. Even though I was once very much at home in that atmosphere, I realized I no longer was.

Although the middle-aged gentleman sitting across from me had a vocabulary full of "colorful" adjectives that were not part of my own language, I struck up a conversation with him, and we found common ground in conversation about gardening and some people with whom we had mutual acquaintance. We had a nice visit for most of the afternoon. I mentioned "the good Lord" once or twice in our conversation, as is common for me, and he blinked as if those words were foreign to him, but he didn't seem to mind my company. When it was time to leave, he promised to get me a bag of some of his green beans he had been telling me about, and I plan to share some of my homemade pepper relish with him.

I realized that we become accustomed to the atmosphere we create around ourselves. If our time is spent in pursuit of the things of God, then the things of this world are going to seem foreign to us. We cannot be a witness to this world if we are so much a part of it that we don't stand out.

That doesn't mean that we should see ourselves as better than the people of this world, but we certainly should *not* fit in.

In fact, as the "end of days" approaches—and I believe it is approaching—those who have made Christ the center of their lives should be standing out more and more...*a light in the darkness...a city on a hill.*

Father, forgive me when I am tempted to "fit in." Guard my heart...keep it pure...don't let me lose the "shock factor." Keep me tuned to your voice and in touch with your *Word* instead of the *world.* I pray that you speak to your own, that you bring us apart from the world and fill us with your love for the world. Give us wisdom and boldness as we see the day approaching. In the name of your Son, Jesus, amen.

John 15:19

If you were of the world, the world would love you as its own; but because you are not of the world, but I chose you out of the world, therefore the world hates you. (ESV)

Romans 12:2

Do not be conformed to this world, but be transformed by the renewal of your mind, that by testing you may discern what is the will of God, what is good and acceptable and perfect. (ESV)

1 Peter 2:9

But you are a chosen race, a royal priesthood, a holy nation, a people for his own possession, that you may proclaim the excellencies of him who called you out of darkness into his marvelous light. (ESV)

John 17:15-18

I do not ask that you take them out of the world, but that you keep them from the evil one. They are not of the world, just as I am not of the world. Sanctify them in the truth; your word is truth. As you sent me into the world, so I have sent them into the world. (ESV)

Galatians 2:20

I have been crucified with Christ. It is no longer I who live, but Christ who lives in me. And the life I now live in the flesh I live by faith in the Son of God, who loved me and gave himself for me. (ESV)

1 Corinthians 6:9-11

Or do you not know that the unrighteous will not inherit the kingdom of God? Do not be deceived: neither the sexually immoral, nor idolaters, nor adulterers, nor men who practice homosexuality, nor thieves, nor the greedy, nor drunkards, nor revilers, nor swindlers will inherit the kingdom of God. And such were some of you. But you were washed, you were sanctified, you were justified in the name of the Lord Jesus Christ and by the Spirit of our God. (ESV)

Romans 13:14
But put on the Lord Jesus Christ, and make no provision for the flesh, to gratify its desires. (ESV)

->>>> ✳ <<<<-

Reflection Time

How has God been speaking to you today? Take time to write it in your journal.

Chapter 108
Sweet Hour of Prayer

This morning, as I came to wakefulness, the Lord said, "Pray, Sherry. I'm answering."

He has been speaking to my heart a lot about prayer lately, and I have been thinking about the "evolution" of my prayer life over the years. It's now so much deeper than it has ever been, and yet, feels like it is so much less than it could be.

I remember kneeling with my sisters beside my bed when I was a small girl and praying, "Now I lay me down to sleep"…and then as a teenager, "Lord if you will just get me out of this, I promise I will never…."

Later as a young adult, my prayers were more like a duty, a check in the "spiritual box," something I was supposed to do as a Christian.

I heard about "prayer meetings" at church, and to be honest, I wasn't really interested. It sounded boring to me. I imagined round-robin-type prayers going no higher than the ceiling and being trapped in the room till everyone was done.

Prayer was the part I yawned through in church, anxious to get to the singing part.

Somewhere along the way, in my quest to really *seek* after God, my prayer life has changed.

I've also noticed a difference in our prayer times during my ladies Bible studies. The time we spent in prayer has been deeper…richer… sweeter…and our prayers are being answered! This week my friend, Jenny, came over to spend the day. We sat down in the sunroom to chat and then decided it would be nice to spend some time praying together. I have no idea how long we prayed, but *wow!* There was no doubt that our prayers were definitely going "higher than the ceiling" and the sweet, holy presence of the Lord was in the room with us.

Yesterday when I woke up, the Lord told me to pray for my Facebook friends list. "That's a lot of people, Lord…."

"Is anything too hard for God?" he responded.

"Well…no…."

I laid my hand on my friends list and began to pray a group prayer. As I prayed, I could literally sense a "heavenly upload" of my friends list beginning to happen.

He led me to pray for healing—spiritual healing, physical healing, mental healing—for broken marriages and hurting relationships. I prayed for the lonely. I prayed for friends who have lost loved ones to death and for friends whose children have gone astray.

My tears began to flow as I prayed for friends going through the fire…too much responsibility…so much on their plates….

I prayed for those struggling with their jobs and finances.

But most of all, I prayed for a hunger to grow in every single person on my list—a hunger for the things of God, a desire to be satisfied with nothing less than *all* of him.

Names and faces from my friends list began to flash through my mind with lightning speed as I prayed, and I knew with *certainty* in my heart that the Lord was aware of each name on my list and intimately acquainted with all their needs.

I posted a short line about that experience on Facebook yesterday: "If you are on my friends list...I prayed for you today."

The response brought me to humble tears, so I think my friends are thinking about prayer too.

Father God, raise your children up to *pray*!! Wake us from our slumber!! You are Almighty God—*all powerful God*—able to meet all of our needs, able to change the direction of our hearts, the hearts of our children, our families, our marriages...you are able to change the direction of *entire nations*!! I pray for a great outpouring of your Holy Spirit on your people, Lord! Turn our hearts toward you. Help us make a *difference*! In the name of The One to whom *every* knee will bow soon and very soon—Your Son, Jesus—Amen.

Hebrews 4:16

Let us then approach the throne of grace with confidence, so that we may receive mercy and find grace to help us in our time of need. (BSB)

1 Timothy 2:1-4

I urge, then, first of all, that petitions, prayers, intercession and thanksgiving be made for all people—for kings and all those in authority, that we may live peaceful and quiet lives in all godliness and holiness. This is good, and pleases God our Savior, who wants all people to be saved and to come to a knowledge of the truth.

Reflection Time

How has God been speaking to you today? Take time to write it in your journal.

Chapter 109
Deceptive Hearts

The world says to "follow your heart" on issues that the Bible would call sin. The problem is, all our hearts tell us different things—and sometimes our own heart changes its mind.

It is very hard not to give our hearts and emotions top priority. So we redefine what the Bible calls sin in order to make ourselves feel better, to keep ourselves comfortable.

It is *because* all our hearts tell us different things that we are not qualified to make the judgment call about what sin is. That is why we always have to use the Word of God as our guide. The Bible defines sin and its consequences very clearly. The consequence of sin is death. It also says that we all have sinned and fall short of the glory of God. Jesus preached forgiveness of sin…unlimited…we are to forgive and forgive and forgive, just as God does.

If we redefine sin, then we don't have to repent of it, but without repentance, there is no forgiveness.

I have found in my walk with the Lord that unconfessed sin leads to separation in my fellowship with him. Once I had experienced that sweet fellowship, I didn't want anything to hinder its flow.

Satan knows that a consequence of sin is separation from God relationally.

So his most successful ploy to keep us from experiencing fellowship with God is to keep us confused about what sin is. Even Christians seem to be confused about sin these days.

Our problem is in our perception of God. We see him more as a concept or theory rather than an all-powerful, living entity.

Or we might believe he exists, but we really don't believe what he says in his Word…his promises…his provision.

It is our human nature to cling to the things we can see, touch, and feel.

God asks us to love him with all our hearts, with all our minds, and with all our strength. That's a tough one.

And yet if we did, we would find that he meets all our desires so much more than the people and things that we cling to. If we did love him like that, it wouldn't be so hard to accept him at his Word, to believe that he can work all things for our good…even painful things.

Simon Peter answered him, "Lord, to whom shall we go? You have the words of eternal life. We have come to believe and to know that you are the Holy One of God."

So, for anyone who reads this….

> I kneel before the Father, from whom every family in heaven and on earth derives its name. I pray that out of his glorious riches he may strengthen you with power through his Spirit in your inner being, so that Christ may dwell in your hearts through faith. And I pray that you, being rooted and established in love, may have power, together with all the Lord's holy people, to grasp how wide and long

and high and deep is the love of Christ, and to know this love that surpasses knowledge—that you may be filled to the measure of all the fullness of God. Now to him who is able to do immeasurably more than all we ask or imagine, according to his power that is at work within us, to him be glory in the church and in Christ Jesus throughout all generations, for ever and ever! Amen. (Ephesians 3:14-21, NIV)

1 John 1:8-10

If we say we have no sin, we deceive ourselves, and the truth is not in us. If we confess our sins, he is faithful and just to forgive us our sins and to cleanse us from all unrighteousness. If we say we have not sinned, we make him a liar, and his word is not in us. (ESV)

John 14:23-24

Jesus replied, "Anyone who loves me will obey my teaching. My Father will love them, and we will come to them and make our home with them. Anyone who does not love me will not obey my teaching. These words you hear are not my own; they belong to the Father who sent me."

Acts 3:19

Repent therefore, and turn back, that your sins may be blotted out. (ESV)

Acts 26:18

To open their eyes, so that they may turn from darkness to light and from the power of Satan to God, that they may receive forgiveness of sins and a place among those who are sanctified by faith in me. (ESV)

1 John 1:9

If we confess our sins, he is faithful and just to forgive us our sins and to cleanse us from all unrighteousness. (ESV)

Reflection Time

How has God been speaking to you today? Take time to write it in your journal.

Chapter 110
Complete Family

Yesterday, we enjoyed a lovely day with our friends, Greg and Jenny. We went to watch a movie, dine out, and shop. During the course of the day, our conversation at one point turned to things in the news—all the shootings, the controversial nuclear deal, the uproar with Planned Parenthood and the abortion issue, etc., etc.

When we were on the way home last night, the car was very quiet…we were tired from the day.

I stared out the car window sleepily, watching the beautiful moon across the river. A few lazy clouds drifted across its golden glow as the stars began to appear.

"What a beautiful world you have given us, Lord," I thought, "and so many gifts to enjoy in it…the love of family and friends…. How have we messed it up so badly?"

A Scripture from Genesis came to my mind: "The Lord regretted that he had made human beings on the earth, and his heart was deeply troubled." (Genesis 6:6, NIV)

My own heart grew heavy, and I had this strange sense—similar to a feeling I've had before—like when we have moved to a new house, and I look around one last time as I close the door to the old house....

When we arrived home, I went to close up the chickens for the night. I looked for the moon over the hilltop as I breathed deeply of the warm summer evening and listened to the peaceful sound of the crickets.

My thoughts turned again to the moonlit ride home.

"Father, I don't understand how this world is still here. Your Word says you are coming back again and you will make all things new...why didn't you do that a long time ago?"

He spoke to my heart. "Well, Sherry...*you* wouldn't have been here a long time ago...."

Wow!

I thought about how I felt after I had my first two sons. I loved them with all my heart, and yet my family didn't feel complete... until after my third child.

I had never thought of it that way. The Lord has been waiting for *his* family to be complete—those of us who are here now wouldn't have been here a long time ago.

Once time as we know it is done, the "family" will be complete.

I woke up in the middle of the night with that same sense I'd had the night before—the "when we have moved to a new house, and I look around one last time as I close the door to the old house" sense.

I believe the time is short. The "family" is almost complete. Jesus is coming back soon. When he does, the expiration date will have run out. Are you ready?

Dear God, please prepare the hearts of all your family to receive you. Help those that are already in the fold to remain steadfast and watchful as we see the day approaching. In Jesus's name, amen.

→⇒⟩⟩ ❋ ⟨⟨⟨←

Matthew 24:30-31

Then will appear the sign of the Son of Man in heaven. And then all the peoples of the earth will mourn when they see the Son of Man coming on the clouds of heaven, with power and great glory. And he will send his angels with a loud trumpet call, and they will gather his elect from the four winds, from one end of the heavens to the other.

Matthew 24:37-44

As it was in the days of Noah, so it will be at the coming of the Son of Man. For in the days before the flood, people were eating and drinking, marrying and giving in marriage, up to the day Noah entered the ark; and they knew nothing about what would happen until the flood came and took them all away. That is how it will be at the coming of the Son of Man. Two men will be in the field; one will be taken and the other left. Two women will be grinding with a hand mill; one will be taken and the other left. Therefore keep watch, because you do not know on what day your Lord will come. But understand this: If the owner of the house had known at what time of night the thief was coming, he would have kept watch and would not have let his house be broken into. So you also must be ready, because the Son of Man will come at an hour when you do not expect him.

Reflection Time

How has God been speaking to you today? Take time to write it in your journal.

Chapter 111
Watch and Pray

I woke up at 3 a.m. and lay there wide awake for a few minutes. Usually I pray when I wake up early like that, but I felt like God wanted to show me something, so I tiptoed downstairs. Thinking maybe he wanted to show me an especially beautiful moon, I went to all the windows, looking for a glimpse. I opened the front door and realized it was raining…so, no moon. I headed out to the sunroom (which Al now calls the "War Room," since seeing the movie with the same title). I sat down and waited, looking out at the night sky.

Usually I have my iPad when I go to the War Room. It contains my prayer list and my praise and worship music, and it's what I do my writings on. But I had left it upstairs, so I just sat in silence. I became fidgety after a few minutes of gazing out at the night sky, which was barely visible through the hedge of towering pines.

I hadn't been to the War Room for a few days. My last session in prayer was pretty intense, and it literally wore me out. Very often, when I pray for those on my prayer list, the tears roll down my cheeks as I am touched by each need, but when I had gone in there a few days ago to pray for our nation, a burden unlike any I had ever experienced had overwhelmed me to the point that I literally sobbed and wailed as I prayed.

I didn't like my heart rending like that. I felt like I would rather go back to my morning routine of the last few years: reading my devotions, listening to my worship music, praying for my loved ones, and studying for my Bible study lessons. (Hmm…I just noticed all the instances of *my* in that sentence.)

Anyway, back to the sunroom…fidgeting…sitting in silence… waiting.

I prayed for a few needs that crossed my mind.

"What is it God? Why am I down here?"

No response.

I sighed and tried to quiet my thoughts.

After a few minutes, he spoke to my heart just three words. "Watch and pray."

I waited for a bit. "Is that it?"

Sensing nothing else, and beginning to feel sleepy, I padded barefoot back upstairs one step at a time, slowly, trying to keep the old stairs from creaking. I climbed back into bed and, grabbing my iPad and headphones, flipped to YouTube and typed in Watch and Pray. I clicked on a beautiful old song by that title, and as I listened to the words, I was overcome with emotion.

Father, forgive me for wanting my Christian walk and prayer time to be about soft chairs in beautiful surroundings with yummy smelling candles and soft praise and worship music. That is the comfort zone I have created for myself while a lost and dying world wails and groans. Forgive me when I want to shut my ears and protect my heart from their pain. Give me courage to battle in intercessory prayer for those the enemy has in his clutches…for Christian brothers and sisters throughout the world who have to give their very lives for their faith…for thousands of refugees who are being forced from their homes with *nothing* to call their own…for my own nation, which becomes increasingly divided every day on a multitude of issues…for your children who no longer read the Bible for themselves and are being led astray by false teachings…for friends and loved ones who do not know you as Savior.

Forgive me for not wanting to step out of my comfort zone, for not wanting to rend my heart…forgive me…forgive me. Strengthen me in prayer. Let me approach your throne boldly. Help me to lay my requests at your feet and leave them there. In the name of your Son, Jesus, amen.

Luke 21:36

Watch ye therefore, and pray always, that ye may be accounted worthy to escape all these things that shall come to pass, and to stand before the Son of man. (KJV)

Reflection Time

How has God been speaking to you today? Take time to write it in your journal.

Chapter 112
Present Your Requests to God

I was barely coming to wakefulness this morning when the Lord spoke to my heart: "What if I told you that everything you brought to me in prayer this morning, I would start working on, and you could just relax and enjoy your life?"

Wow! I felt so special! Feeling like someone had just told me I had won the lottery, I tried to get my sleep-addled brain to remember everything on my prayer list. I began to pour out names and needs to God like I was on a time clock counting down.

I paused for a moment, furrowing my brow and mentally tapping my head, trying to think of who I'd forgotten (before the offer ran out), when bits and pieces of Scripture began to cross my mind.

> *If we ask anything according to his will, he hears us.*
> *Rejoice in the Lord always…Do not be anxious about anything….*
> *…present your requests to God…And the peace of God, which transcends all understanding….*

Wait a minute…those are promises for everyone every day!!

I could almost hear God chuckle.

Ok. Haha. Good one, God!

Father God, sometimes I make the easy things difficult, don't I? You want your children to live happy, fulfilled lives. Your promises say that if we bring our requests to you and leave them in your capable hands, trusting you to take care of them, you hear us and give us peace in return. Keep me ever mindful of your promises. In Jesus's name, amen.

1 John 5:14-15

This is the confidence we have in approaching God: that if we ask anything according to his will, he hears us. And if we know that he hears us—whatever we ask— we know that we have what we asked of him.

Philippians 4:4-7

Rejoice in the Lord always. I will say it again: Rejoice! Let your gentleness be evident to all. The Lord is near. Do not be anxious about anything, but in every situation, by prayer and petition, with thanksgiving, present your requests to God. And the peace of God, which transcends all understanding, will guard your hearts and your minds in Christ Jesus.

Hebrews 4:16

Let us then approach God's throne of grace with confidence, so that we may receive mercy and find grace to help us in our time of need.

Sherolyn Porter

Reflection Time

How has God been speaking to you today? Take
time to write it in your journal.

Chapter 113
A New Name

Our Bible study lesson tonight was about Jacob wrestling with the angel.

Jacob's name meant "Deceiver," and he spent a lot of his life living up to that name. Yet even when Jacob wasn't where he should have been spiritually, God was faithful to him.

It made me think about my own walk with God. Most of my spiritual growth has come from times of "wrestling."

I have wrestled with patience. I have wrestled with mercy…and doubt. I have wrestled with anxiety, depression, pain, and chronic fatigue. I have wrestled with insecurities over all of the above. And I have wrestled with the idea that God has the power to take all my struggles away, but he doesn't always do it. Why not? Because, God's goal is not to make my life "cushy."

God allows the struggles because his goal is to make me an overcomer.

When the Bible said that the angel "could not overpower Jacob," it didn't mean that Jacob was stronger than the angel. It meant that Jacob didn't quit. Jacob held on to the angel and wouldn't let him go until the angel blessed him. Then the angel asked him a strange question. "What is your name?" The angel knew his name, but he wanted Jacob to say it.

"My name is Jacob (Deceiver)."

When the wrestling was over, not only was Jacob a different person, but God gave him a new name.

If I made an honest assessment of myself—if what I struggle with was actually my name—what would it be? "Much Afraid?" or "Much Too Tired?" or "Unmerciful?"

When I assess these things and then strive to bring them into alignment with who God's Word says I am, then I am wrestling. I am overcoming.

Revelation 2:17 says, "To the one who is victorious, I will give some of the hidden manna. I will also give that person a white stone with a new name written on it, known only to the one who receives it."

Someday, our Father will give us a new name, just between him and us. Only he knows the things we have had to wrestle to overcome. How sweet that name will be.

Father, I thank you that you never give up in us. Even when we are faithless, you remain faithful. Your Word says that when you begin a good work in us, you are faithful to complete it. Help me to cooperate with that process. In Jesus's name, amen.

James 1:12

Blessed is the one who perseveres under trial because, having stood the test, that person will receive the crown of life that the Lord has promised to those who love him.

James 1:2-4

Consider it pure joy, my brothers and sisters, whenever you face trials of many kinds, because you know that the

*testing of your faith produces perseverance. Let persever-
ance finish its work so that you may be mature and
complete, not lacking anything.*

Reflection Time

How has God been speaking to you today? Take
time to write it in your journal.

Chapter 114
The "Autumn" of Time

Autumn is my favorite season. I look forward to sweaters and hot tea, campfires on the patio at night, homemade soups and breads.

Autumn is also a season I love to decorate for. I anticipate, with the excitement of a child, filling my home with the warm, rich colors and smells of fall: brightly colored silk-leaf garlands on the mantels, pumpkins and gourds on my tabletops, and the scents of cinnamon and pumpkin spice suffusing the air.

Strangely enough, as I decorated this year, I became pensive and thoughtful.

I began thinking about the "autumn" of time. Sometimes when I'm out shopping or running errands, I look at the people around me and wonder if anyone else feels it too—this sense of "winding down," of saying goodbye to the ways we've always known…the feeling that something is about to change.

If I were eighty years old, that feeling wouldn't seem so foreign. But I'm not. There should be a lot of life left ahead of me.

Six months ago, my thoughts of the future consisted of taking our first cruise…or loading up the camper and traveling up the east coast in autumn…or heading out west to see the Grand Canyon…or spoiling the grandchildren (I don't yet have).

It seems that these days, more of my focus is to spend time with the Lord, praying for the strength and protection of his children… praying for those who do not yet know him. Don't get me wrong. I am enjoying my family and friends more than I ever have, but the sense that "our time here is short" grows stronger by the day.

Father God, I pray that you would open ears to hear and eyes to see. I pray for a tendering of hearts. Autumn is the season of harvest, and I pray that *this* autumn there will be a great harvest of souls. I pray that you would give all your children an increasing burden for the lost and a new boldness to share the good news. Most of all, I pray for a great outpouring of your love on your children. May it overflow from us and be a sweet aroma to all those with whom we come in contact. Even so, come quickly, Lord Jesus. Amen.

Acts 17:30–31

The times of ignorance God overlooked, but now he commands all people everywhere to repent, because he has fixed a day on which he will judge the world in righteousness by a man whom he has appointed; and of this he has given assurance to all by raising him from the dead. (ESV)

Matthew 24:44

Therefore you also must be ready, for the Son of Man is coming at an hour you do not expect. (ESV)

Luke 21:36

But stay awake at all times, praying that you may have strength to escape all these things that are going to take place, and to stand before the Son of Man. (ESV)

2 Peter 3:10–13

But the day of the Lord will come like a thief, and then the heavens will pass away with a roar, and the heavenly bodies will be burned up and dissolved, and the earth and the works that are done on it will be exposed. Since all these things are thus to be dissolved, what sort of people ought you to be in lives of holiness and godliness, waiting for and hastening the coming of the day of God, because of which the heavens will be set on fire and dissolved, and the heavenly bodies will melt as they burn! But according to his promise we are waiting for new heavens and a new earth in which righteousness dwells. (ESV)

2 Timothy 3:1–5a

But understand this, that in the last days there will come times of difficulty. For people will be lovers of self, lovers of money, proud, arrogant, abusive, disobedient to their parents, ungrateful, unholy, heartless, unappeasable, slanderous, without self-control, brutal, not loving good, treacherous, reckless, swollen with conceit, lovers of pleasure rather than lovers of God, having the appearance of godliness, but denying its power. (ESV)

Reflection Time

How has God been speaking to you today? Take time to write it in your journal.

Chapter 115

J Have Been Crucified With Christ

J have been going through something…maybe the stress of the last few months…maybe this cold virus that has worn me down.

The last ten days or so have been a time of soul searching for me. The anxiety that has plagued me off and on for much of my adult life became especially heightened. One morning, in utter frustration, I asked the Lord, "What is going on with me? Why is this a constant battle? I feel like I am not living in the victory that you mean for me to have."

I got in the shower and let the warm water wash over me, sadly wishing my fears could just wash down the drain with the soap suds. As I stood there, heavy hearted, the warmth of the water not reaching my weary soul, the Lord began to speak: "Your earthly father never allayed your fears. In fact, he was the cause of your fears. You keep praying for me to remove the spirit of fear…what you need to ask for is the revelation of the Spirit of adoption that I have already given to you."

"Spirit of adoption?" I resolved to look it up when I got out of the shower.

"For ye have not received the spirit of bondage again to fear; but ye have received the Spirit of adoption, whereby we cry, Abba, Father." (Romans 8:15, KJV)

I knew I had emotional baggage from my childhood, growing up with an alcoholic father, living with constant uncertainty and fear. I never felt safe or protected. I was afraid to hope in promises made in sober moments, because they would always be broken....

My father died at the young age of fifty-five. My mother had remarried about twelve years earlier, and I was blessed with a wonderful stepfather who never let us down, but some childhood wounds remained.

I hoped, with the revelation I had just received, that my deliverance from fear was as good as done. However, the days following were full of emotional upheaval unlike any I have ever experienced. The ensuing spiritual warfare left me wondering about my sanity. I embarked on an emotional roller coaster; fear, grief, terror, and even rage seemed to come at me from every direction, with blows that left me shaking and exhausted. My heart pounded for hours on end. I couldn't eat but a few bites at a time. My body was wracked with pain and my mind with confusion. I tried to put on the armor of God. I listened to Scripture. I prayed. And I cried ever so many tears. I contacted a counselor, but she couldn't see me professionally because of our friendship; when she suggested others, I hesitated.

"Abba, what am I to do?" His response was, "This is for me to do. You just need to trust and cooperate with me in the process." Finally, I confessed to some friends what I was going through and asked for prayer. I worried that they too would think I was losing my mind. But what I received from them was encouragement. They prayed over me, they sang over me, they laid hands on me and anointed me with oil. They gave me encouraging Scripture, and they gave me love. And I tried to trust and listen for Abba's voice. One night was especially bad. I just lay in bed, and as the tears ran in endless streams down my face, all I could do was whisper into the darkness that threatened to suffocate me, "I am his. I am sealed. I am safe."

God told me when the emotions came not to run but to be still and let them wash over me and then to offer them up to him. The onslaught of emotions seemed as endless as the tears at first. As I offered them up to Abba, he showed me where forgiveness of others was needed and where confession and repentance was needed on my part. Although I slept peacefully each night during this process, every morning it began again. Gradually, however, the intensity began to lessen.

This morning when I woke up, I felt the familiar heaviness began to settle around me. Wearily, I began to offer it up to the Lord. I felt relief for a few moments, but then a new heaviness settled around my heart. He showed me that this particular heaviness involved my children and my reluctance to let them go. "Offer them up to me," he said. In my mind's eye, I lifted them up, but when he reached to take them from me, my grip tightened.

He tugged ever so gently, and my grip tightened further. I let them go partially but kept a piece for myself. Its edges were sharp and felt like a thorn in my heart. "Abba, I kept a piece," I confessed. "It hurts."

"What you refuse to turn over to me becomes an idol," he said. Then I had a vision of the walk-in closet in the bedroom of my childhood home. Its walls were slanted as they often are in older homes. Clothes hung on the hanger bars, and shoes were stacked in the corner, along with some toys.

"Abba, why are we here?" I questioned.

"You have had many dreams about this closet over the years," he said. "What were your dreams about?"

I thought about it. In my dreams, I was always looking for my clothes, but the only ones in the closet were from different ages in my childhood—nothing that would fit me now.

"It's time to stop clinging to things that no longer fit who you are now," he said.

I lay there in silence with my eyes closed, thinking about that. Suddenly, my chest began to feel like it was being flattened, growing thinner and thinner, until it felt as flat as a board. I felt a pain like a large nail right in the middle of it. Then I had a vision of Jesus on the cross, nails in his hands and feet and a large one though his chest. "But Lord," I said, "You never had a nail in your chest…."

He said, ever so softly, "The nails in My hands and feet did not hold me to that cross. The one in My chest held me there."

"But where did that one come from?" I asked.

"That one is yours," he replied. I gasped.

"The love in my heart for you…*that* is what held me on that cross."

The Scripture came to my mind, "I have been crucified with Christ and I no longer live, but Christ lives in me. The life I now live in the body, I live by faith in the Son of God, who loved me and gave himself for me." (Galatians 2:20, NIV)

I'm sure my trials and lessons are not over, but today has been easier. My emotions have settled…the muscles in my body are more relaxed than they have been for a long time—like the tears have all been cried out of them—and there is a stillness in my soul that seems almost foreign to me. I pray for the Lord to replace all that I have offered up to him with peace and joy.

Galatians 2:20

I have been crucified with Christ and I no longer live, but Christ lives in me. The life I now live in the body, I live by faith in the Son of God, who loved me and gave himself for me.

Reflection Time

How has God been speaking to you today? Take time to write it in your journal.

Chapter 116
A Dangerous Current

One year when our daughter, Autumn, was small, we went to the Outer Banks for vacation. Each of our three children had brought a friend, and we had planned to meet some of our old high-school friends as well. One day we all packed a picnic, loaded up chairs, towels and umbrellas, and headed down to the beach.

Autumn and her friend were playing with Al and me in the shallow water. The tide was out, and a huge sand bar some distance away was exposed. It looked like a small island, and other people were walking out to it, as the water was no deeper than waist high. The girls and I had our boogie boards, and we floated and kicked our way lazily out to the sandbar to look for shells, joining other beach goers who were headed in that direction.

Al walked alongside the girls, guiding their boogie boards with a hand on each one. We strolled around on the giant sandbar, the girls playing in the sand, looking for shells and splashing joyfully in the water. After a while, realizing that we were the only ones left on our small island, we too began to head back to shore.

We weren't very far from the sandbar, when we noticed that the tide had begun to come in without our realizing it, and the water had become much deeper. Not only was it deeper, but the current was frighteningly strong, and it was not carrying us back to shore but out to sea. The water quickly became deep enough that I could no longer touch the bottom. I hoisted myself on my boogie board and tried to paddle to shore. Autumn and her friend were laughing and talking on their boogie boards, blissfully unaware of the danger, as Al walked between them holding them tightly. Al and I looked at each other as he began to feel the strength of the dangerous current also, and I saw alarm cross his face. This frightened me even more, because my husband does not get easily alarmed.

He was soon over his head and began to kick his feet, holding onto the girls as he struggled to guide them to the safety of the mainland. The three of them were quickly being pulled away from me toward the open waters. I was kicking with all my might to try to get to shore and becoming increasingly exhausted. My heart began to pound; panic threatened to steal my breath, and I could see fear and the beginning of fatigue on the face of my husband as he struggled to keep the two girls on the boogie boards and swim them to safety.

I looked at the people on the shore; everyone seemed oblivious to our plight. I began to pray for protection and strength. My legs felt like rubber, and I could see Al and the girls were very far away from me at that point, although he was making headway toward the beach. I finally made it to shore and saw that they had made it to the beach as well, several hundred yards down. I collapsed on the sand exhausted.

Reunited, we walked back to our spot on the beach, and Al began to tell our friends about our experience.

The fear of our close call haunted me for the rest of the day, and that experience instilled a fear of the ocean in me. I had experienced firsthand that, beneath its beautiful waves, there were strong, deceptive currents that could have led to our deaths.

Reflections From the Sunroom

I lay back on my beach chair and closed my eyes. I began to think about our culture and how its ever-changing beliefs have caught many in its deceptive current. The Bible is no longer the "mainland" by which we set our sights. Those who try to stand on its truths are struggling against a strong deception that is deep and wide. Those who don't have their eye on the mainland are completely unaware of the current's danger, and some who *are* aware have just worn themselves out in the struggle. I admit, I too have found myself weary at times, tempted to go with the flow.

Sometimes I feel weary about guiding my children through the deceptive, seemingly harmless currents of this world. I see many other Christian parents who do not seem worried about guiding their children away from the mainstream currents (sexual immorality, abortion, occultism, drugs and alcohol, etc., etc.) of our society. Many Christians are floating along with the current themselves, deceived by it or afraid of being labeled *intolerant* if they stand up against it. Jesus said in the last days that many would be deceived—even the elect if it were possible. These dangerous currents are not that hard to recognize if the mainland of God's Word is used as a guide.

If we are not consistently reading his Word and listening for his voice, we are in danger of being swept away, little by little, before we even realize it.

Sometimes we are in defiance when we step out into the water… sometimes it happens quite innocently…but we are always in peril when we trust the direction of the current without keeping our eyes on the mainland.

I was talking to the Lord about it last night as I got ready for bed.

"Father," I said, "sometimes I feel lulled by the current, very much alone in my struggle to keep my eyes on the mainland. And the currents…they don't always seem so dangerous—those caught up in them do not seem afraid—and I'm tempted to just relax and float along. People think I'm old fashioned and weird…dogmatic. They mistake my concern about drifting away from your Word as judgmental."

He whispered, "He who stands firm to the end will be saved."

I got into bed and pulled up a video about end-times events that a good friend had emailed to me.

A few minutes into it, the speaker began talking about being caught up in the currents of our society—drifting away from the truth of God's Word—and then he said, "But he who stands firm to the end will be saved."

Father, thank you for encouraging me when I question. Forgive me for being tempted to give up instead of standing firm when the current is strong. Help me to keep my eyes firmly on you. Give me boldness to shout out warnings to those who don't realize the current is dangerous. Help me to always speak the truth in love. In Jesus's name, amen.

Matthew 10:22
You will be hated by everyone because of me, but the one who stands firm to the end will be saved.

Isaiah 66:5
Hear the word of the LORD, you who tremble at his word: "Your own people who hate you, and exclude you because of my name, have said, 'Let the LORD be glorified, that we may see your joy!' Yet they will be put to shame."

Galatians 6:9

Let us not become weary in doing good, for at the proper time we will reap a harvest if we do not give up.

Matthew 24:13

But the one who stands firm to the end will be saved.

Matthew 24:23-25

Then if anyone says to you, "Behold, here is the Christ," or "There He is," do not believe him. For false Christs and false prophets will arise and will show great signs and wonders, so as to mislead, if possible, even the elect. Behold, I have told you in advance. (NASB)

Reflection Time

How has God been speaking to you today? Take time to write it in your journal.

Chapter 117
The Testing of My Faith

I'm sitting in my chair, listening to worship music and watching the autumn wind tease the leaves off the trees. Spinning and twirling in the sun against the backdrop of the beautiful blue sky, they look like brightly colored butterflies sailing on the breeze, blissfully unaware that this is their final dance.

I wish I could exhibit that carefree joy no matter what my circumstance.

For the past six weeks, I have been struggling with the frustration of my physical limitations and how they are imposing upon me. I caught a cold a couple of months ago, and it set off a relapse of the chronic fatigue/fibromyalgia that I have had since my early twenties. This happens periodically when I am exposed to a virus, and it leaves me ill and feeling very weak for months at a time. I love to be busy, and I absolutely rail against having to be still. Even if I take the stairs slowly, one at a time, I am still worn out when I reach the top. I struggle with guilt when I cannot help others or take care of my family like I want to. I struggle with anger at myself for my discouragement, as there are so many worse off than I am, and I bring them before the Lord in prayer.

It has been a painful lesson regarding areas of my faith that need strengthening.

My recent prayer and worship time has been the result of discipline rather than the joy that it usually is, but I will continue because "Whom have I in heaven but you? And earth has nothing I desire besides you. My flesh and my heart may fail, but God is the strength of my heart and my portion forever."

Our next Bible study is going to be about the life of Paul. I'm sure that is not by accident. I pray that the Lord can make me like Paul through this trial…that I can learn to be content whatever my circumstance and to give thanks in everything.

Father God, I thank you for the many blessings you have given me. Forgive me when I invite myself to a pity party. I pray that you would grow me through my trials. Help me to submit to being made into the image of your Son. Grant me the serenity to accept the things I cannot change, the courage to change the things I can, and the wisdom to know the difference. In Jesus's name, amen.

→⟩⟩⟩ ❊ ⟨⟨⟨←

1 Thessalonians 5:16-18

Rejoice always, pray continually, give thanks in all circumstances; for this is God's will for you in Christ Jesus.

James 1:2-4

Consider it pure joy, my brothers and sisters, whenever you face trials of many kinds, because you know that the testing of your faith produces perseverance. Let perseverance finish its work so that you may be mature and complete, not lacking anything.

Sherolyn Porter

1 Peter 4:12-13

Dear friends, do not be surprised at the fiery ordeal that has come on you to test you, as though something strange were happening to you. But rejoice inasmuch as you participate in the sufferings of Christ, so that you may be overjoyed when his glory is revealed.

Matthew 7:24-25

Therefore everyone who hears these words of mine and puts them into practice is like a wise man who built his house on the rock. The rain came down, the streams rose, and the winds blew and beat against that house; yet it did not fall, because it had its foundation on the rock.

Reflection Time

How has God been speaking to you today? Take time to write it in your journal.

Chapter 118
Trust the Father

This morning I read a beautiful, poignant, heart-wrenching post from a father who is sitting with his son as the son goes through daily chemo treatments. His son has Down's syndrome, so he doesn't quite understand why he is suffering. Father and son have a very close relationship, and the father is with him every step of the way, holding his hand and holding him when he cries. The son trusts the father and leans on his strength.

As I prayed for them, I began to cry. Others on my prayer list began to cross my mind, and I prayed for them too with an ache in my chest and tears streaming down my face: a friend who is ill yet trying to care for a dying parent…another friend who also suffers with fibromyalgia and chronic fatigue and is trying to raise her grandchildren with limited resources…friends who are battling cancer and the fear that goes along with it…friends who grieve the loss of their children or spouses…friends who grieve the loss of their health.

I am touched by their pain because I have experienced my own, so when I lift them up in prayer, my prayers are fervent and heartfelt.

As I prayed this morning, I thought about how God sent his Son to Earth to experience the human condition, to be acquainted personally with the sufferings we experience. He left a perfect place—willingly—to do that. He died in our place for our sins, so that when this temporary life on Earth is over, we can be with him forever in a place where there will be no more suffering, no more sickness, no more tears.

And his job now, as he sits at the right hand of the Father, is to pray for us. He understands our pain and suffering because he experienced it, so his prayers are heartfelt and sincere.

If we allow him, he can use our sufferings to make us into his image…make us tender…give us understanding so that we can be used for a greater good—one we may not see or understand now.

Sometimes we are healed quickly, and sometimes we are healed in the midst of a long struggle through which we must persevere, but he has promised never to leave us or forsake us. Nothing can remove us from his love.

Father, help me to be like this young man going through chemo. He doesn't understand his suffering. But he trusts in his father who is right beside him, holding his hand. In Jesus's name, amen.

→>>>> ❈ <<<<-

Hebrews 4:14-16

Therefore, since we have a great high priest who has passed through the heavens, Jesus the Son of God, let us hold fast our confession. For we do not have a high priest who cannot sympathize with our weaknesses, but One who has been tempted in all things as we are, yet without sin. Therefore let us draw near with confidence to the throne of grace, so that we may receive mercy and find grace to help in time of need. (NASB)

Revelation 21:1-4

Then I saw "a new heaven and a new earth," for the first heaven and the first earth had passed away, and there was no longer any sea. I saw the Holy City, the new Jerusalem, coming down out of heaven from God, prepared as a bride beautifully dressed for her husband. And I heard a loud voice from the throne saying, "Look! God's dwelling place is now among the people, and he will dwell with them. They will be his people, and God himself will be with them and be their God. 'He will wipe every tear from their eyes. There will be no more death' or mourning or crying or pain, for the old order of things has passed away."

Reflection Time

How has God been speaking to you today? Take time to write it in your journal.

Chapter 119
Hope Painted Like a Pony

I sat on the porch rocker earlier this evening watching the autumn leaves drift lazily down from the trees. My pony came to the fence in the meadow across the yard, and upon seeing me began to nicker.

We haven't seen each other for a while because I've been too weak to walk to the meadow or the barn. Although it isn't far at all—no more than a few hundred feet from the house—the distance has seemed impossibly daunting to me lately.

I stared longingly at him, and he nodded his head as if to say, "You can do it, friend."

I rose up out of the chair and went inside to get an apple. He was still waiting and watching when I returned to the porch, as if he knew I couldn't resist.

I walked carefully down the porch steps and slowly across the yard as he followed me up the fence line. I sighed contentedly as we met, and I ran my fingers through his mane. I stared into his liquid brown eyes and then closed my own, breathing deeply of his wonderfully warm, horsey scent.

He took the apple from my hand and crunched it happily, the juice from it running through my fingers and making my hands sticky. He teasingly nudged me as if looking for more treats, and we stood there and enjoyed each other's company for a while.

I rested my legs and then decided they might be strong enough to carry me to the chicken coop. I could tell my hens had missed me too, as they ran to the front of the pen when they saw me coming. I tossed them some grain and listened to their contented clucking.

I turned to go back to the house, enjoying the sight of a few dark clouds against the backdrop of the muted sunset-colored sky. I could not have been more content at that moment, so grateful my legs were strong enough for that short walk and so thankful to see the beautiful sunset.

I made it to the house with legs so tired, they barely carried me up the stairs.

Now I am propped up in bed with the window wide open, enjoying the cool night air wafting through my room. The evening breeze is accompanied by the sound of crickets and the fresh damp smell of an unexpected rain shower. I can hear my pony in the meadow, nickering in the dark. I'm sure he can see me by the light of the bedside lamp through the window facing the meadow.

Thank you, God, for the hope you gave me tonight...initiated by the nicker of a beautiful, painted pony. In Jesus's name, amen.

→⟫⟫⟫ ☀ ⟪⟪⟪⟵

Jeremiah 29:11

"For I know the plans I have for you," declares the LORD, "plans to prosper you and not to harm you, plans to give you hope and a future."

Isaiah 40:29-31

He gives strength to the weary and increases the power of the weak. Even youths grow tired and weary, and young men stumble and fall; but those who hope in the LORD will renew their strength. They will soar on wings like eagles; they will run and not grow weary, they will walk and not be faint.

Reflection Time

How has God been speaking to you today? Take time to write it in your journal.

Chapter 120
The Spark of Life

J woke up thinking about some things I'd like to do today…even imagined myself doing them: the load of laundry sitting by the bedroom closet that needs put away (has needed put away for over a week); the spinach and lettuce in the greenhouse that needs picked; quilt blocks that have been sitting in the corner of my sewing room for months, waiting to be sewn together; the pattern pieces of a cute little sleeveless dress lying on the sewing room table…all the beginnings of projects, waiting for energy to seep back into their creator. I happily imagined myself doing all of it.

Then I got up to let the dogs out, and my legs were not as strong as my mind imagined them to be. Fighting back a twinge of disappointment, I went downstairs and opened the front door for the dogs, who could barely contain their excitement to be outside.

My senses were beautifully permeated by the smell of the fallen autumn leaves mingled with the dampness of the cool morning air. The sight of the trees robed in finest reds and golds made my breath catch in my throat. I was overcome with gratitude that I could actually engage with the beauty of it this morning. Although this beauty always surrounds me, some days it cannot awaken my soul. Some days it is like looking at a photograph that someone else has taken: there is no life in it.

But today, I felt the spark of life. So today, I pray for the energy to take some photos of my own and capture this glorious autumn day before the breath of winter blows it away.

Father God, I pray for enough strength in body and mind to enjoy your creation today and also to enjoy some creation of my own. You are the giver of life. You give power to the faint, and to them that have no might you increase strength. They that wait on you shall renew their strength. They shall mount up with wings as eagles; they shall run and not be weary; they shall walk and not faint. I thank you for the life I have in me today. Bless it and help me to keep my mind on you and your promises, in Jesus's name, amen.

Isaiah 40:28-31

Hast thou not known? hast thou not heard, that the everlasting God, the LORD, the Creator of the ends of the earth, fainteth not, neither is weary? there is no searching of his understanding. He giveth power to the faint; and to them that have no might he increaseth strength. Even the youths shall faint and be weary, and the young men shall utterly fall: But they that wait upon the LORD shall renew their strength; they shall mount up with wings as eagles; they shall run, and not be weary; and they shall walk, and not faint. (KJV)

Reflection Time

How has God been speaking to you today? Take time to write it in your journal.

Chapter 121
A Guardian Angel Named Luke

I have a guardian angel of the four-legged variety named Luke. He is fourteen years old. His eyes are growing dim with age, but they are still kind and very expressive. He loves me unconditionally, and he has seen more of my tears than any other living creature on this earth. My tears are safe with him. He does not judge or make me feel guilty. His warm presence and silence are always comforting to me. Sometimes it seems as if he can read my thoughts, and when I am weary and sad, he will just press his forehead against my own and leave it there for a length of time, as if to silently offer me strength.

He was our first family pet but assigned himself specifically to me when I became very ill nine years ago and was bedridden or wheelchair bound for three long months. Although typically mild mannered, if a visitor other than family approached my bed during that time, Luke would place himself between me and them and growl fiercely. Since that time he has been "my dog," and the other family members had to get their own pets. He always measures his steps to mine, whether I am having good days or really difficult ones.

When climbing the stairs, if I can do three before I rest, then Luke does three; if I can only do one, Luke does one. He used to run as fast as a deer. He is getting arthritic now, and sometimes his legs tremble too, but he still follows me everywhere I go.

He knows when I am having a "good day," and when I step outside, he leaps and pounces and runs in circles as fast as his arthritic legs can carry him.

My Heavenly Father has taught me a lot about his own love through my furry friend.

Sometimes when I can't feel my heavenly Father's presence in the midst of my storm, I lean on his promises that say he will never leave me or forsake me, that he is an ever-present help in time of trouble, that he hems me in behind and before, that He protects me and guards me in all of my ways....

I have a sense of what those promises mean because of my furry friend.

I dread the day when I will no longer have my Luke, but I believe the Lord will have him waiting for me when I cross to the other side.

Father, I thank you for expressions of your love encompassed in earthly vessels. I thank you for my faithful friend, Luke, and his comfort to me here on this earth. Help me to show unconditional love to others and be empathetic to their weaknesses also. In Jesus's name, amen.

Proverbs 17:17a
A friend loves at all times.

Reflection Time

How has God been speaking to you today? Take time to write it in your journal.

Chapter 122
The Light of Hope

Several times this week, the Lord has brought to my mind a favorite childhood memory—one that I cherish. If I close my eyes, I can still smell, see, and feel the moment as if I were experiencing it right now.

This memory is of a Christmas Eve candlelight service. I was probably ten or eleven years old. The air was brisk and cold, and the sky filled with countless stars as we walked through the old, wooden double doors of the small, country church. The rich smell of old wood from the pews lining the aisles mixed with the scent of fresh pine filled my senses as we were given unlit white taper candles. The church was dark, except for a few lighted candles in the front, which gave it an ethereal glow, and the hushed silence in the congregation was respectful and reverent. As the service began, someone took the lighted candles and began to light the candles of the people sitting at the end of the pews. They in turn lit the candle of the person next to them and so on.

As the strains of "O Holy Night" flowed from the piano and people began to sing, I indeed felt the holy presence of God. As more and more candles were lit, the church became illuminated in a soft glow. At times, whether by draft or by accident, someone's candle began to go out, and the person next to them would relight it with their own. One tiny flame would become a much larger flame as the candle shared its light.

I think that night, as a young child, was my first personal encounter with the holy presence of God.

This week has brought to my attention many people with heartbreaking needs to pray for. Some of them have been going through difficulties for a long while.

I believe that is why the Lord has brought that childhood memory to my mind.

Some of their candles are flickering…some have gone out. I have felt the glow of my own candle grow dangerously dim these last few months, but thankfully I have precious friends in the Lord who have been tirelessly willing to share their light to strengthen my own.

As God's children, we cannot grow weary of this—even when some candles have trouble staying lit—because we need them all for God's church to have a Holy glow.

I believe that is what we are called to do as children of God: bear one another's burdens, lift one another up, share the light of hope.

Some of us are blessed with good candles and are not facing the winds of adversity.

Some may have lights that don't shine as quite as brightly, but we are called to share the light that we have, and when we do, our own flame will burn brighter.

Father, I thank you for the friends who have been faithful to pray for me. Help me to be faithful in my prayers for others, to persevere in prayer and not to lose heart. Keep my heart compassionate and close to your own. In Jesus's name, amen.

-->>>> ❄ <<<<-

John 13:34-35

A new command I give you: Love one another. As I have loved you, so you must love one another. By this everyone will know that you are my disciples, if you love one another.

Ecclesiastes 4:9-10a

Two are better than one,
because they have a good return for their labor:
If either of them falls down,
one can help the other up.

Ephesians 6:18

And pray in the Spirit on all occasions with all kinds of prayers and requests. With this in mind, be alert and always keep on praying for all the Lord's people.

John 13:12-17

When he had finished washing their feet, he put on his clothes and returned to his place. "Do you understand what I have done for you?" he asked them. "You call me 'Teacher' and 'Lord,' and rightly so, for that is what I am. Now that I, your Lord and Teacher, have washed your feet, you also should wash one another's feet. I have set you an example that you should do as I have done for you. Very truly I tell you, no servant is greater than his master, nor is a messenger greater than the one who sent him. Now that you know these things, you will be blessed if you do them."

Sherolyn Porter

Reflection Time

How has God been speaking to you today? Take time to write it in your journal.

Chapter 123
True Light

"The true light that gives light to everyone was coming into the world. He was in the world, and though the world was made through him, the world did not recognize him. He came to that which was his own, but his own did not receive him." (John 1:9-11, NIV)

Written two thousand years ago and yet still true. He is here and we rush right past him; we don't even know we are looking for him. He longs to show us that he is *everything* we need and all that we are looking for: healing, love, acceptance, comfort, peace, security, strength. He is all the things we wear ourselves out trying frantically to obtain…and sometimes selling our souls in the process. Security is not found in the pursuit of wealth. Unconditional love is rarely found in other human beings. Acceptance is certainly not found in a succession of empty relationships that steal away our hearts piece by piece. We search for elusive peace in a bottle, or medication, or fancy vacations. We seek security in the fortresses that we build for ourselves—fortresses that can be washed away or blown apart in disaster or times of personal crisis.

The King of glory—our hearts' desire—isn't found in the greatest achievements of man. He was found in a manger, announced by the angels to the lowly shepherds. We miss him because he did not arrive as our definition of a hero. He did not arrive in the midst of glitz and glamour, surrounded by Hollywood stars, nor will he be found there now.

He is simplicity in all of his great complexity. He is found in the stillness.

Don't waste any more time in the pursuit of things and people that will always leave you empty in the end. Seek him while he may be found.

He's right here…a breath away…a prayer away.

Father God, give boldness to those of us who have found the light, and help us to share it. Help us not to be afraid of the darkness and those who want to put out that light. Remind us that the light will prevail, no matter what. Help your children of light, your children of the day to rise up in the truth that we know. Keep us in your Word…remind us to make time for you daily, for you are our strength and shield…you are a very present help in times of trouble. In Jesus's name, amen.

→→⟫⟫ ❋ ⟨⟨⟨←

Isaiah 55:6

Seek ye the LORD while he may be found, call ye upon him while he is near. (KJV)

John 1:1-5, 9-13

In the beginning was the Word, and the Word was with God, and the Word was God. He was with God in the beginning. Through him all things were made; without him nothing was made that has been made. In him was life, and that life was the light of all mankind. The light shines in the darkness, and the darkness has not over-come it....

The true light that gives light to everyone was coming into the world. He was in the world, and though the world was made through him, the world did not recog-nize him. He came to that which was his own, but his own did not receive him. Yet to all who did receive him, to those who believed in his name, he gave the right to become children of God—children born not of natural descent, nor of human decision or a husband's will, but born of God.

Reflection Time

How has God been speaking to you today? Take time to write it in your journal.

Chapter 124
Give Your Pain to Jesus

My husband and daughter went to church. I am sitting in the sunroom, comfortably clad in my PJs, watching the trees bend as the wind howls. My little fireplace puts off a comforting glow as I watch the birds finish off what's left in the feeders. Al will have to fill them up tonight, as winter is scheduled to make an appearance with high winds and plummeting temperatures. I am not too happy about it. I have this fantasy of living where it's eternal springtime.

But...this is the season of winter. I already feel isolated from people because I've not been well for months; the coming frigid weather will isolate me from the outdoors as well.

The last few months have been a time of "enforced" rest for me. I have had to give up a lot of things I love: my Monday night Bible study that I have enjoyed for years; taking care of my family; even reading my Bible, because it hurts to hold it. These are things that, in my mind, define who I am as a person.

I'm thankful to have an iPad and the Internet. I can listen to audio Bible, sermons on YouTube, and praise and worship music.

During this listening time, the Lord has had a lot to say to me, and I am still struggling with him about some of it.

One day, I was in more pain than usual and feeling very discouraged about it. As I was praying, I asked Jesus to take my pain from me. Suddenly, I had a vision of him hanging on the cross, bruised and beaten, and he looked at me and said clearly, "Give it to me."

In my mind's eye, I shrank back, clutching my pain tightly. He so clearly was suffering...how could I put more pain on him? He spoke again, insistently. "Give it to me."

I slowly backed away. "I cannot." He looked at me sadly. Then the vision faded.

I was in a quandary. I did not want this pain, but I didn't want to hang it on the suffering man on the cross. I examined my heart and realized the man in the vision was not the Jesus I wanted to see. I wanted the conquering hero, the one sitting at the right hand of the Father, the one who was already past the suffering of the cross. *That* is the one I wanted to take my pain.

Another day, the Lord spoke to my heart: "Why would someone not receive a gift that was being given to them?"

"I don't know, Lord. People love to receive gifts"

"But if someone won't receive a gift," he persisted, "what would be the reasons?"

I thought about it.

He whispered to my heart, "They might not think the gift is for them, but for someone else...or they might think they are not deserving of the gift...or they might not trust the giver...or all of the above...."

"Well, wow...that's some deep stuff, Lord...and I've got a feeling it all applies to me to some degree."

I felt his smile.

I listened to the book of Job one day. Now *that's* a book that puts suffering in perspective.

I've never much liked the book of Job. It has always made me very nervous to think that God allows suffering.

I guess it goes along with my "living in eternal springtime, bypass the suffering of the cross" mentality.

But the fact is Christ suffered…and sometimes God's children suffer.

It could be a consequence of our own foolish choices, but many times, it's because we live in a fallen world, where it rains on the just and the unjust.

If we do not trust God in our suffering, well then, our suffering is futile, and that's a sad place to suffer.

The Bible is not silent about suffering. It is not a fantasyland, feel-good storybook where God's followers live in the "land of eternal springtime." (Well, not yet anyway. That happens at the end of the book.)

Although the Bible is full of stories of suffering, it is also full of promises—promises that we can hold on to in the midst of our suffering, promises that if our suffering is bathed in trust, it will not be in vain.

Most of what I've had to do in this time of trial is listen…and pray. I have also had to ask for prayer…a LOT…and it's been very hard for me to do. But I could not have survived this time without it. When I ask for prayer, I am strengthened—in my body and in my faith.

Father God, I am so ready for this trial to be over, but help me to trust you until it is. Help me to trust you enough to put my pain on you, in the place that you ordained to take it. Help me to trust that your promises are for me and that your love for me is all it takes to make me deserving of your promises. Help me to wait on your timing and to receive whatever it is you have for me. Enable me to rest in you until then. In Jesus's name, amen.

⇢⇛ ❋ ⇚⇠

Job 23:10

But he knows the way that I take;
when he has tested me, I will come forth as gold.

1 Peter 5:10

And the God of all grace, who called you to his eternal
glory in Christ, after you have suffered a little while,
will himself restore you and make you strong, firm and
steadfast.

Isaiah 43:2

When you pass through the waters, I will be with you;
and when you pass through the rivers, they will not
sweep over you. When you walk through the fire, you
will not be burned; the flames will not set you ablaze.

2 Corinthians 1:3-4

Praise be to the God and Father of our Lord Jesus
Christ, the Father of compassion and the God of all
comfort, who comforts us in all our troubles, so that we
can comfort those in any trouble with the comfort we
ourselves receive from God.

Romans 8:18

I consider that our present sufferings are not worth
comparing with the glory that will be revealed in us.

2 Corinthians 4:17

For our light and momentary troubles are achieving for
us an eternal glory that far outweighs them all.

Romans 8:35

Who shall separate us from the love of Christ? Shall trouble or hardship or persecution or famine or nakedness or danger or sword?

Reflection Time

How has God been speaking to you today? Take time to write it in your journal.

Chapter 125
Your Name Shall Be Joy

I haven't felt well enough to write for a while, but also, the truth is I have felt so discouraged, I didn't feel like anyone wanted to hear my musings. I catch a glimpse of myself in the foyer mirror sometimes as I pass, and my face is drawn, my eyes dark and sad…I glance away quickly.

Last week, I looked up some articles about Christians with no joy, and they left me feeling broken.

Most had the theme of, "If you don't have joy, you're not really a Christian." Ouch.

The Lord gently brought me back to the book of Job—not the first time in this long siege….

Job did not have joy, but what he had was hope—hope in the God he had known before his time of testing.

This week I went to the visitation for a friend's father who had passed away. He was a believer, and as I saw him lying there, I thought, "He's the lucky one." I immediately felt ashamed. It wasn't that I wished to be dead; I just know his suffering is over and he has received a new body.

I have so many blessings in my life—a great husband, children, and home; friends and family who love me—but for the past four months, I have been either too weak or in too much pain to enjoy them.

I have many interests as well—writing, sewing, cooking, reading, and Bible study—but the pain has not allowed me to do much of any of those things. Many days, I sit and stare out the window. Some days I struggle with depression…and sometimes anxiety. My friend, Peggy, visits on Tuesdays—the highlight of my week—and on the weekends, my family is home.

I am eating a very healthy diet, taking supplements, listening to encouraging Scripture and teachings, praying…and yet progress is maddeningly slow.

Sometimes you can do all the right things to the best of your ability, and yet circumstances remain unchanged.

I have sat by my window and watched the vivid colors of autumn turn to the frigid gray of winter. On a rare sunny day, I turn my chair to catch the sun and let its rays wash over me. I imagine what heaven will be like. Light and warmth…no more pain….

I pray for those who have troubles much worse than my own, pray for their strength to endure, but most of all I pray for them to be aware of the presence of God.

Because in those moments, when I can truly rest in his presence, the other things I'm missing out on…they just don't matter so much.

We've had a lot of conversations, he and I, over the last four months. He has showed me some areas of my heart that need attention. He is a gentle teacher: I am, many times, a distracted and sometimes petulant student.

I'm choosing to believe this time of rest is for a reason, that God will work it for my good.

This afternoon I was in more pain than usual but finally managed to take a nap in the sunroom chair.

As I was coming to wakefulness, I heard his gentle voice: "Do you really want me to take you, daughter?" I immediately remembered the thought I'd had in the funeral home.

I paused. "No, not really."

"Why not?" he questioned.

"Well, because…I want to bring joy to people."

I startled myself. Where in the world did *that* come from? The last thing I am feeling right now is joy…I certainly don't have it to give away.…

I heard his voice faintly, fading away like a distant breeze.

"Your name shall be Joy."

I must not have heard him right. "Wait…what?"

I sure didn't see that one coming. Seems like that would take a miracle.…

Father God, help me to hold on to your promises. Give me strength to endure, to persevere. Be with those who are undergoing fiery trials in this hour. Father, pour down your Spirit on your children. Help us to lift up the fallen, to always rest in your peace, and to trust in your goodness, for in your presence is fullness of joy. In Jesus's name, amen.

James 1:2-4

Consider it pure joy, my brothers and sisters, whenever you face trials of many kinds, because you know that the testing of your faith produces perseverance. Let perseverance finish its work so that you may be mature and complete, not lacking anything.

Romans 15:13

May the God of hope fill you with all joy and peace as you trust in him, so that you may overflow with hope by the power of the Holy Spirit.

Philemon 1:7

Your love has given me great joy and encouragement, because you, brother, have refreshed the hearts of the Lord's people.

Psalm 27:6

Then my head will be exalted
above the enemies who surround me;
at his sacred tent I will sacrifice with shouts of joy;
I will sing and make music to the LORD.

Isaiah 35:10

And those the LORD has rescued will return.
They will enter Zion with singing;
everlasting joy will crown their heads.
Gladness and joy will overtake them,
and sorrow and sighing will flee away.

Psalm 30:5a

Weeping may stay for the night,
but rejoicing comes in the morning.

Psalm 16:11

You make known to me the path of life; in your presence there is fullness of joy; at your right hand are pleasures forevermore. (ESV)

Reflection Time

How has God been speaking to you today? Take time to write it in your journal.

Chapter 126
Heal the Wounds but Leave the Scars

I was awakened in the darkness of early morning by a soft tone telling me that there was a message in my inbox. Although I'd had a restful sleep, rolling over made me wince in pain. Sighing, I breathed yet another prayer for healing as I reached for my iPad. There was a request for prayer from a dear soul who has had way too much to deal with lately. As I prayed for her situation, with tears streaming down my cheeks, it struck me that the pain of others touches me so much more deeply because of my own pain and struggles.

"Lord," I said, "I want healing so badly, but I believe you have brought good out of my pain. I pray that you would heal my wounds, but leave the scars—not so tender that I get distracted and self-absorbed by them, but tender enough that another's pain can still touch them and gently remind me so that I am able to pray more fervently."

I prayed for my friend, and then the Lord brought many others to mind, so I lifted them up as well. Later in the morning, while fixing breakfast, the Lord reminded me of when he appeared to the disciples in the upper room after his resurrection, and how he addressed the doubts of Thomas by showing him his scars. And it hit me....

The power that raised Christ from the *dead* still left the scars.

That resurrection power could have restored completely—to perfection—but it left the scars.

The Bible says that Jesus sits at the right hand of the Father, that he lives to make intercession for us. The one who prays to the Father on our behalf kept his scars to remind him of the pain we face, of the rejection we face…the loneliness…the grief….

He remembers what it feels like, and so he is able to pray fervently for us. Wow!

Father forgive me when I expect healing to leave no trace of pain. Help me to remember that you work all things for my good…and sometimes the ultimate perfection is found in the scars. Open the eyes of my heart Lord. I want to see you. In Jesus's name, amen.

John 20:24-29

Now Thomas (also known as Didymus), one of the Twelve, was not with the disciples when Jesus came. Sothe other disciples told him, "We have seen the Lord!"

But he said to them, "Unless I see the nail marks in his hands and put my finger where the nails were, and put my hand into his side, I will not believe."

A week later his disciples were in the house again, and Thomas was with them. Though the doors were locked, Jesus came and stood among them and said, "Peace be with you!" Then he said to Thomas, "Put your finger here; see my hands. Reach out your hand and put it into my side. Stop doubting and believe."

Thomas said to him, "My Lord and my God!"

Then Jesus told him, "Because you have seen me, you

have believed; blessed are those who have not seen and yet have believed."

Hebrews 4:14-16

Therefore, since we have a great high priest who has passed through the heavens, Jesus the Son of God, let us hold fast our confession. For we do not have a high priest who cannot sympathize with our weaknesses, but One who has been tempted in all things as we are, yet without sin. Therefore let us draw near with confidence to the throne of grace, so that we may receive mercy and find grace to help in time of need. (NASB)

Reflection Time

How has God been speaking to you today? Take time to write it in your journal.

Chapter 127
Steadfast Under Trial

I received some prayer requests today from people who are in the fire and facing desperate situations. Their faith is being sorely tried and tested. I could think of several more going through difficult trials. Sometimes in our walk with the Lord, circumstances can throw us from the mountaintop into the midst of a stormy sea. The hands that have been lifted in praise become hands that can only cling to a life preserver, trying to remain above the waves.

John the Baptist announced Jesus to the world. Jesus said of John that there was no one greater among men. And yet that same John sent a message from the prison cell, "Are you the one who is to come, or should we expect someone else?" (Luke 7:19, NIV)

When Jesus knew Peter was going to deny him because of fear, he said, "Simon, Simon, behold, Satan has demanded permission to sift you like wheat; but I have prayed for you, that your faith may not fail; and you, when once you have turned again, strengthen your brothers." (Luke 22:31-32, NASB)

When we are in the fire, the enemy loves to come at us with accusations that our faith is weak or our God is weak.

There are times when the struggle is fierce, when we cannot even focus to read the Word…when our praise seems empty and our doubts seem huge.

Sometimes all we can do is just hold on, and that is the highest form of praise—when we choose to believe that he is God, even though our mountains don't seem to move and the seas don't part in front of us.

During those times, we ask for prayer, and we should ask for it over and over again.

Those who love us can pray for our strength to endure, for our faith to not fail; they can help us lift our hands until we are strong enough to lift them on our own again.

Father God, please give strength to those who are being tested; give them strength to endure, to persevere. Enable them to be aware of the presence of the Comforter. You have promised to work *all* things for our good. Help us to rest under the shadow of your wings. Remind us to pray for those in the fire. In Jesus's name, amen.

Psalm 42:5
Why are you cast down, O my soul, and why are you in turmoil within me? Hope in God; for I shall again praise him, my salvation. (ESV)

Psalm 3:4
I cried aloud to the LORD, and he answered me from his holy hill. (ESV)

Psalm 34:17
When the righteous cry for help, the LORD hears and delivers them out of all their troubles. (ESV)

Reflections From the Sunroom

Psalm 50:15

And call upon me in the day of trouble; I will deliver you, and you shall glorify me. (ESV)

Proverbs 3:5-6

Trust in the LORD with all your heart, and do not lean on your own understanding. In all your ways acknowledge him, and he will make straight your paths. (ESV)

Psalm 146:5-6

Blessed is he whose help is the God of Jacob, whose hope is in the LORD his God, who made heaven and earth, the sea, and all that is in them, who keeps faith forever. (ESV)

2 Corinthians 1:10

He delivered us from such a deadly peril, and he will deliver us. On him we have set our hope that he will deliver us again. (ESV)

James 1:12

Blessed is the man who remains steadfast under trial, for when he has stood the test he will receive the crown of life, which God has promised to those who love him. (ESV)

James 1:2-4

Count it all joy, my brothers, when you meet trials of various kinds, for you know that the testing of your faith produces steadfastness. And let steadfastness have its full effect, that you may be perfect and complete, lacking in nothing. (ESV)

Romans 8:28

And we know that for those who love God all things work together for good, for those who are called according to his purpose. (ESV)

→⟩⟩⟩ ❊ ⟨⟨⟨←

Reflection Time

How has God been speaking to you today? Take time to write it in your journal.

Chapter 128
Love is Not Self-seeking

I had my feelings hurt today. I told the Lord about it and about those who had hurt me. He listened and comforted me. As I sat down to read my Bible and devotions tonight, both the Bible passage and unrelated devotional reading were about love. For a moment I felt vindicated. I had not been shown love today…but as I continued to read, I felt like the accusers who dropped their stones and turned away as Jesus knelt and began to write in the sand.

Yes, love is patient and kind, but love also is not self-seeking… it is not easily angered…it keeps no record of wrong.

Father, I thank you that you are a gentle teacher. I thank you that I can pour out my heart and my hurts to you; you listen without condemnation, and then you gently show me truth. Please help me to love. In Jesus's name, amen.

1 Corinthians 13:4-6
Love is patient, love is kind. It does not envy, it does not boast, it is not proud. It does not dishonor others, it is not

self-seeking, it is not easily angered, it keeps no record of wrongs. Love does not delight in evil but rejoices with the truth.

Reflection Time

How has God been speaking to you today? Take time to write it in your journal.

Chapter 129
Under His Wings

God is anxious to talk with us.

Today I sat down in the sunroom to pray and listen for his voice.

I gazed out the windows at a winter wonderland. As the birds darted from the feeders to the pine branches, laden heavily with snow, they would dislodge an occasional cascading waterfall of sparkling white crystals.

I love to watch the birds. I have learned about their fiercely protective parenting from raising chickens. The Lord turned my mind to a few years ago when we lived on a farm, and the chickens would sit on their eggs patiently and tirelessly to hatch their baby chicks. It was very thrilling for us. Usually....

Sadly, however, a predator once got into the hen house during the night and killed our favorite white hen. She could have escaped, but she refused to leave her eggs, and the predator killed her on the nest. My heart broke at the sight, and I marveled at her fiercely protective loyalty.

When a hen was sitting on her eggs, the only way we could tell if a chick had hatched was to listen for its peeping. Under their mother's wings, we couldn't see them at all.

The Lord began to speak to my heart about his protection.

"I can keep you at peace only when you are at rest by trusting me. When you are struggling, you are out from under My wings, My place of protection. Rest is trust. Focus on me.

"This is an important act of obedience. Under my wings, the distractions and the dangers are hidden from your sight. There is only me…my shield over you…My love."

Father, I thank you that you speak to us through the things you have created. Help me to remain in your rest and your love…under the shadow of your wings. In Jesus's name, amen.

Matthew 23:37

Jerusalem, Jerusalem, you who kill the prophets and stone those sent to you, how often I have longed to gather your children together, as a hen gathers her chicks under her wings, and you were not willing.

Psalm 91:4

He will cover you with His pinions, and under His wings you may seek refuge; His faithfulness is a shield and bulwark. (NASB)

Deuteronomy 32:11

Like an eagle that stirs up its nest, that hovers over its young, He spread His wings and caught them, He carried them on His pinions. (NASB)

Psalm 17:8

Keep me as the apple of the eye; Hide me in the shadow of Your wings. (NASB)

Psalm 36:7

How precious is Your lovingkindness, O God! And the children of men take refuge in the shadow of Your wings. (NASB)

Psalm 57:1

Be gracious to me, O God, be gracious to me, for my soul takes refuge in You; And in the shadow of Your wings I will take refuge until destruction passes by. (NASB)

Reflection Time

How has God been speaking to you today? Take time to write it in your journal.

Chapter 130
The Lord Looks at the Heart

Have you ever bought something based on the outward appearance of it and then found that the quality was poor? It makes you angry and disillusioned. That happened to me with my last appliance purchase. Unfortunately, the outward appearance did not reflect the true quality of the product. It was superficial. Those appliances sure did look great in the showroom and in my kitchen, but their performance left much to be desired. On my next appliance purchase, I resolve not to be swayed by outward appearances but to do research on the inner workings before I commit.

As humans, we place way too much emphasis on outward appearances and not enough on the hidden parts. Yet the hidden parts are where the performance or the "fruit" comes from.

When God asked the prophet Samuel to anoint a king from the house of Jesse, even Samuel first overlooked God's choice. Had he not listened to God's voice, one of Jesse's older sons would have been chosen. They were strong and handsome and had the appearance of making a good king. Yet God, who knows each heart, chose the youngest son, David, a shepherd boy who had not even been brought in from the field for the selection process.

If I do not listen for God's voice, I can easily make the wrong selection. God gives me plenty of information in his Word to use as a guide.

Father God, forgive me when I make decisions without consulting you. Help me not to judge strictly by outward appearances but to trust your leading, because only you see the inward parts. Give me wisdom to discern and judge by fruit. In Jesus's name, amen.

1 Samuel 16:6-13

When they arrived, Samuel saw Eliab and thought, "Surely the LORD's anointed stands here before the LORD."

But the LORD said to Samuel, "Do not consider his appearance or his height, for I have rejected him. The LORD doesnot look at the things people look at. People look at the outward appearance, but the LORD looks at the heart."

Then Jesse called Abinadab and had him pass in front of Samuel. But Samuel said, "The LORD has not chosen this one either." Jesse then had Shammah pass by, but Samuel said, "Nor has the LORD chosen this one."

Jesse had seven of his sons pass before Samuel, but Samuel said to him, "The LORD has not chosen these."

So he asked Jesse, "Are these all the sons you have?"

"There is still the youngest," Jesse answered. "He is tending the sheep."

Samuel said, "Send for him; we will not sit down until he arrives."

So he sent for him and had him brought in. He was glowing with health and had a fine appearance and handsome features.

*Then the L*ORD *said, "Rise and anoint him; this is the one."*

*So Samuel took the horn of oil and anointed him in the presence of his brothers, and from that day on the Spirit of the L*ORD *came powerfully upon David.*

→→⟩⟩⟩ ❄ ⟨⟨⟨←

Reflection Time

How has God been speaking to you today? Take time to write it in your journal.

Chapter 131
Winter Season

It's late afternoon, and I'm resting in the big, overstuffed chair facing the windows of the sunroom. The fireplace glows, and I'm snuggled under a big comfy blanket. I'm so thankful that this is the first time I've had to rest today; not so long ago, I was having to rest way more than I was able to be up.

The view from the windows still speaks of winter: the trees are bare and the sky is a cold, steely gray. Yet my spirit gladdens with the anticipation and certainty that spring is just around the corner.

I am ready for some springtime, not only in the physical realm but in my soul as well. The last ten months have been difficult and trying, not just for me but for many people that I care about. "Winter season" started long before the cold weather hit last year. I guess it's appropriate for hope and the warmth of springtime to begin in my heart and soul before winter's end.

As I write, the sun breaks through the clouds with a confident brightness and warmth, as if to lend confirmation to the hope that has begun to bud within my heart. Healing is on its way.

God's Word tells me that, to everything there is a season and a time for every purpose under heaven.

So what have I learned from this season of winter in my soul?

I have learned how to press in to the Lord, to cry out to him for comfort, and to rest in him while I wait. I have learned that faith is the substance of things hoped for even when there is no evidence to be seen. I have learned compassion for others who are going through fiery trials. I have enjoyed strengthened relationships from friends and family who have proven themselves not to be "fair weather," and I have received strength from their persistent prayers.

I have learned to be more patient with myself and have a newfound gratitude and thankfulness to be able to do the smallest tasks that most people take for granted.

God has shown me that the best relationship with him is one of partnership. He has taught me to ask for wisdom and then listen for his voice. He has taught me that there is a part I must play and to trust that he will do what I cannot.

And so I welcome spring. In the dead of winter, I embrace it.

The substance of things hoped for…the evidence of things not seen.

Father God, I still don't like trials…don't like being in the fire… but I am thankful for the lessons I learn there. I am thankful for your love, that you never leave me or forsake me and that you work all things for the good of those who love you. I thank you for friends who stick closer than a brother. I pray that I may comfort and encourage others with the comfort and encouragement that I have received. In Jesus's name, amen.

Ecclesiastes 3:1
To every thing there is a season, and a time to every
purpose under the heaven. (KJV)

→»»» ❋ «««←

Reflection Time

How has God been speaking to you today? Take time to write it in your journal.

Chapter 132
Prodigal

I have been restless in my spirit lately. A loneliness of sorts has permeated my being. It must have snuck in when I was sick and lacking in social contact for months. Even God has felt distant to me.

I have been asking the Lord to help me figure out what was going on with me.

Last night at dinner, we were having the age-old discussion that families have had since time began: children perceiving that one child is the "favorite." So I asked my three grown children, "Who do you think is my favorite?" Hilariously, each child pointed to a different child. So there you have it. They are *all* my favorites.

As a parent, that argument has always seemed ridiculous. I love all my children. However, I remember as a child thinking one or the other of my sisters was the "favorite."

There are times as a parent when I seem to relate more to one child than another, and that is usually because one is reaching out to me more at that particular time. As they get older and busier with their lives, they need me less...but even then, they sure notice if one of the other siblings seems to be getting more attention.

This morning, I was listening to the story of the prodigal son. The youngest son asked his father for his inheritance, and then he traveled a long way from home, squandering it as he went. When he had nothing left to give anyone, all of his friends disappeared.

Coming to his senses, he realized how destitute, hungry and lonely he was, and the only thing that made sense was to return to his father. The father's position never changed through all of this. He was in the same place…just waiting for the son to return. The oldest son, who had all of the father's attention during the younger's absence, was quite jealous when the prodigal returned. The father reassured him that he was always with him and everything he had was his.

As I came out to sit in the sunroom for my quiet time this morning, I realized how inconsistent that quiet time in my special place has been. For a long time, I was too sick to spend time there. I was in bed a lot, and when I finally began to feel better, I was so excited about getting to do all the things I had missed during my illness that I spent much of my time doing those things…and neglected my quiet times in the sun room.

As I settled down in my quiet place, listening to some sweet praise and worship music and talking to God about what was on my heart, I realized that my Father had never moved. I was the one who had put the distance between us. And even if fair-weather friends fade away, he is always there. I am always "his favorite"…just as all his children are.

Father God, I thank you for your faithfulness. If I put my hope in anything other than you, at some point I will be disappointed. I thank you that you are always here waiting for me to come to you. Forgive me when I wander away. I thank you that I can bring you any hurt or disappointment, and you gently comfort and teach me. In Jesus's name, amen.

Luke 15:20

So he got up and went to his father. But while he was still a long way off, his father saw him and was filled with compassion for him; he ran to his son, threw his arms around him and kissed him.

Reflection Time

How has God been speaking to you today? Take time to write it in your journal.

Chapter 133
Desire of My Heart

Al and I went for a walk on a little trail in the woods behind our house tonight. He said he wanted to show me a waterfall. My steps were slow, and my legs trembled from so many months of inactivity. Al measured his pace with mine and held my hand for extra support.

As we headed into the woods, I breathed deeply of the spring breeze, laden with the smell of damp earth and trees beginning to bud with the promise of new beauty. A feeling of overwhelming gratitude washed over me as I remembered a conversation I'd had with the Lord this winter when I was sick in bed for months. I told him how discouraged I was, not only with that particular sickness but with the fibromyalgia that has plagued me for years and limited my physical activity. I remembered saying, with tears running down my face, "Lord, I just want to be able to walk in the woods with my husband." I would even imagine it while I was lying there in bed.

Tonight, as I walked hand in hand with the love of my life and stopped to rest by that beautiful little waterfall under the mossy pines, it felt like a wonderful gift—from my God and from my husband.

Father God, I am sorry that I complain so much. Thank you for your patience with me. Help me to count my blessings...there are so many things to be thankful for even when I don't feel well. Thank you for answering the desire of my heart tonight. In Jesus's name, amen.

Psalm 27:13-14

I believe that I shall look upon the goodness of the LORD in the land of the living! Wait for the LORD; be strong, and let your heart take courage; wait for the LORD! (ESV)

Psalm 37:34

Wait for the LORD and keep his way, and he will exalt you to inherit the land; you will look on when the wicked are cut off.

Proverbs 3:5-6

Trust in the LORD with all your heart, and do not lean on your own understanding. In all your ways acknowledge him, and he will make straight your paths. (ESV)

Isaiah 30:18

Therefore the LORD waits to be gracious to you, and therefore he exalts himself to show mercy to you. For the LORD is a God of justice; blessed are all those who wait for him. (ESV)

Isaiah 40:31

But they who wait for the LORD shall renew their strength; they shall mount up with wings like eagles; they shall run and not be weary; they shall walk and not faint. (ESV)

Reflections From the Sunroom

Lamentations 3:25

The Lord is good to those who wait for him, to the soul who seeks him. (ESV)

Micah 7:7

But as for me, I will look to the Lord; I will wait for the God of my salvation; my God will hear me. (ESV)

Reflection Time

How has God been speaking to you today? Take time to write it in your journal.

Chapter 134
Finding Peace in a Puddle

This morning, after I let the dogs out, I paused and sat down on the front-porch steps for a few minutes. It had rained during the night and was still sprinkling a bit. A puddle underneath the truck in the driveway caught my eye. It held a reflection of the hyacinth bush that was on the other side of the truck. I was mesmerized by how beautifully perfect and crystal clear the reflection was. Sitting there, with the raindrops cool on my skin in the humid morning air, I felt impressed by the Lord to go sit in the rain on the back patio. I strolled around the side of the house to the patio and settled comfortably in a chair. My mind quieted, and I began to enjoy the feel of the rain on my skin, the sweet smell of the spring flowers, and the cacophony of bird song.

I thought of the reflection in the puddle again, and the Lord began to speak to my heart. The puddle doesn't strive and worry, doesn't reach for the sky to grab the rain. It cannot reflect the heavens until the heavens fill it. It just waits, allowing itself to be filled from above…and when it is filled, it reflects what is above.

So, I too, need to be still. I need to rest and wait, allowing God to fill my spirit…and when he has, I will reflect Christ. I won't have to strive to show him to others; the reflection of Christ in me will be beautiful and clear for everyone to see.

I have struggled for months, frustrated by my limitations, feeling worthless, begging for God to remove my obstacles, begging for strength, fussing with him about my weaknesses…but in those few moments of stillness this morning, I found some peace. I'm hoping I can remember how I got to that place of peace. I'm sure it won't be the end of my striving, but this morning, the peace was quite lovely.

Father God, help me to trust and rest when my physical limitations weary my soul as well as my body. Take my discouragement and replace it with your peace. In Jesus's name, amen.

Isaiah 30:15a

This is what the Sovereign LORD, the Holy One of Israel, says: "Only in returning to me and resting in me will you be saved. In quietness and confidence is your strength." (NLT)

Psalm 91:1-2

Whoever dwells in the shelter of the Most High will rest in the shadow of the Almighty. I will say of the LORD, "He is my refuge and my fortress, my God, in whom I trust."

Reflection Time

How has God been speaking to you today? Take time to write it in your journal.

Chapter 135
The Bride of Christ

I remember when I fell in love...I couldn't wait to spend time with that special someone. The more I got to know him, the more I loved him. Everything else faded into the background when we were together...my focus was solely on him. When we couldn't be alone together, I anxiously counted the moments until we could, and I purposely created opportunity for that to happen.

The Bible says we are the bride of Christ, yet too much of the time, our relationship with Him is more like an arranged marriage. We remain distant strangers instead of enjoying the romance that we were meant to treasure.

If we believe that Jesus is God's Son and that he died for our sins, and we repent of our sins and accept him into our hearts, our eternal destiny is secured. We go to heaven when we die. That fact alone is unfathomably wonderful, but we don't have to wait until we die to experience God's kingdom. I want to fall in love with Jesus in the here and now.

Christianity isn't supposed to be just a list of duties to fulfill until we reach our final destiny. Christianity is about the engagement to the bridegroom, getting to know him here before the wedding supper in heaven someday.

In all honesty, giving that relationship priority was a struggle at first; it was a fidgety, distracted time that I had to discipline myself to attend to. There are times I still fight distraction.

Practicing his presence is a lost art, but I don't want to miss out on it.

Father God, continue to draw me close to you. Give me a hunger to know you intimately. Make your Word come alive to me. Help me to live in your kingdom in the here and now. In Jesus's name, amen.

Psalm 16:11

You make known to me the path of life; you will fill me with joy in your presence, with eternal pleasures at your right hand.

Revelation 19:7–9

"Let us rejoice and exult and give him the glory, for the marriage of the Lamb has come, and his Bride has made herself ready; it was granted her to clothe herself with fine linen, bright and pure"—for the fine linen is the righteous deeds of the saints. And the angel said to me, "Write this: Blessed are those who are invited to the marriage supper of the Lamb." And he said to me, "These are the true words of God." (ESV)

Isaiah 54:5

For your Maker is your husband, the LORD of hosts is his name; and the Holy One of Israel is your Redeemer, the God of the whole earth he is called. (ESV)

--»»» ✳ «««--

Reflection Time

How has God been speaking to you today? Take time to write it in your journal.

Chapter 136
Narrow the Focus

One of the positives of living with chronic illness is that it has taught me to narrow my focus. When an everyday job such as cleaning the kitchen seems to be more than I can handle, I've learned to concentrate on just one small part of the task at a time. For instance, I will clean just the section of the counter by the coffee pot and then turn my attention to the area by the sink. Instead of being overwhelmed by a whole flight of stairs to climb, I just look at the two in front of me. In the garden, I concentrate on a one-foot section of weeding and refuse to look at a whole garden of weeds.

There are times when the cares of life can overwhelm us. That's when it helps to narrow our focus. There is a story in the Bible about the disciples at sea during a terrible storm. In the midst of the wind and the waves, they see someone walking on the water. They were frightened until they realized it was Jesus. Peter said, "Lord, if it's you, tell me to come to you." Jesus said, "Come." Peter jumped out of the boat and began walking on the water towards Jesus. He did just fine when his focus was on Jesus. When his attention turned from Jesus to the waves crashing around him, he began to sink. He cried out for the Lord to save him…and he did.

When life overwhelms me and my prayer list seems long with very few answers, I have to narrow my focus. At those times, I just have to think about the Lord and who *he* is and not what is going on around me. In the book of Psalms, David has to do that quite often. Many times a psalm will start out with a list of overwhelming troubles that David is in a panic about. When he takes his mind off the problems and begins to contemplate the character of God, peace is not far behind.

Father, help me to narrow my focus when the storms of life threaten to overwhelm me. Your Word says that nothing can separate me from your love. Quiet my fearful thoughts and help me to concentrate on your faithful character. Help me to remember that sometimes you calm the storm, but when you don't, you can calm your child. In Jesus's name, amen.

Matthew 14:25–31

Shortly before dawn Jesus went out to them, walking on the lake. When the disciples saw him walking on the lake, they were terrfied. "It's a ghost," they said, and cried out in fear.

But Jesus immediately said to them: "Take courage! It is I. Don't be afraid."

"Lord, if it's you," Peter replied, "tell me to come to you on the water."

"Come," he said. Then Peter got down out of the boat, walked on the water and came toward Jesus. But when he saw the wind, he was afraid and, beginning to sink, cried out, "Lord, save me!" Immediately Jesus reached

out his hand and caught him. "You of little faith," he said, "why did you doubt?"

Romans 8:38-39

For I am convinced that neither death nor life, neither angels nor demons, neither the present nor the future, nor any powers, neither height nor depth, nor anything else in all creation, will be able to separate us from the love of God that is in Christ Jesus our Lord.

Reflection Time

How has God been speaking to you today? Take time to write it in your journal.

Chapter 137
A Cloudy Shade of Gray

Last week, our family went on vacation to the beach. One morning, I arose before dawn and saw my beautiful soon-to-be daughter-in-law sitting on the deck, watching the sunrise. She invited me to join her, and I grabbed a sweatshirt and a cup of hot tea and settled in a deck chair beside her. The ocean air was warm enough to be comfortable, and the sound of the waves brought the day to a peaceful awakening.

It was not quite 6 a.m. and most of the household were still sleeping. I cradled the mug of warm tea in my hands as I breathed deeply of the scent of the sea and relaxed to the peaceful sound of the ocean waves crashing upon the shore. Amanda and I sat in companionable silence.

To the north, we could see the beginnings of a storm that was forecast to roll in, but there was still breathtaking beauty in the cloudy sunrise. I noticed that where the clouds were gathering, it was difficult to tell where the ocean met the sky. The colors melted together and got lost in one another. But as I looked toward the light where the sun was beginning to rise, it was easy to tell the difference.

The Lord began to speak to my heart.

"Like the blending of a multitude of colors, the different opinions of man get mixed together in a cloudy shade of gray. Many in the world are not looking toward the light of my Son, so it is difficult to tell where earth meets heaven. To them it all looks the same. Men call good *evil* and evil *good*. Where the lines cannot be discerned is where souls get lost. Just as Amanda invited you to share the sunrise, you must keep calling out to others, directing their attention to the beauty of the light. The light is *truth*. It can be found only in my Word, not in the opinions of man."

Father God, forgive me when I want to retreat from speaking your Word to others. You call us to come apart and rest in you, but we are not to stay there. Help me to let the light of your Son shine through me. Everything this world needs is found in him: peace, love, wholeness, and healing. Make me an instrument of your peace and truth. In the name of Jesus, amen.

1 John 1:5-9

This is the message we have heard from him and declare to you: God is light; in him there is no darkness at all. If we claim to have fellowship with him and yet walk in the darkness, we lie and do not live out the truth. But if we walk in the light, as he is in the light, we have fellowship with one another, and the blood of Jesus, his Son, purifies us from all sin. If we claim to be without sin, we deceive ourselves and the truth is not in us. If we confess our sins, he is faithful and just and will forgive us our sins and purify us from all unrighteousness.

Sherolyn Porter

Reflection Time

How has God been speaking to you today? Take
time to write it in your journal.

Chapter 138
So Many Changes

We were thrilled when our oldest son got engaged at the beach last week. I believe the woman he has chosen will be a great helpmate.

This week brought another surprise, in the engagement of the youngest, our beautiful daughter, Autumn. Her new fiancé, Tyler, is the answer to the prayers I have prayed since she was a baby in my arms. He is a good man with godly values. They do not want a long engagement, so wedding plans are already underway.

My emotions have been on a roller-coaster ride. I go back and forth between joy at the new additions to our family and sadness at the change our lives will be undergoing. My life has revolved around my children for many years.

I know that God calls his children to leave one place for another, but for some strange reason, I am always surprised by the next stages in life.

Father God, I thank you for the blessing of good helpmates for my children. Please hold me close, because you know how scary change is for me. Help me to embrace all that you have for us. In Jesus's name, amen.

Ephesians 2:10

For we are his workmanship, created in Christ Jesus for good works, which God prepared beforehand, that we should walk in them. (ESV)

Hebrews 11:8

By faith Abraham obeyed when he was called to go out to a place that he was to receive as an inheritance. And he went out, not knowing where he was going. (ESV)

Ephesians 5:31

Therefore a man shall leave his father and mother and hold fast to his wife, and the two shall become one flesh. (ESV)

Reflection Time

How has God been speaking to you today? Take time to write it in your journal.

Chapter 139
The Purpose for Which You Have Been Created

$\mathcal{L}$ife has been topsy-turvy at our house lately. So many changes are coming our way. Two of our three children will be getting married; it's hard to believe one can be so happy and so sad at the same time. I've been incredibly busy which is good, but sometimes I get very nostalgic and weepy. Autumn jokes that I cry at least four times a day…a song…a picture…a commercial…you never know what will set me off.

I took to motherhood like a duck takes to water. Once I held those children in my arms, I knew I was created to be their mother. It felt like they were my purpose for being on this earth.

So in the busyness of preparing for these upcoming changes, a little thought has nagged at the back of my mind: "What's going to happen when it is all said and done, when this whirlwind of preparation is over and they begin their own story?" I really didn't want to think about it.

I have poured out my heart to the Lord for weeks—in thanksgiving for the wonderful helpmates he has brought into their lives and in sorrow at the chapter of my life that is closing.

We have had two weeks of vacation in the midst of the wedding planning, plus Autumn's college graduation and a family birthday party. I am just now getting the house put back together.

Feeling a little sad, I was folding up the tissue and gift bags from all the celebrations to store away. I stacked the bags neatly and then slowly and carefully smoothed out the tissue paper, my thoughts a million miles away.

As I folded the tissue paper, the top gift bag caught my eye. I don't know whether it had held a birthday gift for me or a graduation gift for Autumn, but in large print was a Scripture verse that had somehow escaped my attention before:

"Perhaps this was the very moment for which you have been created." (Esther 4:14, paraphrase)

It was one of those instances where I heard the voice of the Lord speaking loudly and clearly, like he does so many times, through very ordinary things—this time through beautiful words on a lovely gift bag.

My thoughts snapped into focus. How strange to see these words at a time in my life when I feel like my purpose is disappearing through my fingers like grains of sand.

I felt the Lord speaking to my heart. "I know the number of your days, the hairs on your head; as long as you are alive, I have a purpose for you, a reason that you were created. That purpose will change with different seasons, but there is always a purpose. Every day, there is a purpose." His voice faded away.

Father, help me not to grieve when a purpose that I have put my very heart and soul into comes to an end. Help me to listen for your voice and step into the next thing you have planned for me. Help me to trust that you work all things for the good of those who love you and are called according to your purpose. Thank you for your love, help, and guidance. In Jesus's name, amen.

Reflections From the Sunroom

—»»» ※ «««—

Proverbs 19:21

Many are the plans in a person's heart, but it is the
LORD's purpose that prevails.

Exodus 9:16

But I have raised you up for this very purpose, that I
might show you my power and that my name might be
proclaimed in all the earth.

Job 42:2

I know that you can do all things; no purpose of yours
can be thwarted.

Romans 8:28

And we know that in all things God works for the good
of those who love him, who have been called according
to his purpose.

Ephesians 1:11

In him we were also chosen, having been predestined
according to the plan of him who works out everything
in conformity with the purpose of his will.

—»»» ※ «««—

Reflection Time

How has God been speaking to you today? Take
time to write it in your journal.

Chapter 140
Committing My Children to God

I have prayed for the people who would marry my children since they were new babies. This year, I am seeing the fruit of those twenty-plus years of prayer come to fruition. This has certainly been the "year of love" in our household. My oldest son, Alan, got engaged when we were on vacation at the beach. He dropped to one knee in the sand, with all the family present, and asked Amanda to be his bride. As I watched him there, offering his heart forever to the love of his life, I remembered when he left home to live on his own in Philadelphia a few years before. He was lonely and having a difficult time, and I begged the Lord to bring him back. The Lord encouraged me instead to pray for his perfect will in my son's life. It was very difficult for me, but I learned to pray that way. Now I realize that, had he not stayed in that city, far from home, he would never have met his bride to be. Amanda is perfect for my son in so many ways. She is beautiful, energetic, hardworking, kind, and compassionate.

I watched her cover her mouth, with tears running down her face, as she said "yes" to my son, and I thanked God for his faithfulness to my family.

A week later, Tyler, the fine young man who had been dating our youngest daughter, asked for her hand in marriage. They didn't want a long engagement, so we began planning the wedding immediately. The Lord had encouraged me the year before to pray for his will in Autumn's life, particularly for her relationships. Then, along comes Tyler, a young man with godly values. He's also strong, handsome, hardworking, and patient (except when it comes to wedding dates), and he is perfect for my Autumn Rose.

I joked with Autumn a few days later. "Both you and your brother got engaged within a week of each other. I feel like I am dreaming! Since this is my dream, I'm going to say that your brother Andy (my middle child and a confirmed bachelor) is going to bring home a girl for me to meet this week." Autumn laughed.

A couple hours later, Andy came to the house and said, "Mom, there's a girl I want to bring home to meet you guys on Thursday." My mouth dropped open. I literally had to pinch myself.

He told me that she had picked him up for their first date, and when he got in the car, she'd had the radio tuned to the Christian station. "My mom is gonna love you," Andy had said.

Then he went on to tell me, "You kind of know who she is...."

It was a girl I had mentioned to him about five years previously. Al and I had been eating dinner at a local restaurant, and while waiting for our food, I noticed how sweet one of the girls working the counter was. She was so kind and polite to every customer, treating them with the utmost respect, no matter their age or gender or whether they were dressed nicely or shabbily. I was struck by her sweet, gentle mannerisms. She was beautiful in a quiet and unassuming way, and I looked at her left ring finger and noticed it bare. "Hmmm," I had thought, "I think Andy needs to come eat at this restaurant."

I told him about her and he rolled his eyes. A few weeks later when he had his wisdom teeth removed and was miserably trying to eat, he decided to go to the restaurant for some soup. His waitress was so sweet to him and noticed immediately that he was in pain.

Andy was impressed with her too and told me he had met the girl I was talking about. "You better snap her up, buddy," I said. "A sweet, beautiful girl like that will not remain single for long." But my handsome, blue-eyed son is never in a hurry when it comes to relationships, so by the time he was ready to ask her out, she was in a relationship…which lasted the next four years. I continued to pray for God to bring him the perfect girl…and now four years later and single again, the sweet little waitress, now turned banker, Kassy, was coming to meet us for the first time. When we met in person, I was not disappointed. Their relationship is new, but I have high hopes. She is beautiful, sweet, and kind, with eyes the color of a summer sky…just like my Andy's.

Father God, it is definitely going to be a year of change. Help me in this letting-go process. You know how I drag my feet when it comes to change. I thank you for your faithfulness to my children. I ask for your perfect will in their relationships, and that you will be at the center of them. In Jesus's name, amen.

Genesis 2:18

*And the L*ORD *God said, "It is not good that man should be alone; I will make him a helper comparable to him."*
(NKJV)

Psalm 103:17

But the love of the LORD remains forever with those who fear him. His salvation extends to the children's children. (NLT)

1 Corinthians 13:4-7

Love is patient and kind. Love is not jealous or boastful or proud or rude. It does not demand its own way. It is not irritable, and it keeps no record of being wronged. It does not rejoice about injustice but rejoices whenever the truth wins out. Love never gives up, never loses faith, is always hopeful, and endures through every circumstance. (NLT)

Reflection Time

How has God been speaking to you today? Take time to write it in your journal.

Chapter 141
Freedom

I settled down comfortably on the front-porch rocker amidst cushions of red white and blue. It was very chilly for a morning on the fourth of July. The skies were heavy with the promise of rain, and the faint, cool breeze carried the earthy, country fragrance of the corn growing in the field below. The birds were singing so sweetly to the background of the trickling waterfall. A soft rain began to fall…what a good morning for a hot cup of tea and some time with the Lord.

I thanked him for so many answered prayers, some that I have been praying for a very long time.

I thought about the meaning of this day, a day that stands for declared freedom….

There are many things that can hold people captive besides an oppressive government.

People can be held captive by relationships, fear, illness, religion, and false doctrines and ideologies.

Other things that can hold us in a cage of misery and oppression and keep us from experiencing freedom are sin, guilt, unforgiveness, bitterness, and anger.

The biggest mistake people make is to think that freedom is the absence of boundaries.

To live safely in the boundaries ordained by God...*that* is where the truest freedom lies.

I think of the freedom that Jesus died to give us. When he became a sin offering for us, the veil was torn that separated man from God. There are no hindrances now to a relationship between God and man except those we create ourselves.

God, thank you for Jesus and the Holy Spirit who can free us from everything that imprisons us. Living within the boundaries set by your Word is the truest freedom man can experience. In Jesus's name, amen.

Psalm 16:5-9

Lord, you alone are my portion and my cup;
you make my lot secure.
The boundary lines have fallen for me in pleasant places;
surely I have a delightful inheritance.
I will praise the Lord, who counsels me;
even at night my heart instructs me.
I keep my eyes always on the Lord.
With him at my right hand, I will not be shaken.
Therefore my heart is glad and my tongue rejoices;
my body also will rest secure.

2 Corinthians 3:16-18

But whenever anyone turns to the Lord, the veil is taken
away. Now the Lord is the Spirit, and where the Spirit
of the Lord is, there is freedom. And we all, who with

unveiled faces contemplate the Lord's glory, are being transformed into his image with ever-increasing glory, which comes from the Lord, who is the Spirit.

Galatians 5:1

It is for freedom that Christ has set us free. Stand firm, then, and do not let yourselves be burdened again by a yoke of slavery.

Reflection Time

How has God been speaking to you today? Take time to write it in your journal.

Chapter 142
Whatsoever Things Are True

I went out to close up the chickens for the night. The sun had set, and darkness was stealing across the sky. My heart was heavy with the weight of all the controversy and racial tension in the news the last few days. I hate that skin color is a barrier to relationships.

As I crossed the yard, I enjoyed the smell of freshly mown grass and the wildflowers at the border of the meadow down below. I watched the fireflies rising up to light the darkness and stopped for a moment, thinking wistfully of simpler times…days long ago, running barefoot through the grass and catching fireflies. I stood perfectly still for a few moments, letting the peace of the evening wash over my body and allowing the little messengers of light to gladden my heart.

As I came back in the house and headed upstairs to get ready for bed, I heard the soft ding of a text message on my phone. As I read the words from one of my very best friends, Vonnie (who happens to be a black woman), it felt like one of those moments ordained by our Creator. The message read, "Just thinking…wouldn't it be nice to run around barefoot in the grass and catch fireflies."

I texted back that I had been having the same thoughts at the same time and that I loved her. She responded that she missed me. I felt our hearts unite, despite the separation of many miles and the difference in the color of our skin.

The Lord whispered a verse from Philippians in my ear: "Whatsoever things are true, whatsoever things are honest, whatsoever things are just, whatsoever things are pure, whatsoever things are lovely, whatsoever things are of good report; if there be any virtue, and if there be any praise, think on these things." (Philippians 4:8, KJV)

Father, I thank you for that little miracle...you know my heart even when I don't say a word. I want so badly for the world to know you, to know my "Papa." So kind and good...so loving. I thank you for your message coming through in the text of a friend: that love conquers all. In Jesus's name, amen.

Reflection Time

How has God been speaking to you today? Take time to write it in your journal.

Chapter 143
Until the Rains Come

I went to out to feed the horses in the early morning hours before the heat of the day set in. The humidity was oppressive with the promise of another scorcher; the brief shower from the night before had left no evidence in the parched and cracked earth. As I opened the shed door to get the horse feed, a solitary flower caught my eye. It was delicate and beautiful…the most vibrant shade of blue. Fascinated, I took a picture with my phone's camera, hoping I could discover what type of flower it was at a later time. I looked around but saw nothing else like it.

I fed the horses and then headed for the house.

Later in the evening, Autumn and I took the truck and went to get hay. Before she backed the trailer into the field, I grabbed a small hand trowel with the intent of digging up that beautiful, tiny blue flower before it was crushed by the big truck tires. Sadly it was nowhere to be found, although I saw a brown, dried up little bud in the same location. I tried to dig it up just in case it had been the beautiful blossom from this morning, but the ground was as hard as concrete, and my little spade refused to break the crusty earth.

Hot and tired, I gave up and headed toward the air-conditioned house. My wilted ferns greeted me on the porch, and ignoring them, I opened the door and stepped into the cool darkness of the old house. I decided to call it an early night, as I was weary and zapped from the heat. I made my way upstairs, thinking that my garden was probably as wilted as the ferns.

The enthusiasm I'd had in early spring for flowers and growing things was nowhere to be found.

"It's too hard to keep all this stuff alive in this heat," I grumbled to myself. "It's just wearing me out. I'm tempted to just let it go... too much work."

I sat down with my iPad and checked my messages, finding several prayer requests that touched my heart: people who are going through a difficult time, overwhelmed by relationship issues or health issues, and others just ready to throw up their hands and say, "It's not worth the effort."

The Lord spoke to my heart in a whisper: "At times, life and relationships are like trying to keep your plants lush and green in a hot dry summer. The work it entails doesn't seem worth the effort, but you must persevere until the rains come again."

I prayed for those caught in a season of heat and drought, those who are weary and beginning to despair. I asked the Lord to strengthen them and help them endure. I prayed for a glimmer of hope—like that delicate blue flower rising from the parched earth to help them hold on until the rains come again.

Father, I thank you for the glimmers of hope you give in the midst of a long, dry season. Help me to persevere when it seems the rains will never come again. In Jesus's name, amen.

-»»» ❋ «««-

Romans 5:3-5

Not only so, but we also glory in our sufferings, because we know that suffering produces perseverance; perseverance, character; and character, hope. And hope does not put us to shame, because God's love has been poured out into our hearts through the Holy Spirit, who has been given to us.

James 1:2-4

Consider it all joy, my brethren, when you encounter various trials, knowing that the testing of your faith produces endurance. And let endurance have its perfect result, so that you may be perfect and complete, lacking in nothing. (NASB)

James 1:12

Blessed is a man who perseveres under trial; for once he has been approved, he will receive the crown of life which the Lord has promised to those who love him. (NASB)

Romans 12:12

Be joyful in hope, patient in affliction, faithful in prayer.

Reflection Time

How has God been speaking to you today? Take time to write it in your journal.

Chapter 144
Opening a New Chapter

As if we didn't have enough going on, in the midst of wedding planning, my husband and I have been looking to purchase an investment/retirement home in the mountains of Tennessee.

Our close friends, John and Teresa, with whom we travel to Tennessee, had already bought some property and were planning to build a home for retirement later. We had begun to look online last year and had made numerous trips this summer to look at houses, but with no success. We would drive for hours, only to be disappointed when we arrived, because the properties were not what we expected or we were unable to get in to see them because the home was rented. At this point, I was ready to give up.

When we were young newlyweds, we had always dreamed of owning a log cabin someday, so that is what we had been looking for. However, every cabin we had looked at in the last six months, though beautifully furnished and attractively built with big logs and massive stone fireplaces, did not feel like home to me.

As we drove to Tennessee yet again, I prayed, "Father, if this is not what we are supposed to do at this time in our lives, please shut the door. I pray that you would make unavailable all the homes we have chosen to see during this trip."

Al drove while I looked up available properties and talked on the phone to our realtor, Eric, who had also become our friend. Surprisingly enough, we were going to be able to get into about seven properties—the most we had ever been able to see. As I was browsing, I noticed a home that had caught my eye earlier in the year, but had been considerably out of our price range. However, recently, the price had been dropped drastically, and although it had none of the criteria we had been looking for, the view was incredible. It was not a log cabin but an older frame home, sitting on top of a mountain. I showed it to Al, who said he had noticed it a few days before when browsing properties and had meant to tell me about it. I called Eric again to see if it would be available to show, and he confirmed that we would be able to see it.

We spent two exhausting days looking at all the homes on our list. Some had beautiful views, but we didn't care for the house. Others, although I loved the house, were missing the peaceful view of the mountains that my heart desired. We also had hoped to find something that was close to where our friends were going to build, and several were an hour or more away from them.

The last house we looked at was the older home on the mountain. We parked in the driveway and walked up the sidewalk, winding through some sparsely landscaped flower beds. As I neared the top of the sidewalk, the sight of the valley far below stopped me in my tracks. The view was not of the peaceful Great Smoky Mountains National Park as I had dreamed about, but it took my breath away. I looked out over valleys and mountain ranges that stretched for miles. The cities far below looked like toy buildings, and it gave me the same feeling in my stomach as when I am looking out of an airplane window. The realtor, seeing my face, said, "You can see for ninety miles up here."

The house itself was about fifty years old and needed some serious updating, but it had large open rooms and many windows. The kitchen floor, boasting of once-elegant marble tile, was now cracked and faded.

The décor was neither warm nor inviting, and the house smelled musty and old; I felt almost as if I was in a museum…but something was drawing me in.

I wandered from room to room, imagining restoring this grand old masterpiece of a home.

Al came up from the basement with a look of disgust, where he had crawled into a dusty, moldy crawl space full of trash, and noticed the dreamy look on my face. His own expression was saying, "Ain't no way."

We thanked the realtors and left the house, heading for the cabin we were going to be sharing with our friends for the remainder of the week. I could not get the house off my mind, and asked Al if we could go back for a second time. The only thing he could remember about the house was the mess he had seen in the crawl space, but he agreed, and I made an appointment for the end of the week before we left for home.

The night before we were to go see the mountain house the second time, I prayed, "Father, I know that house looks like a lot of work, and I will go with my husband's wishes. Give him wisdom to make the right decision, and help me to accept that graciously. But if this is the house for us, I pray that he will see the same things that I saw last time and that he will fall in love with it too."

On Saturday morning, we bid farewell to our friends as they began their journey home, and we went back to meet the realtor at the mountain house. I tried to resign myself to the fact that it was way more work than we needed to take on, especially as we were living three states away.

Al walked through the house as I paused in front of the large windows overlooking the valley. Although the view was breathtaking, it was not the mountain view of the national park that had wrapped itself around my heart on all my trips to Tennessee. I hesitated. Maybe this is not the house we are supposed to get after all.

Just then, Al walked back up the stairs exclaiming, "I can't believe I missed all this! I was so focused on that crawl space...This place is great! Where do we sign?"

I stared at him, dumbfounded.

Eric and his wife, Tiffany, said they would write up a contract and email it to us, and we said goodbye and headed for Ohio.

Father, I thank you for your guidance and for directing our paths. I am so humbled that the Creator of the universe cares about the things that concern me. Thank you for your loving care, and help us to hear your voice in this next chapter of our lives. In Jesus's name, amen.

→→⟩⟩ ✳ ⟨⟨←←

James 1:5
But if any of you lacks wisdom, let him ask of God, who gives to all generously and without reproach, and it will be given to him. (NASB)

Psalm 31:3
For You are my rock and my fortress; For Your name's sake You will lead me and guide me. (NASB)

Proverbs 3:5-6

Trust in the LORD with all your heart, and do not lean on your own understanding. In all your ways acknowledge Him, and He will make your paths straight. (NASB)

Reflection Time

How has God been speaking to you today? Take time to write it in your journal.

Chapter 145
Every Good and Perfect Gift

This last month has been crazy. We are finishing up all the last-minute wedding plans, creating table decorations and flower arrangements, filling goody jars with chocolate kisses, and helping Autumn get ready to move to her new home. In between, we have made trips to Tennessee to oversee renovations of the old home and purchase needed items. We hired a mountain of a man named Ben to remove some trees at the end of the property. Ben is a gentle giant with a heart of gold, much like most of the people I have met from Tennessee.

We were making our last trip to the mountain house before the wedding to check on the status of the renovations. Although I was looking forward to seeing the progress, I couldn't help feeling like I should have been home in case Autumn needed something. Ben had texted me to tell me that most of the trees we had marked had been cut down and to let him know if we needed anything else.

We arrived at the mountain house in the late afternoon. I was so anxious to get out of the car and stretch my legs. As we drove up the driveway, I could see where Ben had cleared quite a few trees.

I walked up the winding sidewalk and stopped at the top to look over the valley. "This view never ceases to take my breath away. Thank you, Father, for blessing us with this property," I said.

"It's not the view you dreamed of," he responded softly.

"No, but it's beautiful and I love it. I know this is the place you picked out for us."

I opened the front door and passed through the foyer into the dining room, heading for the sunroom so I could get a better look at where Ben had been working on the bottom side of the property. As I entered the sunroom, I gasped in disbelief. Tears filled my eyes as I gazed in wonder out the sunroom windows. The trees Ben had removed at the bottom side of the property had hidden a glorious surprise. There before me was the vista I had fallen in love with on my trips to Tennessee: a panoramic view of the Great Smoky Mountains National Park.

"Oh, Father God," I breathed, overcome with emotion. "You knew this was there the whole time."

I wanted to weep in gratitude. I sat down in a chair, unable to move as I gazed at the peaceful mountain ranges I had come to love.

Dear God, you never cease to amaze me. Thank you for hidden treasure…I know that is your specialty. I don't deserve your goodness to me, but I am so grateful for it. In Jesus's name, amen.

James 1:17

Every good and perfect gift is from above, coming down from the Father of the heavenly lights, who does not change like shifting shadows.

Reflections From the Sunroom

Reflection Time

How has God been speaking to you today? Take time to write it in your journal.

Chapter 146
The Veil

Yesterday was the day we had been planning for months: the day of my daughter's wedding. A week before the wedding, the veil we had ordered online arrived, and to our dismay, it was hideous—nothing like the picture portrayed it to be. I was tempted to throw it out.

Knowing it was too late to order another, we purchased some lace, and my mother and I spent hours painstakingly removing the old lace and sewing on the new lace by hand. Although it was a great improvement, I wasn't sure how it would look with the dress, which was still being altered at the bridal shop. I prayed we hadn't made a mistake.

Then, after all the months of preparation, the day arrived. It seemed to fly by at warp speed. We had spent three months planning for the wedding, talking about the wedding, shopping for the wedding…our lives had seemed to center around that special day—a day in the future.

And then suddenly, it was here.

My beautiful daughter Autumn and Amanda, her maid of honor (and my lovely daughter-in-law to-be), submitted to the skillful touch of hair and makeup specialists. I readied the lunch my sister had prepared for us on a nearby table.

Country music played softly in the background and both girls seemed calm and relaxed.

The photographer traveled between Tyler and his family, who were getting ready in another part of the church, and my two daughters, who were becoming even more beautiful right before my very eyes. I watched as she moved here and there, capturing precious slices of life on her camera, priceless moments to be frozen in time: Autumn and Amanda, helping each other into their gowns...my sister pinning a flower on Autumn's grandfather...Autumn's smile as her grandfather kissed the back of her hand...my handsome husband straightening his tie...the look in my son's eyes as he caught a glimpse of his beautiful sister and his own fiancé....

I wanted the day to slow down, wanted to savor every moment, every smile, every hug, every tear. I wished I could bottle it up and keep it like a sweet perfume.

And then the photographer announced, "Five minutes until the mothers walk down the aisle."

My breath caught in my throat. I began to feel anxious. *Not yet...stretch it out just a little longer....*

I made my way to the entrance at the back of the church and watched my handsome soon-to-be son-in-law walk his mother up the aisle.

My legs trembled, and I was overcome with emotion. "Father God, give me strength," I breathed.

And then there was Tyler, my daughter's husband-to-be, smiling down at me and offering me his arm for my turn to walk up the aisle. "Free hug at the end," he whispered. I tucked my hand in the crook of his arm—an arm that felt so strong, much like the arm of my husband. The strength of it reassured me, and I felt my nerves began to settle.

These arms would hold my daughter and keep her safe…these arms would someday cradle my grandchildren….

The Lord reminded me that, even though I had only known this man for a short time, I had prayed for him for most of his life. A memory flashed in my mind…of rocking my baby girl during middle-of-the-night feedings while I prayed over her life, prayed for the man who would someday be her husband, prayed for a godly man, sweet and kind, who would love her deeply.

And now, nearly twenty years later, here he was, the answer to my prayers, walking me down the aisle to the front of the church, where he would turn and wait for his bride.

His bride…my little girl…who would be escorted down the aisle on another strong arm: the arm of her father.

And I marveled at the faithfulness of God….

As father and daughter neared the front of the church, their eyes moist with tears, my own eyes misted in a rush of emotions.

"Who gives this woman?" asked the pastor, and my husband answered softly and clearly, "Her mother and I."

My daughter stepped forward and took the hands of her groom, and yet I felt no loss.

As they looked into each other's eyes, I felt only gain—not the loss of a daughter but the gain of a son—and my heart swelled in gratitude at the faithfulness of God.

The pastor spoke of the love of God and family and the sanctity of marriage.

My daughter's head turned slightly, and the light caught the veil; it shimmered and sparkled like magic in its beauty.

The hours her grandmother and I had spent sewing had been worth it.

I think about all this today as I ride in the car on the way to the Tennessee mountains with my husband of thirty-six years.

Young love and weddings are so romantic, but the true beauty will show up later—when love has had the stitches of time invested in it.

Sometimes life will throw us surprises, and our relationships won't look so good; like the veil that arrived in the mail, sometimes we are tempted to throw them out.

Sometimes our relationship with God isn't what we think it should be, and we wonder if it's worth investing the time.

I remember the words of the pastor again...for better or for worse...for richer and for poorer...till death do you part....

It is time that reveals to us the depths of true love.

It is time that reveals to us the faithfulness of God.

Sometimes, the beauty of the whole cannot be seen when we are just concentrating on the stitches, but it will never be seen without them.

Father God, I commit my baby girl to you. Bless her new husband. Bless their marriage. Help them to put you first always and to grow in love for you and for each other. I thank you for your faithfulness. I love you. I could not do this life without you, Lord. In Jesus's name, amen.

1 Corinthians 13:4-8a

Love is patient, love is kind. It does not envy, it does not boast, it is not proud. It does not dishonor others, it is not self-seeking, it is not easily angered, it keeps no record of wrongs. Love does not delight in evil but rejoices with the truth. It always protects, always trusts, always hopes, always perseveres. Love never fails.

->>>> ❋ <<<<-

Reflection Time

How has God been speaking to you today? Take time to write it in your journal.

Chapter 147
Closing the Book

Al and I reached the mountain home after dark.

The massive log bed awaited me like an old friend. I had to climb on the roughly cut log side-rail to reach the king-sized mattress, and its comforting softness wrapped around me like a big hug. All the hectic wedding preparations of the last few months melted away, and I sank into a restful sleep.

The next morning, I made my way out to the deck just before sunrise. I settled into a chair and gazed at the mountains, timeless in their beauty, and sighed in contentment.

The words from a song my father used to sing to me ran through my mind: "…Then sings my soul…."

It was so still. The only sound I heard was the whisper of a gentle breeze as it rustled the leaves. I imagined not much had changed around this lofty perch in many years.

But this quietness, which would seem to be the theme of this new phase of my life, was foreign to me. Quietness had not been the norm in my life for twenty-nine years.

Twenty-nine years of motherhood to two sons and a daughter…the changes that had taken place flashed through my mind like photos on a slideshow:

Rocking babies and reading storybooks…coloring books and play dough…constantly stepping on Legos and toy cars…dress-up boxes and silly songs….Then came school days with homework…countless t-ball, baseball, and floor-hockey games…soccer, basketball, and barrel-racing competitions…a houseful of children and their friends that transitioned into a houseful of teenagers and their friends (many of which came to feel like my own children)…thousands of meals cooked and eaten…thousands of hugs, kisses, and I love yous….

I cherished every second, never wanting it to end.

With a loving mom's sadness at the departure of her youngest child, I needed a place to regroup, and the peaceful mountain home was the perfect spot.

So, there I sat in the quietness, the sun warm on my skin, as the breeze caressed my face. I gazed at the Great Smoky Mountains with their strong majestic peaks, and I felt my spirit settle into peaceful stillness.

It seemed as if the first book of my life was ending.

The sequel would have fewer characters living in the old house… just my husband Al and me.

I was grateful we had survived the first book of our lives together.

I have lived most of our marriage with chronic illness and the bone-crushing pain, fatigue, anxiety, and depression that sometimes went along with it. I knew the additional efforts it had taken on the part of my husband, and I know without a doubt that the only way we had survived and raised a beautiful family together was due to the faithfulness of God.

I am keenly aware of my weaknesses—physically, mentally, spiritually— and I know I don't have what it takes to do what I've done...but God's grace has been sufficient.

All our children joined us for a few days on the mountain, and I shed some tears when they had to leave, but for most of those last two weeks in our mountain retreat, it was just Al and I. And it was lovely. Although the change in our lives had made us sad, we laughed a lot and enjoyed each other's company.

As we traveled back home a few days later, I felt a little hesitant about returning. Home seemed to have a new definition now.

I closed my eyes and talked to the Lord...thanked him for all his help...asked to know him even better in this next book of my life...and then I asked, "But Lord, what am I going to do now?"

He placed a picture in my mind: an image of the mountains, strong, steady, unchanging, reminding me of his own characteristics. And then I heard his answer:

"You're going to write a book...."

Deuteronomy 7:9

Know therefore that the LORD your God is God, the faithful God who keeps covenant and steadfast love with those who love him and keep his commandments, to a thousand generations. (ESV)

Psalm 36:5

Your steadfast love, O LORD, extends to the heavens, your faithfulness to the clouds. (ESV)

Psalm 89:8

O LORD God of hosts, who is mighty as you are, O LORD, with your faithfulness all around you? (ESV)

Sherolyn Porter

Psalm 119:90

Your faithfulness endures to all generations; you have established the earth, and it stands fast. (ESV)

->>>> ❋ <<<<-

Reflection Time

How has God been speaking to you today? Take time to write it in your journal.

Afterword

It had been three years since the beginning of my journalings... eight months since God had spoken to me about writing a book.

I had spent a good bit of time assembling my reflections from the sunroom, turning each spiritual excursion tapped out on computer keys into printed pages. It was a bit overwhelming. I believe God called me to write this book...I'm just not sure why.

When I reach for a book, I am usually looking for answers from someone who has identified a problem and figured out a solution, a formula or some series of steps to help another arrive at a higher level of knowledge. In fact, my library is full of such books, especially spiritual ones.

So what qualified me to write a book, especially on spiritual things?

I am certainly no expert....

The fact is, I'm still very much on the journey...still looking for answers...still asking God the questions and trying to hear his response.

There are times when he is as close as my next breath, when I can bask in all that I know is truth, times when he is as real to me as the ground I am standing upon. How I wish I could say that those times are an everyday occurrence, but they do happen more and more these days.

Many times, the greatest revelation of the faithfulness of God comes when looking back. I have become keenly aware of this as I have edited my last three years of writings to put into this book. *Reflections From the Sunroom* is a "book of remembrances." I know that I have made it this far not because I am wise or have life's questions and answers figured out or because I am strong. Instead, my book of remembrances has reminded me all too well of my weaknesses, but it has also reminded me of his strength, his provision, and his faithfulness.

One thing I have become sure of in this desire to know the Father better, this quest for hidden treasure: he is very anxious to talk with us, and he is just looking for a willing heart that desires to hear him. So, I continue on the journey. I have found enough of the treasure to know that I want more.

I hope my journey has encouraged you to draw closer to the Father on your own pilgrimage through life. He loves you immeasurably and desires fellowship with you.

My prayer for us still—for myself as well as for you, dear reader—is from Ephesians 3:

> I pray that out of his glorious riches he may strengthen you with power through his Spirit in your inner being, so that Christ may dwell in your hearts through faith. And I pray that you, being rooted and established in love, may have power, together with all the Lord's holy people, to grasp how wide and long and high and deep is the love of Christ, and to know this love that surpasses knowledge—that you

may be filled to the measure of all the fullness of God. (Ephesians 3:16-19, NIV)

In Jesus's name, amen.

In his love,
Sherolyn Porter